International e-Business Marketing

International e-Business Marketing

Richard Fletcher, Jim Bell and Rod McNaughton

Australia · Canada · Mexico · Singapore · Spain · United Kingdom · United States

International e-Business Marketing
Copyright © Thomson Learning 2004

The Thomson logo is a registered trademark used herein under licence.

For more information, contact Thomson Learning, High Holborn House, 50–51 Bedford Row, London WC1R 4LR or visit us on the World Wide Web at: http://www.thomsonlearning.co.uk

British Library Cataloguing-in-Publication Data
A catalogue record for this book is available from the British Library

ISBN 1-86152-945-7

First edition 2004

Typeset by LaserScript, Mitcham, Surrey

Printed in Great Britain by TJ International Ltd, Padstow, Cornwall

Contents

List of figures

List of tables

List of case studies

The nature of e-business

1 Introduction: e-business, marketing strategy and the international environment

Learning objectives

After studying this chapter, you should be able to:

- Explain how Internet-based technologies affect organizations, markets and industries.

- Discuss the meaning of the terms e-business and e-commerce.

- Relate e-business to the broad themes of globalization, organizational change and market orientation.

- Define the scope of an e-business implementation.

- Discuss differences between the dot.com era and current business approaches to e-business.

- Demonstrate familiarity with broad patterns in the adoption of e-business in business-to-business and business-to-consumer markets.

- Understand why this book focuses on the intersection of the international environment, e-business and marketing, and the importance of this interface between domains of study.

The Internet

A technology changing the boundary of the firm

The Internet and related technologies offer an unprecedented opportunity for firms to overcome geographic barriers to expansion into foreign markets. Smaller firms can particularly benefit from the ability to gather information, promote themselves, and service customers in new markets for relatively little expense (Quelch and Klein, 1996). A number of possible effects of the Internet on the marketing environment suggest that firms will experience fewer barriers to internationalization, and be able to market globally at an early stage of development. The impacts of the Internet include:

- reduced importance of economies of scale
- lower marketing communication costs
- greater price standardization
- reduced information float time
- temporal asynchronicity
- increased contact between buyers and sellers
- changes in intermediary relationships.

Several studies of Internet use by small firms conducted in the mid-1990s found that the use of Internet technologies by the existing population of small firms is rather limited, the most frequent impediments being lack of knowledge and skill (e.g. Hamill and Gregory, 1997; Hamill, 1999). While this is changing, and varies by country, adopting the Internet into their business strategy remains a problem for many firms, especially smaller firms with limited resources.

A key theme of this book is change, particularly change in marketing activities in an international context. New information and communications technologies (ICT), create opportunities and challenges for organizations, their markets and industries. The influence of the Internet goes to the heart of why firms exist, and is causing a massive restructuring of firms and how they relate to their markets. Coasian economics (Coase, 1937), and more recently Transaction Cost Analysis (TCA) (Williamson, 1975), argue that firms exist because of market imperfections, and that coordinating the processes required to manufacture goods or provide services is sometimes accomplished more efficiently within an organization than through market exchange. The process of exchange gives rise to transaction costs that may cause market failure in the sense that the market is an inefficient means of mediating exchange. Transaction costs are those relating to search and information gathering, the costs of monitoring and enforcing contracts, and coordinating access to resources and the processes that transform resources into goods or services.

According to the logic of TCA, when transaction costs are low, and markets competitive, there is little incentive to substitute internal organization for market exchange. In contrast, when the market is unable to impose pricing or behavioural constraints, firms are expected to internalize transactions to reduce the cost of exchange. A limit on integration is imposed by the fact that organizations themselves are not perfect, and transaction costs also exist within corporate structures. These are often referred to as organizational or bureaucratic costs, and include investments in legal, administrative and operating infrastructures. The Internet lowers transaction costs in three ways:

1. *Search costs*: the Internet increases the amount of information available to both buyers and sellers, and makes information available in a convenient and timely manner.

2. *Contracting costs*: the Internet makes it easier to compare and negotiate prices and other terms, and to keep in touch with and monitor the performance of partners in business relationships.
3. *Co-ordination costs*: the Internet reduces the costs of sharing information, and can automate and integrate many business processes.

Because of these changes, the boundary between the firm and its environment is changing. Markets are becoming more efficient and agile. E-business challenges managers to overcome the inertia of the bureaucracy and culture within their organizations. Firms must become more flexible and responsive to compete with a more dynamic market for exchange. Managers must increasingly deal with exchanges in the marketplace over which they have little control, rather than between subsidiaries, units and employees over which they have administrative authority.

E-business is a major management challenge. E-business strategy is not simply a matter of choosing between technologies. Rather it involves managing a process of change in the firm, and creating strategies either to anticipate or respond to transformations in markets and industries. Internet-related technologies are strong agents of change. If a firm in a value chain starts doing business electronically, soon companies up and down the value chain must address their own e-business strategy or risk substitution in the activities of the chain.

What is e-business?

The popular business press often uses the terms e-business and e-commerce interchangeably. There is little agreement in academic literature as to the meaning of these terms. Figure 1.1 distinguishes between the terms based on the extent to which transactions cross firm boundaries – specifically exchanges with customers. In this definition, e-commerce involves electronically mediated exchanges with customers, while e-business refers to the application of ICT to processes within the firm, and possibly to transactions with suppliers as well.

Figure 1.2 illustrates an alternative view. In this model, e-business is an inclusive term referring to all uses of ICT within the business context. This includes communication, information and data exchange, advertising, and

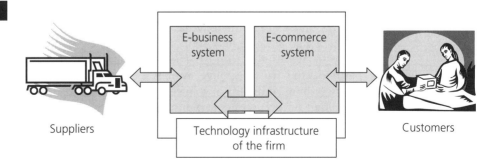

Figure 1.1

E-business and e-commerce systems

Suppliers

E-business system

E-commerce system

Technology infrastructure of the firm

Customers

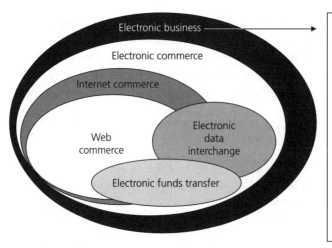

Figure 1.2

Relationship between e-business and e-commerce

Source: Huff, Wade and Schnebergers (2002: 4)

secure exchanges of funds, with suppliers, internal customers (within the firm), or external customers (in the market).

A focus of this book is marketing activities, so it emphasizes information exchange, communication, and exchange with external customers. However, it is not possible to separate these activities from the impact of the Internet on business processes and dealings with suppliers. E-business is about more than just selling and buying using the Internet. This book promotes the view that all business is e-business, because Internet-related technologies have the potential to transform all aspects of business activity. E-business is not just about adopting the technology. It is central to business strategy, and involves redefining business models to take account of changes in transaction costs to find new ways of conducting business that increases value for the stakeholders of the firm.

The scope of e-business initiatives

The extent to which firms adopt ICT technologies and incorporate them into their business model varies significantly. The potential of the Internet to affect a firm or its market depends on a number of factors including product characteristics, market characteristics, and organizational design. Figure 1.3 shows a way of defining the scope of an e-business initiative. Scope is measured on four dimensions – who, what, where and why. An initiative near the centre of the circle has limited scope, and aims to reduce the costs of business processes within the firm. An extensive initiative would involve the firm and its partners, and try to achieve numerous objectives to transform the conduct of business in an industry or market.

As part of their strategic planning processes, firms must decide on the scope of their e-business initiatives. The availability and capabilities of a technology does not mean it should be adopted. Firms in different contexts will experience different benefits from e-business, and need to balance the costs of investment in

Figure 1.3

Scope of e-business
initiatives

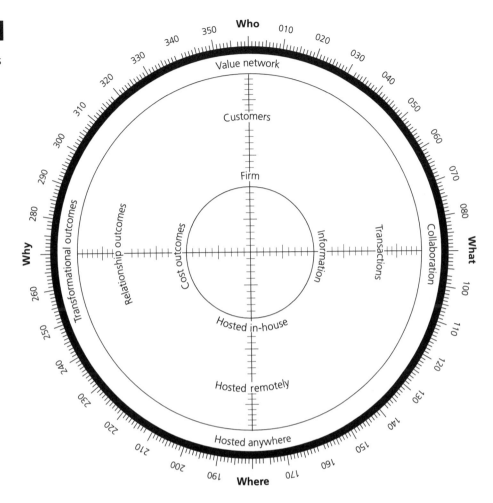

Source: Sawhney and Zabin (2001: 16)

e-business infrastructure, software and training against benefits from reduced costs, improved communications, relationships, or expanded markets. Figure 1.4 suggests that e-business initiatives are like a ladder, with each rung representing an expansion in both scope and affect. At the bottom of the ladder is the use of the Internet to share information. The first rung is the automation of business processes. The next step is the integration of processes and relationships with partners. Finally, at the top is the transformation of industries and markets.

The scope of e-business involvement correlates loosely with firm size. In large organizations, ICT is essential to the effective management of interdependence (Rockart and Short, 1989). Interdependence, and consequently organizational performance, depend on the accurate and timely delivery and use of information. Traditionally, subsidiaries and functionally isolated departments led to 'many islands of optimised IT applications' (Talvinen, 1995: 14) that could not communicate with each other. The common communication protocol used by the Internet provides a connecting infrastructure, bridging these islands and making integration possible.

Modern organizational design is a balance between the specialization benefits of departmentalization, and the effort involved in coordinating the interdependencies that occur between functions (Mentzas, 1996). Interdependencies relate to specific tasks, information, decision making or organization objectives. Without proper coordination of activities, performance is affected and organizations become chaotic. Management practices like Just in Time (JIT) and Total Quality Management (TQM) that advocate the elimination of resource buffers and slack increase the importance of coordination.

Example *Megazyme*

Megazyme was established in Australia in 1989 by Dr Barry Cleary and Angela Kennedy AMD, but moved to Ireland in 1996 using Internet technologies to facilitate this relocation by establishing continuity for customers. They develop and manufacture a range of diagnostic test kits and reagents for the cereals, food, feed and fermentation industries. Many of their test kits have been validated as standard methods by international scientific bodies. This stamp of approval has formed the foundation of Megazyme's global marketing strategy. Almost all (97 per cent) of Megazyme's business is with overseas customers, 40 per cent of which trade via the web site. Their products are ideal for selling by this method, as they are the only provider of 90 per cent of their product range, and the products are light and easy to ship while commanding a high price on each item ordered.

They view the Web as the most important marketing tool of the twentieth century and take full advantage of the new channels for marketing and distribution that it offers. Megazyme first developed their website in 1994, 5 years after inception and it now attracts 4 to 5 new customers weekly. The web site represents very good value for money costing under £5000 to develop and around £1000 per year to maintain. In comparison, the last printed brochure cost £30,000 to produce and is static while the web site is constantly updateable. One of the prime objectives of the site is to give customers more and better information about Megazyme's products. Users can download technical data booklets about each product on the site. The booklets are presented in Acrobat Reader format, which allows complete control of the booklet's layout. Customers can order goods via the website using a set of forms, offering options for the currency to be used in the transaction. Various payment options are offered, for example, through cheque or wire transfer. They also provide conventional payment options by phone and fax for those who do not wish to order via the web. Using the Fed-Ex they offer a next day delivery service to Europe and the USA. Customers may track and identify the immediate status of their shipments on the home page by typing in their AWB (airway bill) number.

Megazyme's marketing techniques include both online and offline strategies. Offline, they advertise the website in specific targeted technical journals. This is also prominently displayed on business cards and all collateral material. The domain name is very distinctive and easy to remember, which helps to establish a strong online identity. They have worked hard at targeting keywords that will picked up by the leading search engines: to ensure that their site will be well positioned in search results. In addition, they have encouraged other companies and scientific organizations to provide links to their website. Megazyme track user statistics so they are able to identify who is using the site and so constantly refine their marketing strategies.

Figure 1.4

The ladder of
e-business initiatives

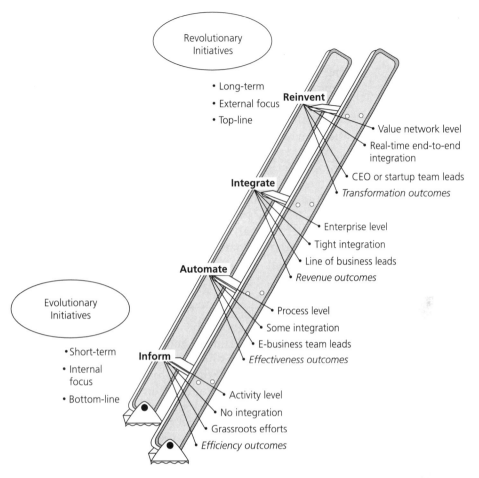

Source: Sawhney and Zabin (2001: 54)

Integration can also benefit the new product development process (Despande and Zaltman, 1982; Song, Neely and Zhao, 1996). Interfunctional coordination can drastically cut new product development time and eliminate alternatives that are not feasible. This can help to minimize the cost of new product development and allow the process to function more smoothly. By soliciting input from a number of departments, firms can increase the number and diversity of new product ideas creating a competitive advantage in innovation. Integration between corporate functions also improves customer service. In particular, development of a market orientation relies on all departments and personnel striving to service customers to the best of their abilities (Narver and Slater, 1990). Because of this, interfunctional coordination is one of the key components of a market orientation.

Computer networks like the Internet have several characteristics that make them ideal for the role of coordination and information dissemination. They have the capacity to store large amounts of information for long periods with perfect recall, and can quickly transmit large amounts of information accurately and without the usual distortions of human communication (Huber, 1990). As a result, geographically dispersed departments, personnel or firms can share files quickly and accurately with each other. Legacy information can be stored for long periods, creating a corporate memory that is independent of particular employees. Networking also allows mangers to communicate with and coordinate a large number of personnel from a central location while promoting decentralized decision making. This 'one-to-many' type of communication offers savings in both time and resources (Migliarese and Paolucci, 1995).

While large firms benefit from improved integration and reduced coordination costs, smaller firms also benefit from incorporating e-business into their strategy. E-business initiatives vary in cost from hundreds of dollars to hundreds of millions of dollars. At the lower end, the Internet has reduced the barriers to entry in many industries. Smaller firms can advertise, reach larger (even international) markets, access lower cost inputs, and cooperate with channel and other partners for lower costs than would traditionally be the case.

The dot.com era

Business rhetoric about the Internet, the importance of e-business, and the transformation of business models, changed significantly after the crash of the markets for shares in technology firms in 2000. Table 1.1 lists some of the differences before and after the market crash.

Before the stock market crash in April 2000, cyberspace was teeming with start-up Internet-based firms experimenting with permutations of technology and business practice. Backed by private equity investments, each was betting that its model would result in rapid growth, and make its founders wealthy. Managers in traditional as well as 'pure-play' Internet companies can learn from the experimentation of this era. Pure-play Internet business models are 'naked' straightforward attempts to apply marketing principles to create value for customers and for the owners of firms. These companies' business models

Table 1.1		Dot.com era	Post dot.com
Differences in business rhetoric between the dot.com and post-dot.com eras	Focus	Technology	Business
	Key performance measure	Revenue growth	Earnings
	Financing	Private equity	Debt and boot strapping
	Players	Entrepreneurial start-ups	Traditional larger firms
	View of competition	Perfect markets	Imperfect markets – importance of brands and network effects
	Business model	Pure plays	'Clicks and bricks'
	Role of intermediaries	Disintermediation	Strengthening intermediaries
	Legal and regulatory environment of marketspace	Ungoverned	Increasing regulation

Source: Adapted from Laudon and Traver (2001: 32)

are naked in the sense that it is easy to see the business processes that drive revenues. The processes that drive earnings (in contrast to revenue) in traditional firms are less obvious.

The dot.com crash raised questions about how long investors are willing to wait for signs of profitability. Firms cannot go on forever spending more than they earn from their customers. The acceptance of ongoing losses during the dot.com era related to the rapid and continuing growth of the Internet community. Large fixed expenditures can be rationalized if the size of the market continues to expand. If expenses remain fixed but revenue continues to go up, eventually a solid business model will generate a profit as the market grows. Marketing is no longer seen as a fixed expense. It turns out that online brands need constant nurturing and the cost of acquiring customers can be high. This stems from the ease with which customer loyalty is contested on the Internet, and the constant flow of new Internet users whose mind share must be acquired.

During the dot.com era the executives of Internet companies argued that the quality of the revenue stream is more important than profitability. If expenditures relate to building a quality service that delivers true value to customers, and each customer is delivering a reasonable revenue stream, it is only a matter of time before a firm will become profitable. On the other hand, if a company's expenses relate primarily to acquiring customers and it does not make very much from each customer, then it will sink deeper into trouble as the Internet grows. So far, few pure-play Internet companies have managed to accelerate revenue and exceed their expenses. These include AOL, Yahoo! and eBay.

Marketing accounts for a large proportion of the expenditures in a pure-play Internet company. Traditional valuation methods based on bottom-up approaches such as discounted cash flows, or comparative ratios such as price/earnings, or price/addressable market are inadequate on their own to value Internet companies. Internet businesses are frequently based on new market entry or transformational change strategies and growth assumptions vary widely. In this situation traditional valuation methods are too static and do not reflect future growth options.

During the dot.com era, the concept of 'option value' started to replace the traditional notion of the 'present value' of customer relationships. Market values were based on net future expectations, which account for both discounted cash flows and future opportunities. The idea was that customer relationships could be monetized and levered in yet to be imagined ways by an innovative company. In traditional firms, the biggest expenses are tangible facilities and equipment that are credited on the balance sheet and expensed over time. In contrast, marketing is the biggest expense for Internet companies. These costs are not credited on the balance sheet and are expensed all at once. The result is a firm with little book value and no earnings. The argument advanced by Internet executives was that marketing expenditures create market-based assets that can be every bit as valuable as those shown on the balance sheets of traditional firms. In fact, while depreciating physical assets tend to decrease margins over time, network and other effects of strong customer relationships may result in increasing margins.

In hindsight, this argument is spurious. If the market for Internet companies were rational, the market capitalization per customer should represent the present value of the total profit expected over the lifetime of an average customer. At the height of the market bubble, the lifetime value of current customers of Amazon reached $US1400 for Yahoo! $US2038 and for eBay $US1952. The market was betting that:

- these firms would continue to grow and take a leading share in the burgeoning online market
- marketing costs per customer would fall as the market stabilized
- the market-based assets these companies are building can be leveraged to generate revenues in new ways (Amazon, as an example, sells tabs on its web site to affiliate retailers).

Supply and demand drove the extraordinary market valuations of the dot.com era. Overwhelming media attention and a constant flow of promotion by newly listed Internet firms created demand for Internet investments. Too much money chased too few sound Internet-based businesses. Many Internet companies rushed to make an initial public offering and entered the market with relatively small floats. Investor demand quickly bid up their immediate post-offering price only to have them fall later to levels below the issue price. Many of these firms are no longer in business.

Current business rhetoric focuses more on 'bricks-and-clicks' models that combine traditional firms and distribution channels with Internet business models. Popular business periodicals now devote more attention to how the Internet is transforming large companies than it does to new start-ups. Traditional methods of valuing firms, and emphasis on earnings records, and a cautious venture capital community characterize the current financial market.

Example   *Markus Cohen*

Markus Cohen, who has over 35 years' experience as a barrister and solicitor, left a large firm in Toronto in 1992 to set up his own firm, The Virtual Law FirmTM. This firm is an Internet-based operation, and is run from a small office in Toronto, servicing a distributed list of international clients. Markus Cohen owns the firm, with one part-time employee who looks after office management and executive assistance responsibilities, a once a month part-time bookkeeper, and 15 to 20 regular associates across North America who are subcontracted on a project by project basis.

At present, Markus Cohen estimates that between 80 to 85 per cent of its revenue is from US markets, 1 per cent from outside North America and the balance from within Canada.

Approximately 70–75 per cent of The Virtual Law FirmTM legal services is related to Franchise law while the balance of 30–35 per cent is related to Trademark law. Franchise law related services are almost entirely business-to-consumer, whereas Trademark law related services are mostly business-to-business, that is to other law firms. With the majority of its clients located in the USA much of the work for which The Virtual Law FirmTM is contracted is to Canadianize American legal documents.

As a concept, this firm is unbounded by geographic or organizational borders, which enables it to expand and contract in size as suits its clients' requirements. This means it offers its clients the best experts available, not just the best experts available within a specific city,

▶

country or single firm. To sustain this model and because it retains no lawyers, the Virtual Law FirmTM recruits lawyers in other firms to subcontract on the firm's contracts. Therefore in a sense it functions as a meta-firm; a firm of subcontracted firms and lawyers. This business model enables the Virtual Law FirmTM to operate efficiently with minimal employer–employee commitments and yet offer its clients a quality service with broad expertise over a large service area.

This firm demonstrates how high quality professional services can be marketed internationally through the Internet and how a small virtual firm can sufficiently increase its profile with a simple web site and Internet presence to compete against larger, established law firms. Among its strengths, it uses basic Internet technologies to recruit potential associates and develop online research services, to broaden its markets, increase the speed yet decrease the costs of its communication, and improve the efficiencies of its core services.

Although the services it provides are no longer considered as cutting edge as in 1992, the firm's early strategic decision to adopt e-commerce practices enabled it to develop a stable client list and strong footing in international markets, which continue to generate revenue. The web site continues to drive new leads, and on average two per month lead to new sales.

Marketing and the Internet

Figure 1.5 shows the growth in online transactions over the last decade. Figure 1.6 divides these data into business-to-business and business-to-consumer components. These two figures show that:

- the e-economy is entering the rapid growth phase of the adoption curve
- online sales have continued to grow despite the collapse of many dot.com companies
- some countries outside the USA are now adopting e-business more rapidly than the USA

Figure 1.5

Global e-commerce revenues

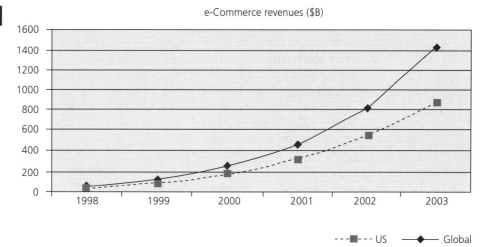

e-Commerce revenues ($B)

- - ■ - - US ——◆—— Global

Source: eMarketer B2B Report (2000)

Global B2B versus
B2C e-commerce
revenues

B2B versus B2C revenues ($B)

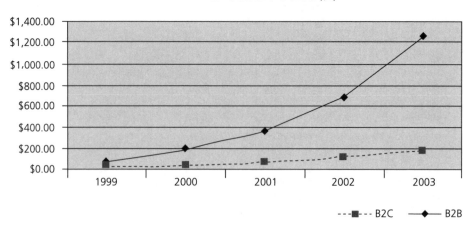

Source: eMarketer (2000)

- business-to-business (B2B) transactions are a much greater proportion of e-business activity than is business-to-consumer (B2C) transactions.

E-business has so far been more influential in the B2B domain because of greater penetration of computer use among businesses than households, the characteristics of B2B products and services are better suited to online sales, and the much larger volume (and value) of B2B transactions. The characteristics of the Internet as a medium for communication, transactions and distribution of digital products mean that online marketing has a significant effect on marketing strategy. Key characteristics include: ubiquity, global reach, universal standards, richness, interactivity, information density and customization/ personalization (Laudon and Traver, 2001).

The common thread that ties these characteristics together is the concept of 'value'. These characteristics can be levered to increase service levels, convenience, accessibility, responsiveness, decrease costs and add information or services around a core offering. The value creation process has evolved within most societies to be organized primarily within privately owned and joint stock firms. The concept of the 'firm' provides a boundary that distinguishes patches of relatively denser social relationships from those that exist in the marketplace. However, relationships also exist between individuals in different firms, and between firms in terms of cross-ownership, alliances, and buyer–seller relationships. It is increasingly common that groups of firms become closely associated with each other in networks that facilitate co-production, or co-marketing. There are also boundaries in the external environment, a key one being international borders. How firms and individuals span these boundaries is a crucial issue. The Internet has the potential to expand all of these boundaries.

A challenge for marketers is that value is increasingly linked to intangible assets such as knowledge, brands and relationships. Further, these intangible assets often exist outside the firm, and arise from the co-mingling of the firm with entities in the external environment. The key issue faced by marketers is the identification of those activities that add or leverage intangible assets to create value for shareholders and customers. New skills are often required because the assets to be managed lie outside the boundaries of the firm. Market-based assets contribute to firm performance through faster penetration, price premiums, brand extensions, lower sales costs and improved loyalty. In turn, performance enhances firm value through improved cash flows and reduced volatility.

The role of marketing stands out in the e-economy because the core of Internet business models are intangibles such as information or a unique position that allows disintermediation or reintermediation of relationships between buyers and sellers. Organizing customers into a community and acting as a broker within the resulting market creates a unique competitive advantage. Internet companies that facilitate B2B transactions, for example, typically have negotiation at the centre of their business model. Variations include forward auctions in which one seller entertains bids from many buyers, reverse auctions in which one buyer considers offers from many sellers, and exchanges in which many buyers and sellers interact to determine a market price. These models create value by revealing the supply and demand for goods, speeding up the selling process, and extending the spatial reach of buyers and sellers.

Creating value through brokerage is not new, but the allure of the Internet is that market leaders enjoy a cost advantage over traditional firms and overcome many geographic constraints. Thus, Internet business models are potentially scalable to serve global markets quickly and with less fixed investment than is possible with traditional technologies. Scale can also create barriers to entry for potential new competitors. For example, Amazon.com's close relationships with book distributors, and AOL's use of a proprietary network to limit subscriber switching.

In some Internet businesses, network effects aid scalability and speed. Each new customer personally gains while increasing the value of the whole network. An example is PlanetAll – an online contact manager. (PlanetAll was acquired by Amazon.com. Amazon incorporated parts of PlanetAll's technology, and then closed the company.) As new customers enter their contacts, the network grows and the overall value of the database increases. When business contacts, friends and family are all using the same contact management system it is easy to update addresses, notify contacts of significant events, and the like. This creates convenience and value for the customer and is a barrier to switching that reinforces the company's position.

Internet business models often find further advantage in rethinking the money chain: who pays and who captures value. Many Internet business models attempt to change the structure of an industry by shifting traditional notions of who should pay, and how value is created. Buy.com, for example, distributes consumer electronics at cost. Rather than extracting a profit from the purchasers of products, it generates revenues from advertising, sponsorship and companion selling of ancillaries.

The basic lesson is that online marketing enhances the ability of a firm to create intangible assets. Figure 1.7 presents a model that maps a path from investment in market-based assets to firm value. This model has three main components: market-based assets, customer value and firm value. Sustainable Internet business models create value for customers. A customer value-based strategy is implemented through the creation of market-based assets consisting of intellectual assets (knowledge about the market), relational assets (outcomes of relationships with stakeholders including channel members, customers, and other players including channel and brand equity), and the interaction between these two asset forms. Market-based assets accumulate by developing knowledge, skills and resources that are unique and difficult to imitate. Assets are built or acquired through various forms of investment, including staff time spent in relationship building, databases, advertising and promotion, corporate image management and sponsorship.

Market-based assets can create value for a firm by building strong barriers to entry that divert competitors to higher cost or less effective strategies, leveraging the asset, and deploying the asset to create customer value. Each firm's business model is unique in both the character of assets and the way they are deployed. The ways in which market-based assets can create value for customers include lowering search costs, better matching of performance requirements and price, improved service, trust, innovative new products and risk reduction.

The marketing literature postulates that firms providing customer value will have more satisfied customers who demonstrate stronger brand loyalty. This can have a number of effects on cash flow that both increase incoming cash and decrease outgoing cash. For example, loyal customers are less likely to switch and require less ongoing marketing effort to retain. Thus, there is a growing pool of customers who by word of mouth act as marketing agents that help to attract new customers. Loyal customers will pay price premiums, adopt line extensions more readily, refer products more readily, and have lower sales and service costs. The overall effect of these processes is to speed receipt of cash, widen the gap between incoming and outgoing cash (for marketing related expenditures), and reduce working capital and fixed capital requirements. All

Figure 1.7

A model of market-based assets and firm value

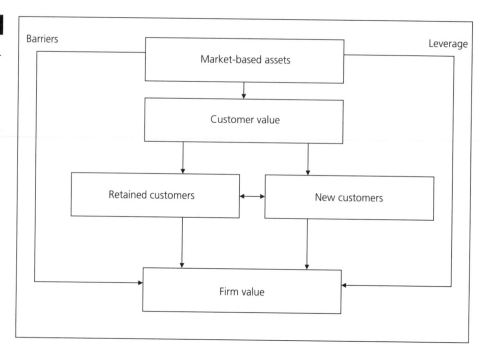

else being the same, this should create higher earnings and reduce the volatility of a firm's cash flow.

A tour of Amazon.com's web site illustrates most of the elements in this model. The core of Amazon's model is the market-based assets of an extensive database of customer characteristics and purchase patterns, a strong brand, and channel equity with suppliers. These assets are levered through affiliate arrangements with other retailers. They are also employed to create value for customers through easy search facilities, extensive stock, home delivery, gift suggestions, security and low prices. Amazon customers become marketers through the 'recommend this selection to a friend' function. Customers are encouraged to buy more through companion selling, and cross-selling between books, CDs and other merchandise. Amazon's site constantly recommends additional products based on the customer's preferences and the purchase patterns of other customers. The potential success of this model is rewarded with a high market valuation even in the frequent absence of profits in quarterly earning reports.

The internationalization of Internet companies

It might be supposed that because of their high skill level Internet start-ups are in a superior position to capitalize on the new marketing conditions, and that the preponderance are therefore 'global from inception'. Indeed, the ability to build market share rapidly is cited as a key to protecting an Internet business model. Internet companies are inherently global – a web site readily reveals key aspects of a business model to opportunists looking for a good idea to copy. Internet companies do not have the luxury of gaining experience and stability domestically before defending themselves internationally. Many Internet companies have found that 'squatters' register foreign versions of their URL soon after the first press release announcing their founding. Others have found overseas companies that have copied the look and feel of their site, sometimes even pirating parts of their web sites.

However, many pure-play Internet companies have a domestic focus, while among those that have internationalized, there are a number of different patterns. The internationalization of Internet companies is by no means a deterministic, or even a homogeneous process. Internationalization pathways reflect different strategies that relate market scope to timing advantages in an attempt to lever value from the business model. Some Internet companies such as the ill-fated luxury clothing retailer Boo.Com pursued high cost multi-country launches. Other key players pursued strategies of acquisition or joint ventures to expand globally. Amazon.com, for example, only generates about 25 per cent of its revenues from overseas sales and is limited by the high cost of shipping overseas from its US base. Amazon clones sprang up in many countries. Amazon acquired many of these companies, including the leading online booksellers in both the UK and Germany, and has opened subsidiaries in other countries. Other companies are using joint ventures to stake their international claim. eBay, for example, joined with NEC for its Japanese auction site. Yahoo! has joint ventures that support its portals in Japan, the UK, France, Germany and Korea.

Aspects of the international environment, including differences in legal and regulatory regimes, the state of the communications infrastructure, and differences in culture including language and perception of the benefits of the Internet, cause unevenness in the adoption and use of e-business. While the Internet is a means to reach out to global markets, the world is not homogeneous in its acceptance of the Internet, or its expectations of e-business. There is a tendency to emphasize the standardization effect of the Internet, but the ability to customize and personalize the Internet experience is the key to successful localization of business models within global markets.

A model of international e-business marketing

Figure 1.8 shows the organization of this book. The unique position of this book is the combination of e-business with marketing strategy and the international context. The next two chapters provide insight into e-business models, and the impact of Internet technologies on the practice of international marketing. Chapters 2 and 3 constitute the 'e-business' component of the model in Figure 1.8. Chapters 4, 5 and 6 discuss components of international marketing strategy – foreign market entry, competitive strategy and networks. These chapters are the 'marketing strategy' component of the model. Chapters 7 through 9 describe the 'international environment' dimension, and provide

Figure 1.8

A model of international e-business marketing

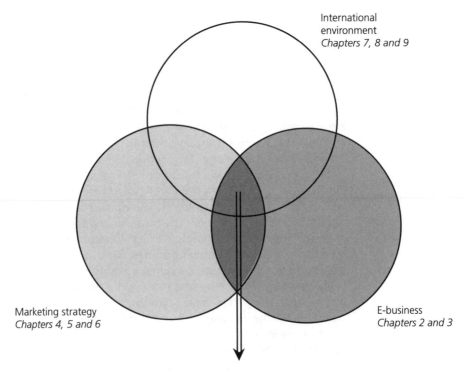

International environment
Chapters 7, 8 and 9

Marketing strategy
Chapters 4, 5 and 6

E-business
Chapters 2 and 3

International e-business marketing
Chapters 10, 11 and 12

information about the international context in which e-business is conducted. This includes differences in the legal, political and cultural contexts. Finally, at the intersection of these three domains is the practice of international e-business marketing. The last three chapters describe marketing tactics in the online environment related to product development, pricing, distribution and promotion in international markets.

Questions

1. What are transaction costs?
2. What does the statement 'the Internet expands the boundaries of the firm' mean?
3. Discuss differences in meaning between the terms 'e-business' and 'e-commerce'.
4. Does the widespread failure of pure-play dot.com companies indicate the death of B2C e-business models? Why or why not?
5. How can the Internet be used to create or help to lever intangible assets?
6. In what ways have Internet-related technologies changed the practice of marketing?
7. Is the Internet a force contributing to global standardization or specialization?

References

Coase, R. (1937) 'The nature of the firm', *Economica* 4, 386–405.

Despande, R. and Zaltman, G. (1982) 'Factors affecting the use of market research information: A path analysis', *Journal of Marketing Research* 19: 14–31.

Hamill, J. (1999) 'Internet editorial: Export guides on the net', *International Marketing Review* 15 (5): 434–6.

Hamill, J., & Gregory, K. (1997) 'Internet marketing and the internationalisation of UK SMEs', *Journal of Marketing Management* 13 (1–3): 9–28.

Huber, G. P. (1990) 'A theory of the effects of advanced information technologies and organisation design, intelligence, and decision making', *Academy of Management Review* 15 (1): 47–71.

Huff, S. L., Wade M. and Schneberger, S. (2002) *Cases in Electronic Commerce*, 2nd edn. New York: McGraw-Hill Irwin.

Laudon, K. and Traver, C. G. (2001) *E-commerce: Business, Technology Society.* Pearson: Addison-Wesley.

Mentzas, G. N. (1996) 'Team co-ordination in decision support systems', *European Journal of Operational Research* 89: 70–85.

Migliarese, P. and Paolucci, E. (1995) 'Improved communications and collaborations among tasks induced by groupware', *Decision Support Systems* 14: 237–50.

Quelch, J. A. and K. L. (1996) 'The internet and international marketing', *Sloan Management Review* spring: 60–75.

Rockart, J. F. and Short, J. E. (1989), 'IT in the 1990's: Managing organisational interdependence', *Sloan Management Review* winter: 7–17.

Sawhney, M. and Zabin, J. (2001) *The Seven Steps to Nirvana.* Maidenhead: McGraw-Hill.

Song, X. M., Neely, S. M. and Zhao, Y. (1996) 'Managing R&D – marketing integration in the new product development process', *Industrial Marketing Management* 25: 545–53.

Talvinen, J. M. (1995) 'Information systems in marketing: Identifying opportunities for new applications', *European Journal of Marketing* 29 (1): 8–26.

Williamson, O. (1975) *Markets and Hierarchies: Analysis and Antitrust Implications.* New York: Free Press.

Case Study 1 *Pac-N-Save*
Sharon Loane

Founded in 1996, Pac-N-Save Shipping & Moving Ltd of Edmonton, Alberta is a moving, shipping and freight forwarding company. Since 1996 it has grown significantly and now offers residential and commercial shipping throughout North America and overseas. Pac-N-Save estimates that 85 per cent of its markets are for residential moving services and 15 per cent for commercial shipping services. The company's market spread increases each year and it is currently estimated that 70 per cent of customers are based in Canada, 20 per cent in the USA, and 10 per cent overseas. However markets are changing, especially since the web site was redesigned. Pac-N-Save has noticed substantial growth in American markets, particularly US interstate residential shipping. Approximately 80 per cent of the requests for quotations submitted through the Internet originate in the USA or internationally.

Pac-N-Save's original business strategy did not include e-commerce. They ventured into e-commerce under the encouragement of a co-owner, who also operates a digital imaging and web development company. From his experience he saw opportunities in e-commerce for Pac-N-Save to expand markets and gain operational efficiencies. Using e-mail alone, he recognized that the company could reduce communication costs and improve the distribution speed of policy and procedures guidelines to the regional representatives promoting consistency throughout the company for core business. The company later created a web site to expand upon these operations and now views e-commerce as the main thrust of its business plan.

Pac-N-Save uses approximately 50 different inland carriers to ship their customers' goods. They use two principal methods to contract carriers and negotiate individual shipments: through their web sites or e-mail and leveraging their standard rate negotiations; and

through online freight forwarding and bidding services. Normally they use both tactics in tandem to generate a list of comparable estimates and then select the best option according to delivery time and price.

They use several sources for online freight forwarding and bidding sources. These password protected web site services are available only to registered freight forwarders and carriers who pay a membership fee. The systems are similar but slightly different. One is a database of carrier estimates, Pac-N-Save submit a query to the system. The web site then polls the database to find carriers or individual truckers that service the specified route, calculates the cost estimate and returns a collated summary of all the matching results. Other bidding systems are as sophisticated message boards in which Pac-N-Save post shipping requirements and receive estimates directly from independent truckers. These methods easily and quickly generate comparative estimates.

Early in 2000 the Pac-N-Save web site added request for quotation forms, called T-Form mailers, for their users to complete online. After only a few months the requests for quotations increased by 75–100 per week. In combination with the launch of the T-Form mailers, Pac-N-Save also published a toll free number on its web site. Since this time the phone rings constantly. This additional volume is a challenge to manage. It forces the company to become more efficient because it understands the importance of timely service.

One opportunity that came directly from its e-commerce operation was the reselling of extended freight insurance coverage. The carriers provide basic, minimal insurance for loss or damage of shipped goods, they realized that there was a gap in the market for extended coverage to insure the goods at a

▶

higher value. In response it negotiated a partnership with an insurance company to offer extended coverage to their customers through the insurance company's password protected web site. The advantage of this partnership is it provides a value-added service to their primary shipping service generating extra income.

The company operation today is much different than it was two years ago. The development of e-commerce capability extensively changed Pac-N-Save's traditional operations in supply chain management, quotation processing and internal communication. It developed a business partnership that enables it to provide a value-added service selling extended freight insurance coverage. This service would not have been possible without e-commerce. The most immediate benefit of e-commerce was increased sales levels.

The company expects it will continue to increase its number of regional representatives throughout Canada, into the USA, Mexico and overseas.

Questions

1. Is Pac-N-Save a pure-play Internet business model? Why or why not?

2. How does Pac-N-Save create value for customers? Where does its revenue come from? How does the Internet help Pac-N-Save to cut costs?

3. Is this business model sustainable in the long run? What is the e-business strategy of other larger players in this industry?

4. What are the opportunities and challenges that face Pac-N-Save as an increasing proportion of their business comes from the US, and in particular residential moves within the USA?

2

The Internet and its impact on international marketing

Learning objectives

After studying this chapter, you should be able to:

- Define the Internet and its constituent applications.

- Demonstrate familiarity with the evolution of Internet use.

- Appreciate the role of e-business in international marketing.

- Assess the incidence of e-business in world trade and its impact on different sectors.

- Recognize the advantages and disadvantages inherent in the application of e-business in international marketing.

- Differentiate forms of buyer behavior in the international online environment.

- Appreciate how e-business can influence global business strategy.

What is the Internet?

The Internet is a global network of interlinked computers operating on a standard protocol that allows information exchange. It is composed of computer networks and individual computers throughout the world connected by phone lines, satellites and other telecommunications systems (Ellsworth and Ellsworth, 1996). Table 2.1 shows the different services provided by the Internet.

The original users of the Internet were researchers in government and universities. Full commercial connection to the Internet only became available in 1990. The most popular early commercial activities on the Internet were e-mail, advertising and promotion. Until the mid-1990s, applications were mostly text based and marketing involved sending plain text messages. However, the introduction of the World Wide Web (WWW) in 1993 with its

Table 2.1   Different services of the Internet

Services of the Internet (alternate terminology)	Comparison with the 'real word'	Software used	Derived services
World Wide Web (WWW, web)	Library	Browser	File transfer protocol (FTP), mostly integrated in web sites
E-mail (e-mail)	Letter	E-mail software (often integrated in browser) or browser in the case of 'web e-mail'	Mailing list
Discussion groups (discussion forum, usenet, newsgroup)	Message board (non-real time)	Browser	
On Line Chat (IRC, Internet Relay Chat)	Discussion rooms (real time)	Normally specific software	

Source: Freeman and Perez (1986: 6) based on Pattinson and Brown (1996)

graphical interface offered new opportunities. It allowed interactive marketing to an extent not found in traditional media. This offered great potential for direct global marketing.

E-mail

From a marketing point of view, the low cost of e-mail makes it an alternative to relatively more costly telecommunications and postal systems. The ability to edit, copy and forward messages, and additional functions such as a facility to attach files and images create a multitude of possibilities for marketers. Recent developments that allow e-mails to be digitally 'signed' to prove the identity of the sender and encrypted to protect the confidentiality of the content of the message facilitate the use of e-mail for sales and the exchange of sensitive legal or financial information

E-mails are not without shortcomings, including potential loss of messages, especially in times of heavy network traffic. Losses average 1 to 2 per cent of e-mail volume. The sender may ask for a return receipt, which partly addresses this problem. Most e-mail messages contain plain text. Although it is possible to send messages in rich text format (RTF) or hyper text mark-up (HTML), many of those who receive e-mails still do not have the software to read such messages. Another deficiency is the difficulty of finding e-mail addresses. Directories of e-mail addresses are less comprehensive and less readily available than telephone numbers. The need to look up e-mail addresses is catered for by a plethora of web-based directories such as www.whowhere.com; www.bigfoot.com; www.people.yahoo.com. Finally, there is the problem of 'spammers' flooding e-mail users with unsolicited and generally untargeted mass e-mail promotional messages.

The web

The web allows the integration of multimedia features such as text, image and video, providing marketers with a full range of communication media. It is interactive in that its users can receive information and respond to it. The information is contained in web pages that can be both down loaded and edited. The standard web protocol accommodates all major languages. Other advantages include its ability to use automatic alert systems that notify registered users of a site when an opportunity becomes available. For example, travel companies can notify customers when the last-minute price of a destination drops below a given price. The web works on any hardware platform, which is cost effective and facilitates easy interconnection between systems. Networks that deliberately restrict outside access can use the same communication protocols as the WWW. Restricted access networks are 'intranets' (exclusive Internet use within an organization) or 'extranets' (restricted to specific associates of the organization). Access to the web is low cost, a presence on the web can be relatively inexpensive, and extends customer access to 24 hours a day, 7 days a week. Updating web sites is easy and the changes are immediately available to those who log on.

The web is not without its problems, including lack of reliability due to down time and sluggishness when pictures, sounds and videos are involved in the communication. These affect the speed of down loading which if too long, may cause user attrition. As a result, some companies simplify their sites (or offer text-only versions) to allow quick access. Despite its phenomenal growth, the total penetration of the web is still relatively limited, especially in developing countries and among older age cohorts. Frequent changes, updates and the perception that security is inadequate, especially when payment is involved, characterize the technology. Identification systems such as digital signatures are available, but not widely used. Finally, the web is largely a 'pull' medium that requires users to enter a web address in order to receive information or promotional messages. 'Push' technologies that deliver promotions targeted to interested users are being developed.

Adoption of the Internet

The adoption of the Internet has been fastest in countries with high gross domestic product (GDP) and in countries where English is the first language or a widely spoken second language. There have been four waves of adoption of the Internet. Table 2.2 shows these waves and their characteristics. An appreciation of these waves is necessary in order to assess the appropriateness of trading on the Internet with potential overseas partners and customers.

Wave 1

This wave began around 1993 in North America and the Nordic countries. During this period, the Internet evolved from an educational tool to a vehicle for corporate communications and transactions. The following are the characteristics of first wave societies:

Table 2.2			
The four waves of Internet development	Wave 1	The USA, Canada and the Nordics	Characterized by early adoption in universities and government in the 1980s. These countries now are among the heaviest commercial users of the technology.
	Wave 2	The rest of the European Union, Australia, New Zealand, Japan, Republic of Korea, Taiwan, Singapore, Hong Kong and Israel	Characterized by high level of private and public sector interest in developing broad information societies. Extensive commercial use, although focus on consumer applications varies widely.
	Wave 3	Developing countries across South East Asia, China, Brazil, Argentina, South Africa, Egypt, smaller island states such as Tonga, Fiji, Barbados and French Polynesia	Characterized by high levels of interest in initiating and developing business applications of online commerce.
	Wave 4	Least developed countries or other countries that deliberately shun Internet use	Characterized to date by unattractive investment environments. In some countries, there have been attempts to ban the Internet for political and social reasons.

Source: Commonwealth of Australia (1999: 8)

- advanced information societies
- clustering of information technology, telecommunications and content industries
- very high levels of Internet usage
- close cooperation on information technology issues between government, business and the general community to create national competitive strength based on information technology.

Finland has been at the forefront of the Internet since its inception due to the Ministry of Education and the Finnish University and Research Network. The government established incentives for online government and service delivery and developed a supportive domestic legal environment including recognizing digital signatures. There was an immediate flow on to the private sector and Finnish banks began to use the Internet for online delivery in 1994. This gave them an early advantage in online banking compared with most other banks around the world (Commonwealth of Australia, 1999: 103).

Wave 2

The second wave began in 1996 and involved northern Europe, North East Asia, Israel, Singapore, Hong Kong, Australia and New Zealand, and is distinguished from the first wave only by a slower uptake of the Internet for commercial use. The levels of development in these countries are varied. Some, like the UK and Germany, are virtually indistinguishable from first wave countries, while others lag behind in policy development and levels of online penetration. Based on Internet hosts per person, Australia is higher than Canada and Japan lies well behind Australia. Spain, Italy and Korea lag behind Japan. One factor could be the abundance of software in English compared with Japanese, Korean and some European languages. Local factors such as the attachment of large firms in North Asia to existing proprietary electronic data exchange (EDI) networks and the impact of existing systems such as Minitel in France (a free service with text and e-mail capabilities delivered by France Telecom to 17 million households) also affect uptake rates.

Second wave countries differ in their objectives for embracing e-business. Some see it as a vehicle to improve international commercial advantage and to access diverse new content and cultural enrichment. Others, while attracted by the international commercial advantages, wish to limit the social and political influence of the medium. For example, Singapore operates a broadband intranet offering rich locally oriented content, but licensed Internet service providers (ISPs) regulate content provided from outside the system.

Wave 3

This period began in 1998 and involved Internet use by business and social elites in a number of the more developed of the developing countries in South and South East Asia, Latin America, the Pacific Islands and the Middle East. Increasing local language content, improved telecommunications infrastructure, and increased foreign participation in both manufacturing and telecommunications influenced their adoption. These forces will eventually challenge the US-centric character of the Internet, and it will become more of a global tool for trade with a majority of users living outside the USA. The slowing of growth in Internet use in the developed world and the rapid growth in East Asia and Latin America, as well as the rapid increase in Internet hosts in a small number of transition economies such as Brazil, Czech Republic, Thailand and the United Arab Emirates, is further evidence of this change (Commonwealth of Australia, 1999: 100).

Wave 3 countries have little in common apart from a desire to improve competitiveness by using advanced technology. The governments of these countries often downplay social, moral and political aspects of the Internet in the interest of accessing online business benefits and reduce the gap between Internet 'haves' and their situation as Internet 'have-nots'.

The focus on specific business benefits reflects economic circumstances, and not the use of technology to realize productivity gains. In many of these countries, a unit of labour might cost the same or be cheaper than a computer and the ancillary support infrastructure that goes with it (Commonwealth of Australia, 1999: 113).

The transition to an information economy for most third wave countries will be difficult because there are:

- major development problems such as shortage of skills and capital and a large number of competing priorities
- often serious deficiencies in telecommunications infrastructure which is capital intensive to remedy

- problems because the business environment is geared to traditional forms of transaction and change is slow. An example is the requirement in the Philippines that a written signature must validate credit card transactions. In Russia endemic credit card fraud and lack of any legal basis for online trade impedes adoption for online selling.

Wave 4

The latest wave is just beginning, and will affect the least advanced of the developing countries. These countries lack infrastructure to support significant Internet commerce and some governments shun the Internet for political reasons. Some of these countries, however, are very interested in promoting online commodity trading, as most of their exports are commodity related. Also in countries where Internet access is controlled, illicit cross-border online trade occurs to get around the restrictions.

The 'information society' is an abstract issue for many countries with pervasive poverty. Internet security is a problem and necessary infrastructure often non-existent. A computer is only affordable for the elite as it costs from 10 to 15 times the average annual wage. Connecting to an ISP is astronomically expensive. For example, in Bangladesh 20 hours of access a month costs more than twice the average annual income (Commonwealth of Australia, 1999: 121). Some governments ban ISPs and the use of international phone lines to access them. Myanmar requires the registration of all faxes and modems not used in teaching or business, and in Laos the government screens Internet content available to subscribers, censors information exchanged and approves each person, business and piece of equipment connected to the Internet.

The incidence of e-business

E-business is a major aspect of the newest techno-economic paradigm that is related to information and communication. There have been a series of such paradigms in recent centuries, each of which involve the diffusion of new key resources and have resulted in a radical transformation of international markets. Figure 2.1 illustrates the chronology of these overlapping paradigms. The first, early mechanization, began in 1770 and lasted until about 1840. The second, involving the railway and steam power, existed from about 1820 until 1890. The third, involving electrical and heavy engineering, major utilities and financial institutions, went from about 1860 to 1940. The fourth, which has been termed 'Fordist' mass production, went from 1920 to 1990. The fifth paradigm of information and communication commenced in 1980 and is continuing.

There has been much hype surrounding e-business and its application in international marketing due to the borderless nature of the medium. After the dot.com crash in 2000, many people wondered if the rhetoric had outpaced the reality of e-business. Yet adoption of the Internet has been faster than the adoption of any other technology in history. The number of people with Internet access increased from 2.3 million in 1995 to over 600 million in 2002. As of September 2000, there were over 21 million sites on the Internet representing a growth of 180 per cent over the previous three years (Zakon, 2000).

The OECD estimates that the value of Internet commerce should reach US$1 trillion by 2005. While this value is impressive, it represents only 0.5 per cent of estimated retail turnover in OECD countries. Table 2.3 describes the global usage of the Internet in 2002. Another measure of the importance of the Internet

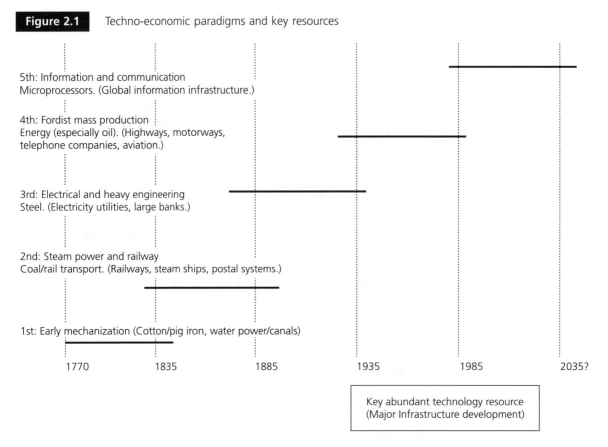

| **Figure 2.1** | Techno-economic paradigms and key resources |

Source: Adapted from Freeman and Perez (1988: 6, based on Pattinson and Brown 1996)

Table 2.3		
Key estimates of global Internet use in 2002	Users	600 to 1000 million
	PCs connected to the Internet	200 to 380 million
	Commerce conducted via the Internet	US$0.5 trillion to $1.5 trillion
	Proportion of global economy affected	1.5 to 4 per cent
	Proportion of online trade across borders	10 to 30 per cent
	Proportion of Internet users making purchases	10 to 20 per cent
	Countries affected	All but least developed

Sources: The Industry Standard (1998); International Data Corporation (1998); NUA Consulting (1998); Forrester Research (1998); Gartner Group (1998); WTO (1998, as cited in Commonwealth of Australia, 1999: 27)

Table 2.4   Worldwide e-commerce growth – online sales

	2000 $	2001 $	2002 $	2003 $	2004 $	% of total sales in 2004
Total ($ B)	657.0	1,233.6	2,231.2	3,979.7	6,789.8	8.6
North America	509.3	908.6	1,498.2	2,339.0	3,456.4	12.8
United States	488.7	864.1	1,411.3	2,187.2	3,189.0	13.3
Canada	17.4	38.0	68.0	109.6	160.3	9.2
Mexico	3.2	6.6	15.9	42.3	107.0	8.4
Asia Pacific	53.7	117.2	286.6	724.2	1,649.8	8.0
Japan	31.9	64.4	146.8	363.6	880.3	8.4
Australia	5.6	14.0	36.9	96.7	207.6	16.4
Korea	5.6	14.1	39.3	100.5	205.7	16.4
Western Europe	87.4	194.8	422.1	853.3	1,533.2	6.0
Germany	20.6	46.4	102.0	211.1	386.5	6.5
United Kingdom	17.2	38.5	83.2	165.6	288.8	7.1
France	9.9	22.1	49.1	104.8	206.4	5.0
Italy	7.2	15.6	33.8	71.4	142.4	4.3
Netherlands	6.5	14.4	30.7	59.5	98.3	9.2
Latin America	3.6	6.8	13.7	31.8	81.8	2.4

Source: Forrester Research (1998)

are the revenues from e-business. Table 2.4 shows that worldwide e-business revenues are expected to grow substantially.

The adoption of the Internet as an instrument of international business differs according to types of products and services (Table 2.5). In particular, there is increasing acceptance of Internet as the main vehicle for trading commodities, manufactured goods and financial instruments in more developed countries. The advent of cheaper, faster and more secure e-business will favour information, telecommunications, financial and personal services sectors. Tables 2.6 and 2.7 describe the differential influence of the Internet by sector.

The Internet and international marketing

The web is an alternative to 'real world' environments, not a simulation of one. Success in web-based transactions requires trust between vendor and customer and security issues still hamper the operation of electronic business. The explosion of electronic business does call into question a number of fundamental principles in international marketing. These include:

- The barriers to internationalization experienced by small and medium sized exporters (SMEs). Firm size is no longer the barrier that it has traditionally been.

| Table 2.5 | Proportion of Internet sales across borders for selected firms |

Firm	Segment and foreign market operations	Online revenue as a per cent of total	International revenue as a per cent of total revenue
CD.Now (USA)	Music	100	35
Music Boulevard (USA)	Music	100	33
Amazon (USA)	Books	100	26
Barnes and Noble (USA)	Books	1	30
NEC (Japan)	Electronic manufactured components	100	35
FastParts (USA)	Electronic components	100	30
Cisco (USA)	Computers	50	17
Dell (USA)	Computers	50	20
TOWER software (Australia)	Database management software	30	60
Sciarbus (Australia)	Shareware	100	90
1800-Flowers (USA)	Flowers	10	15 to 20
Centrebet (Australia)	Online gaming	80	60
Sabre (USA)	Travel	68	18
E*Trade (USA)	Share trading	63	3

Source: OECD (1998)

- Incremental internationalization: the Internet facilitates firms moving quickly into international markets. No longer do firms necessarily internationalize by moving from elementary modes of international behaviour to more advanced modes of international behaviour. In many cases firms move quickly into complex international strategic alliances, aided by Internet-based communication.

- Need for overseas intermediaries: it is easier to both locate overseas customers and deal directly with them, rendering intermediaries such as local agents, less necessary.

- Country screening: firms no longer have to approach international business by moving from familiar countries to those less familiar – information is more readily available and the communication medium is interactive.

The Internet's low cost allows firms with limited capital to become global marketers at an early stage of their development. This is because the Internet can significantly enhance communication with overseas customers, suppliers, agents and distributors. In essence, the Internet is a knowledge medium, a new commercial medium, and a new marketing channel where the flows are bi-directional. An essential element of e-business is connectivity: PCs connect to other PCs to form a network; networks can be local (LANs), and they can be global (as with the Internet, the term means network of networks).

Table 2.6	Sectoral implications of online technology and emerging opportunities for international trade
Information industries	• The publishing, media and printing sector will become increasingly part of the international traded economy as the converged delivery model takes hold. • Electronic book technology in which text can be downloaded over the Internet will help create higher levels of international trade in publishing material. This will complement trade in printed material through online retailing. • Webcasting provides many challenges for traditional broadcasters. Access to broadcast content by consumers will no longer be limited by radio spectrum. Offers to purchase foreign products will be more pervasive than currently. • The publishing and broadcasting of news and advertising will become more internationalized, allowing global brands to become more entrenched and lessening opportunities for censorship and regulation of content.
Telecommunications	• The sale of telecommunications services will increasingly become part of the international economy as consumers take advantage of Internet telephony and other value added telecommunication services delivered through converged delivery mechanisms. • Consumers will be able to access cheaper and more efficient telecommunication services. • The availability of telecommunication services through the Internet will encourage many carriers to invest in new technology such as ISDN and ADSL to extend the usefulness of copper wire technology. • The widespread use of the Internet in telecommunications will encourage many carriers to begin to use Internet protocols in developing new networks.
Services	• Financial and professional services will be treated internationally through the Internet. • Specialized banking, insurance, leasing, equity, derivative and superannuation products could become substantial online traded items. • Providers on online gaming and gambling services, real estate and tourism will gain new markets through the global spread of the Internet
Manufacturing	• The development of contractual manufacturing operations, build-to-order manufacturing and just-in-time inventory control will depend on the application of Internet commerce technology internally and between major trading partners. • The manufacturing sector will become more efficient through applying electronic commerce technology to improve inventory control. In some cases, this will lead to new international trading opportunities. • Automotive components, textiles, clothing and footwear, heavy engineering and processed foods will benefit from more efficient design processes and the ability to provide components for products assembled in other countries. • Internet-based design systems will increase interdependence in supply chains and create opportunities in assembly industries, components and product development.
Consumer markets	• Cross-border sales of consumer items are likely to grow strongly among countries where Internet use is highest. • Markets for mass-produced consumer items are likely to grow strongly among consumers in countries where price differentials and supply problems make online purchasing attractive. European and US merchants are likely to dominate these markets. • Niche markets in high quality textiles, clothing and footwear, and in processed foods, specialty products and health products could emerge into major opportunities

Source: Commonwealth of Australia (1999: 30)

Table 2.7	Industry sector/classification	Comment on impact
Impact of e-business on industry groups	Entertainment and hospitality	Ranked first by output in the final year of the simulation period. This sector benefits from growth in tourism exports and in consumption. Tourism exports grow strongly relative to other exports.
	Transport	This sector owes its high ranking to air transport. Air transport benefits from tourism demand.
	Communication	Cost reductions are achieved in this industry via e-commerce. Demand rises for industry outputs used to facilitate e-commerce activity.
	Banking and finance	Achieves major cost reductions via e-commerce. However, expansion of the sector is limited by low price sensitivities of demand.
	Education Health	Education increases facilitated by higher government revenue. Health expenditure increases facilitated by higher government revenue (a flow an implication of higher levels in activity).
	Food products	Adversely affected in the early part of the simulation period by real appreciation. Later, the sector's exports recover as the real exchange rate weakens. Eventually output will have a positive deviation reflecting growth in consumption.
	Other manufacturing	The output paths for most of these industries are closely related to that of investment. Industries highly exposed to import competition are adversely affected by real dollar appreciation especially in the early years of the simulation period. Industries with considerable export potential will perform well.
	IT and other equipment	Industries in this sector are influenced by a variety of factors. Export-oriented industries (such as agricultural and construction machinery) benefit from e-commerce via increased foreign awareness of their products. The other industries in the sector benefit from stronger investment and consumption, but are harmed by increased competition from imports arising from a stronger real exchange rate.
	Transport equipment	This sector is dominated by the motor vehicle industry. Output is highly sensitive to the real exchange rate. In the early part of the simulation period the industry suffers from import competition brought about by a high real exchange rate. Later, when the real exchange rate fails, the industry shows positive output deviations associated with increased activity in the economy.
	Business services	Achieves major cost reductions via e-commerce. However, expansion of the sector is limited by the strong link between business services and wholesale and retail trade.
	Wholesale and retail trade	The fall in this sector is dominated by the negative result for retail trade. Retail trade contracts as e-commerce permits traditional retailing to be bypassed.

Source: National Office for the Information Economy Report (2000, Table 3)

Characteristics

As a marketing channel, the Internet has the following characteristics:

- an ability to inexpensively store vast amounts of information at different virtual locations
- a powerful and inexpensive means of searching, organizing and disseminating such information
- interactivity and the ability to provide information on demand
- the ability to provide perceptual experiences superior to those from the printed catalogue
- can serve as a physical distribution medium for certain goods such as software
- relatively low entry and establishment costs for sellers (Peterson, Balasubramanian and Bronnenberg, 1997).

The Internet is both a communications and a market intelligence tool. As a communications tool it can help to build and maintain effective communications with foreign customers, distributors and suppliers. The Internet facilitates this by providing a low-cost method (compared with post, phone and fax) of communicating with distant markets. Not only does it transmit in text form but it can also transfer graphics and drawings at high speed. Firms are increasingly forming relationships with international customers, suppliers and agents with the support of electronic communications. Those not prepared to participate are in danger of exclusion from the new international networks. In terms of advertising and promotion, the web is an effective medium because audiences around the world can receive the message transmitted.

The information processing ability of the Internet is a market intelligence tool that acts as a link between firms and the external environment in which they operate. Effective management of information systems can be a powerful source of competitive advantage and the use of the Internet for marketing intelligence enables firms to access information about overseas markets with higher speed and at lower cost. Search engines and electronic surveys provide useful tools for obtaining information on foreign markets. Firms interested in Internet marketing can access a variety of international information sources such as online newspapers and journals, country and industry market research reports, trade lists of suppliers, agents and distributors and contacts in government.

Buyer behaviour in the online environment

There have been many surveys designed to profile Internet users. According to Monnier (1999), most of these surveys show that the typical Internet user is often male, young and has above average levels of both education and income. However, the gap is closing. As Internet penetration increases in a country, this profile expands to embrace other segments of the population. This pattern and profile does not appear to vary much from country to country.

The following sections compare buyer behaviour on the Internet with that in the traditional international marketplace. Fry and Merrilees (2001) examine adoption of innovation in 'marketspace' with that in the marketplace. Instead of the innovator, early adopter, late adopter and laggard, they argue that in marketspace, the relevant categories are e-shoppers, e-security conscious, slow adopters and e-laggards. The e-shopper segment rates the Internet high on entertainment, its usefulness for gathering information and consider themselves comfortable using the Internet. The e-laggards on the other hand are particularly worried about e-security and they tend to be very slow in adopting any new product or technology.

The Internet provides consumers with a new way of searching for information to evaluate products and make purchasing decisions. This information now spans the globe and comes from a diverse range of sources. This leads to a surfeit of information and the ability to separate information search from actual transactions more than was previously the case.

The information provided on the Internet is different in that cues such as touch and smell are not available to influence the purchasing decision. A purchaser of fruit and vegetables from an online grocer is not able to smell or feel the product before buying as would be the case in a fruit and vegetable market. The global information and transaction environment is different with e-business. This is due to the changing structure of global markets for consumer goods and services; the nature of the information search process; and the perception, interpretation and use of information by consumers.

The Internet and the consumer

Information available on the Internet changes the structure of international markets and the organization of physical infrastructure to cope with the flow of information to consumers. Instead of defining markets by political and economic boundaries and by proximity to geographic features, the Internet opens up and reconfigures markets based on Internet access, language and interests. Virtual markets are emerging based on commonality of interests between buyers and sellers and content space. The offering is 'virtual' rather than one consisting of physical or tangible components.

According to Craig, Douglas and Flaherty (2000), there are three categories of products in the Internet environment: physical products, transaction-related products and virtual products (Table 2.8).

Physical products

With physical products (e.g. cosmetics), information search can be conducted online and in many countries, but completion of the transaction either requires the consumer to go to a physical location to purchase the product or for the product to be delivered to the consumer in a given location. In this case, the final stage of the transaction relies on traditional market infrastructure and the merchant relies on physical infrastructure to deliver the goods (e.g. Amazon.com's warehouses in each major geographic region).

Table 2.8	Key dimensions	Physical products	Transaction related products	Virtual products
Internet product typology	Ease of reaching a global segment	Difficult	Moderate	Easy
	Degree of product standardization	Varies	Moderate	Customized
	Role of information	Complement	Enhancement	Equivalent
	Role of infrastructure	Infrastructure constrained	Conforms to infrastructure	Unconstrained by infrastructure

Source: Craig, Douglas and Flaherty (2000: 30)

Transaction related products

With transaction related products (services such as rental cars, air tickets), information search is conducted online but actual consumption is tied to a given time and location. Although delivery of a physical product is not involved, delivery at the time and location requested requires organizational infrastructure such as at the airport check-in desk.

Virtual products

Virtual products (such as music, software, news broadcasts) are digital and there are no physical constraints on their delivery or consumption.

These categories of Internet products differ from each other in a number of ways (Craig, Douglas and Flaherty 2000):

- *Ease of reaching global segments*. This depends on availability of a communications infrastructure to reach the segments wherever they are, a distribution infrastructure to make the product available to customers and the availability of the physical infrastructure necessary to make use of the product (e.g. electricity). Virtual products reduce these problems, providing the computing infrastructure is available. With transaction related products, this is less the case, and physical products remain tied to the market infrastructure.

- *Degree of product standardization*. Unlike physical products, virtual products can easily be adapted to customer groupings and even to individual requirements (e.g. Musicmaker.com creates customized CDs). The Internet will influence the appropriate degree of standardization for transactional and physical products, but opportunities for standardization are likely to be more restricted than in the traditional international marketplace.

- *Role of information*. For virtual products, information is the product and attributes such as price, size and features can be readily determined over the Internet. For transactional products, the Internet provides product enhancement by providing access to information from anywhere in the world (e.g. digital photographs of the appearance of a hotel room). With physical products, the Internet complements information consumers already have about the product and enables a more systematic and detailed evaluation.

These differences are important in structuring international markets for Internet supplied goods and services, in assessing how far consumers can search across national and linguistic boundaries for information and in determining how customers perceive and interpret information.

Example   *Second place and coming-up fast!*

According to Nielsen/Net Ratings, China has the second largest at-home Internet population in the world at the end of April 2002. About 56.6 million people live in households with an Internet connection. While this number is large, it represents only about 5 per cent of households. The country with the largest population of Internet users is the United States with about 166 million people. Japan holds the third place with 51.3 million. The fact that only 36 per cent of homes have a fixed telephone line underscores the vast opportunity that still waits in China. The demographics of Internet users in China resemble that of early users in the United States. Men aged 16–34 dominate Internet access, with 53 per cent accessing the Internet from home, 27 per cent from Internet cafés and 24 per cent from work.

Source: Adapted from ACNielsen/Net Ratings, Quarter 1, (2002)

Another limitation is the willingness of consumers to use the Internet. This will affect segmentation of customers when the Internet is the vehicle for communication and ordering. Many variables, including age, influence this willingness (Table 2.9).

McKinsey Consulting has conducted research to identify segments of online customers. Their segments are as follows:

- *Simplifiers*: spend little time online but account for half of all online transactions. They are experienced Internet users who seek convenience.
- *Surfers*: a small segment that spends considerable time on the Internet. They enjoy novel approaches and controlling the transaction process.

Table 2.9

Internet usage by age group

Age group	Using the Internet %	Bought online during past 12 months %
18–24	73	25
25–34	62	39
35–44	55	34
45–54	55	43
55	36	29

Source: Bristol Group (2000)

- *Bargainers*: classic price shoppers that are excited by the search. The site must appeal on both rational and emotional levels to this group.
- *Connectors*: newcomers to the Internet who use it to connect to others via chat facilities, etc. They seek reassurance when using the Internet.
- *Routiners*: creatures of habit, they visit few sites but spend considerable time at each one.
- *Sportsters*: spend little time online but visit sites mostly focused on sports and entertainment.

Table 2.10 compares these segments.

The Internet and the search process

The Internet extends both the depth and the breadth of the search process by consumers. This is because in addition to company sites, consumers can also access product category sites, retailer sites and consumer-dominated sites such as bulletin boards and chat rooms. With the Internet, the initiative in the search process shifts to the consumer resulting in a topic focused rather than a sequential process-oriented search. The search process is timelier and the costs lower than acquiring information from conventional sources.

The information environment on the Internet differs from that in the marketplace because the majority of sites is located in Western countries, and in general reflect the conventions and symbols of Western culture. As a result, there may be difficulty in both interpretation and retention of information, where communication crosses cultural and linguistic boundaries. This affects the use of the Internet as an international promotion vehicle. The Internet is currently a less culturally sensitive medium than alternative media. Specific areas of concern are as follows:

- *Language*. There is a predominance in the use of English on the Internet (57 per cent of users are English speakers). This implies that non-English

	Table 2.10					
	Segment	Percentage of Internet users	Hours active/ month	Unique domains accessed/ month	Pages accessed/ month	Percentage buying
Online consumer segments	Simplifiers	29	7.1	62	1,021	87
	Surfers	8	30.2	224	4,852	71
	Bargainers	8	8.3	43	1,295	64
	Connectors	36	5.7	54	791	42
	Routiners	15	8.2	32	624	50
	Sportsters	4	7.1	47	1,023	51
	Average	100	9.8	74	1,398	61

Source: McKinsey Marketing Practice, *All Visitors Are Not Created Equal* (April 2000)

speakers have access to a more limited range of information, although there are signs that a global Internet vocabulary is starting to emerge. Use of other languages is impeded by their having a number of spoken dialects (e.g. Mandarin is the written form of Chinese but there are many spoken forms) and the meaning conveyed in the spoken form varying by tonality. Table 2.11 compares the number of people speaking a language with the number of Internet sites in that language.

- *Information misinterpretation.* There is greater scope for misinterpretation and miscommunication of messages on the Internet, especially by non-native English speaking or non-Western consumers.

- *Information credibility.* As 'word-of-mouse' replaces 'word-of-mouth', it is much more difficult to assess the objectivity or biases of the presenter of the information.

- *Product cues.* On the Internet, consumers face truncated cues and the absence of olfactory and sensory cues. This leads to a greater reliance on objective cues such as price and product description. The Internet conveys the later ('digital cues') whereas the former ('non-digital cues') are not communicated on the Internet.

Differences in buyer behaviour in the global electronic environment

In traditional marketplace models, cultural factors explain many geographic variations in behaviour. These factors play a smaller role in virtual markets. In marketspace, cyber culture dominates and local culture acts as a contingency variable that mediates behaviour. Further, information is acquired from geographic locations that are separate from the place in which the resulting transaction will occur. Some related international issues for consumers are as follows:

- *Diffusion of innovation.* Geographic proximity will no longer be as important since the Internet provides a vehicle to communicate the latest developments and a channel to deliver digital products.

Table 2.11	Population speaking (millions)	%	Internet sites (millions)	%
Internet penetration by language				
Mandarin	1,025	35	9.9	6.6
English	497	17	129.0	85.0
Hindi	476	16	–	0.0
Spanish	409	14	9.6	6.4
Russian	279	9	1.4	1.0
Arabic	235	8	0.95	<1.0
Total	2,921	100	150.85	100.0

Source: Adapted from Craig, Douglas and Flaherty (2000: 31)

- *Complexity of evaluations.* Consumers have to evaluate stimuli and make choices based on heterogeneous and often unfamiliar cues (e.g. does the hotel stars rating system mean the same in all countries?).
- *Country of origin effect.* The role of national culture in the formation of values and behavioural norms is likely to decline in importance because of increased exposure to information from other countries. Country of origin will become a less salient cue.
- *Opinion leaders.* Models focusing on the role of personal influence are no longer likely to apply to the same extent. With the proliferation of chat rooms and bulletin boards, the role of such influence becomes more diffuse and depersonalized.

With the Internet, the degree of consumer involvement in the purchase process becomes less and the distinction between high and low involvement goods is not as meaningful. Another factor is that currently consumers using the Internet are different from consumers that do not (in terms of demographics and innovation adoption). This has implications for international market segmentation.

Advantages and disadvantages of applying e-business to international marketing

Because of the unevenness of Internet adoption by country and by sector, there are limitations on its use as a vehicle for international marketing. In deciding whether to undertake international marketing via the Internet, there are a number of factors to consider. These can be categorized into advantages and disadvantages of undertaking international business online. The advantages include being perceived as a firm at the leading edge of the sector in which the firm is involved, facilitation in acquiring components and material from global sources and increased operating efficiency and consequent cost savings. Other benefits are being able to access information on a global basis, improved ability to locate new leads and increase the conversion rate of quotations into firm orders, convenience for clients and access to a new marketing medium.

The major disadvantages relate to the costs of setting up for and operating online, ability for one's competitors to gather data on you from the site, security issues such as hackers, nuisance factors such as junk mail and efficiency factors such as viruses and misuse by employees. In addition it is often difficult to quantify the benefits, the need to keep the site continually updated and the costs of technology and training.

The Internet and infrastructure

The information economy places a premium on the ability to create and trade intellectual property. This in turn depends on the availability of affordable education and training without which a nation's firms will either not adopt electronic business or use it cursorily.

Computer literacy influences the speed of adoption of electronic business in international marketing and electronic business requires an excellent telecommunications infrastructure to operate effectively. This includes PC ownership levels. High levels of PC ownership facilitate Internet access, though Internet cafés can partly offset low levels of ownership. Access on an affordable basis favours developed over developing countries. Countries without this essential infrastructure will miss international business opportunities arising from the Web.

Attributes of the Internet in international marketing

The Internet reduces the impact of time and distance on marketing goods and services overseas. It creates efficiencies in transport and distribution that reduce overhead costs of international trade and these efficiencies make internationally traded goods and services more competitive.

Federal Express (FedEx) dramatically increased the efficiency of parcel delivery by using an Internet-based parcel pick-up and tracking system. This reduces the number of customer telephone inquiries by one million per month. Electronic systems now initiate 68 per cent of all parcel pick-ups. In some cases, Federal Express collects taxes on cross-border shipments of merchandise, creating new opportunities for it to warehouse and ship merchandise on behalf of online traders (OECD, 1998)

By providing a standardized way for businesses to communicate across national boundaries, electronic business reduces the language barrier in international marketing. It also acts as an important tool for gathering and distributing information on international markets and yields efficiencies in processing payments and improving cash flows. The Internet displays any digital item in front of an international audience and creates a so-called 'frictionless' environment for electronic business. It creates a borderless virtual business platform on which suppliers, customers, competitors and other network partners can interact without going through pre-defined channels in the value chain and members of the business network can bypass traditional interaction patterns and form virtual value chains.

Finally, the Internet enables efficient communication with international trading partners. Ford Motor Company installed an intranet across 120,000 workstations in offices and factories across the globe. It reduces the time needed to develop new cars from components manufactured in different countries from 36 to 24 months. Intranets boost productivity in various ways:

- increasing access to common databases
- linking research and development teams around the world in real time
- allowing managers to debate policy directions via video conferencing at a fraction of the cost of attending international workshops
- using video-based systems to train staff in ways that meet their needs, as well as the firm's (Commonwealth of Australia, 1999).

Market penetration issues

The Internet helps smaller firms to access international markets, as it is a cost-effective way for them to trade across international borders. This is because the

Internet overcomes barriers to international marketing usually encountered by small firms such as psychic distance, geographical reach and the costs of researching and doing business at a distance. Because of the Internet, small firms are able to achieve more rapid internationalization and a competitive advantage unrelated to their size. Specifically, with the Internet, scale economies are no longer as important, global advertising by competitors will become less of a barrier to entry and small companies offering niche products will be able to find a critical mass of customers. For small and medium sized exporters (SMEs) a well-designed web site is an attractive, low-cost method of sales promotion to global customers. However, the site needs effective marketing via other media in order to ensure a large number of 'hits'.

Electronic business provides SMEs with the potential to establish small business networks that pool information, share customer orders and collaborate on projects. One initial result of Internet use is that it may influence the selection of countries as firm targets for its initial overseas entry. De facto use of English and the issue of infrastructure are likely to result in targeting the 30 or so developed countries first. In the longer term, the use of the Internet in international marketing is likely to depend increasingly on ability to exploit potential markets where English is not the first language and which are still at the developing stage of Internet use.

The information superhighway

The information superhighway is the concept of a global, high capacity network that will underpin the huge information market. As information can equate to power, the speed at which business can obtain information and get it to a customer may determine success or failure. Nations are contemplating or actively funding national information superhighways in order to improve national competitiveness. One outstanding example is Singapore, which is fully 'wired'. The information superhighway is, however, more than a high-speed mechanizing force as it can fundamentally reshape the way business in undertaken. It can also enhance competitive advantage by delivering increased productivity, reducing both product development cycles and marketing life cycles, and facilitating redesign and re-engineering of the workplace.

Effective management of the information superhighway requires managers to decide whether information is a utility or a strategic weapon within their firm. It affects the disparity between the 'haves' and the 'have-nots. This disparity on a national basis in the new millennium will be a matter of information accessibility rather than just national income.

Underpinning the information superhighway is the telecommunications infrastructure. This platform has revolutionized information collection in a variety of fields. One example is that of airlines, which through their reservations and ticket clearing houses can capture huge amounts of information to study usage, assess financial position and marketing effectiveness on a daily basis. Table 2.12 shows some of the typical applications of information technology.

Table 2.12	Business activity	IT applications
Typical applications of information technology	Advertising	World Wide Web (WWW), e-mail, and fax with client's agreement
	Sales	WWW, telesales (call centres)
	Sales support	Online information services, multimedia
	Customer profiling	Networked client-server databases
	Ordering/invoicing	Electronic data interchange (EDI)
	Payment	Electronic funds transfer/electronic cash
	Customer support	Help desk, e-mail, WWW, fax, bulletin boards, online information services
	Purchasing	Public online information services, WWW, JIT
	Meeting /discussions	Voice and data calls, video-conferencing
	Messaging	Voicemail, e-mail, data pagers, wireless applications
	Answering routine enquiries	Interactive voice response (IVR) systems, fax, WWW
	Project work	Voice and data calls, fax, e-mail, groupware, intranet
	Recruitment	WWW, newsgroups
	Document storage and retrieval	Combined document image and electronic document databases, intranet
	Document distribution	File transfer, e-mail, fax, WWW, intranet
	Software distribution	File transfer, WWW, bulletin boards
	Research and development	Online information services, WWW, virtual conferences, special interest groups

Source: Downey, Boland and Walsh (1998)

The Internet and global business strategy

The international forces that drive firms to use the Internet in their international marketing activities cause them to develop specific strategies that differ from those they have traditionally used when conducting international marketing in the global marketplace.

Drivers of Internet adoption in international marketing

Any firm that establishes a site on the Internet could automatically become a multinational company (MNC). Existing MNCs tend to adopt what Quelch and Klein (1996) term the 'information to transaction model' (i.e. they offer information to address the needs of existing customers). According to Quelch and Klein, start-up companies on the other hand tend to adopt the 'transaction to information' model (i.e. they begin with the transaction and use the medium to build brand image, secure repeat orders, etc.). Figure 2.2 illustrates the two models. Whichever of these two models is used, the specific functions

Figure 2.2

Evolutionary paths
of a web site

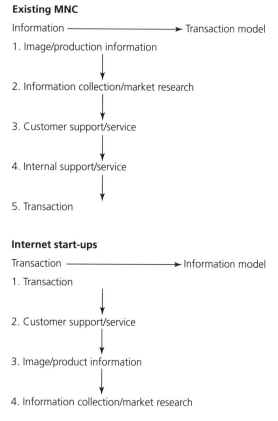

Existing MNC

Information ————————————➤ Transaction model

1. Image/production information

2. Information collection/market research

3. Customer support/service

4. Internal support/service

5. Transaction

Internet start-ups

Transaction ————————————➤ Information model

1. Transaction

2. Customer support/service

3. Image/product information

4. Information collection/market research

Source: Quelch and Klein (1996: 63)

embodied in the web site need to generate revenue or reduce costs. Figure 2.3 shows that the drivers fall into four quadrants.

Quadrant 1 (internal customer focus/cost reduction) This applies to companies that that use the web as a communications tool. They provide customer services in the domestic market and just happen to attract international traffic as well.

Quadrant 2 (internal customer focus/revenue generation) Firms in this quadrant have a similar domestic focus to companies in quadrant one but also offer transactions online. Internationally this enables the firm to reach customers who may be inaccessible via other media.

Quadrant 3 (external customer focus/cost reduction) This quadrant includes firms whose primary motivation for having a web site is attracting an international audience whose involvement benefits all users because of the international scope of operations

Quadrant 4 (external customer focus/revenue generation) These firms go further than those in quadrant three by offering transactions worldwide. Such

Figure 2.3		Primary business impact	
	Focus	Cost reduction	Revenue generation
Drivers of Internet business models	Internal customer	Technical, legal, and administrative support Database management Internal research Company information	Marketing and sales Support/information
	External customer	Customer service transactions	Product information Promotions Database development Market research Transactions

Source: Quelch and Klein (1996: 64)

transactions involve matching buyers and sellers. Global value adding can occur whether companies are targeting existing customers and providing service or attracting new customers.

Impact of the Internet on international marketing variables

When adopting the Internet for international marketing, modifications will be required to marketing mix variables. The Internet will affect the application of marketing mix variables to international markets in a number of ways.

Pricing

Prices can be customized more easily in relation to the consumer's profile and needs, but any artificial difference for satisfying the same need across countries is unlikely to be sustainable. The Internet is likely to lead to increasing standardization of prices across borders and to a narrowing of price differentials due to customer awareness of prices in different countries.

Distribution channels

With the Internet, fewer intermediaries are needed in the worldwide distribution system and less working capital is likely to be tied up in inventory. However, intermediaries can perform a different mix of services made necessary by the Internet. The new role of the intermediary is less likely to lie in handling the physical distribution of goods but rather in the collection, collation, interpretation and dissemination of vast amounts of information.

Creation of new markets

New opportunities exist for firms to make markets by assisting buyers and sellers to locate each other, negotiate terms of trade and in some cases, actually execute transactions. Electronic auctions that create new markets progressively advise sellers as buyers post bids.

New product diffusion

New product announcements on the Internet will spawn immediate demand, and this will mean that immediate availability of goods will become more important. Slow 'test as you go' rollouts from one country to another, will become less common.

Customization

There will still be a need for local adaptation and customization. The ability of the Internet to acquire demographic and purchasing profiles of customers will lead to further customization.

Links between global drivers and the Internet

Feeney and Willcocks (1998) argue that there is a strong link between the forces that drive globalization and the Internet. They attribute this to information technology (IT) having the potential to overcome limits of geography and time and the ambition of global business to harness its worldwide technical resources. The Internet facilitates the coordination of purchasing activities to achieve economies of scale, and provides a coherent response to global customers and is straightforward. This is why global businesses have invested heavily in IT.

However, there is dispute about this link. If IT is a panacea, then why do global business executives spend so much time in airplanes? Why does the volume of useless e-mails bog them down? Why are companies often unable to realize productivity gains from their IT investments? This may be because in some firms IT is not properly used and therefore supports existing activities rather than replaces them. As a result, it adds to workload rather than reducing it. For the successful global firm, management processes need to be redesigned to incorporate IT at its centre, rather than merely add IT to the periphery.

Example	*The future*

Jim Bloomfield, CEO of News Corporation's radio and television broadcasting division, believes that when digital TV begins in Australia his company will revolutionize the business world. He says that digital TV will allow convergence to take place and it will permit the eventual fall of international borders. Convergence, which is the merging of computing, telecommunications and entertainment, will combine the two 'killer' communications applications of the twentieth century – television and e-mail – and push the information age into every Australian living room. It will make redundant regulations covering issues such as cross-media and foreign ownership. The reality is that convergence has not yet happened and few viewers in either the USA or Europe have their set boxes or digital monitors connected to a modem. This is because most people regard TV as an entertainment medium and the Internet as an information or shopping tool. Business is developing technologies to blend the two such as high-speed modems, web-TV and datacasting, but to date consumers do not want TV and the Internet to come through the one box.

Source: Adapted from 'Stand by for the digital TV revolution', *BRW*, 7 May (1999: 77)

Questions

1. Why has e-business been adopted in such a short period compared with other techno-economic paradigms?
2. How will the impact if the Internet on communication change the conduct of international marketing?
3. Why will doing business via the Internet in some countries be more difficult than in others?
4. What are the immediate effects of the Internet on international marketing?
5. How does the Internet reduce the traditional disadvantages faced by small and medium sized exporters (SMEs)?

References

Bristol Group (2000) *E-Business as the Speed of Like*, March, www.bristol.com.

Commonwealth of Australia (1999) 'Creating a Clearway on the New Silk Road – International Business and Policy Trends In Internet Commerce', Camberra: Commonwealth of Australia, pp. 8, 24, 27, 30

Craig, C. S., Douglas, S. P. and Flaherty, T. B. (2000) 'Information access and internationalization – the internet and consumer behavior in international markets', *Proceedings of the eCommerce and Global Business Forum*, 17–19 May, Santa Cruz, CA: Accenture Institute for Strategic Change, pp. 30–31.

Downey, R., Boland, S. and Walsh, P. (1998) *Communications Technology Guide for Business*, Boston: Artech House.

Ellsworth, J. H., and Ellsworth, M. V. (1996) *Marketing on the Internet – Multimedia Strategies for the WWW*, New York: Wiley.

Freeman, C. and Perez, C. (1988) 'Structural crises of adjustment, business cyles and investment behaviour, in G. Dosi, C. Freeman, R. Nelson, G. Silverberg, and L. Soete (eds) *Technical Change and Economic Theory*, London: Pinter, pp. 41–57.

Fry, M. L. and Merrilees, B. (2001) 'Early adopters of e-shopping: Innovators vs slow adopters', Proceedings of the World Marketing Congress, 27–30 June, University of Cardiff.

Forrester Research (1998) www.forrester.com

Gartner Group. (1998) www.gartner.com

Hamill, J. and Gregory, K. (1997) 'Internet marketing and the internationalisation of UK SMEs', *Journal of Marketing Management*, 13 (1–3): 9–28.

International Data Corporation (1998) www.idc.com.

McKinsey Marketing Practice (2000) *All Visitors are not Created Equally*, www.mckinsey.com.

Moen, O. and Servais, P. (2002) 'Born global or gradual global? Examining the export behavior of small and medium-sized enterprises', *Journal of International Marketing* 10 (3): 49–72.

Monnier, P. D. (1999) *Cybermarketing: A Guide for Managers in Developing Countries*, Geneva: International Trade Centre.

National Office of the Information Economy Australia (2000) *E-commerce – Beyond 2000*, www.noie.gov.au/projects/information_economy, Table 3.

Nguyen, T. (2001) 'A study of the internet and the internationalization of firms in transitional markets', Unpublished PhD thesis, University of Technology, Sydney.

NUA Consulting (1998) www.nua.ie

Organization for Economic Cooperation and Development (OECD) (1998) *Social and Economic Impacts of Electronic Commerce*, Paris: OECD.

Pattinson, H. and Brown, L. (1996) 'Metamorphosis in marketspace – paths to new industries in the emerging electronic marketing environment', *Irish Marketing Review* 9: 55–67.

Peterson, R. A., Balasumramanian, S. and Bronnenberg, B. J. (1997) 'Exploring the implications of the internet for consumer marketing', *Journal of the Academy of Marketing Science* 25 (4): 329–46.

Plumley, D. J. (2000) 'Global eCommerce – The market, challenges & opportunities', *Browne Global Solutions* January: 4.

Poon, S. and Jevons, C. (1997) 'Internet-enabled international marketing: a small business network perspective, *Journal of Marketing Management* 13 (1–3): 29–42.

Quelch, J. A. and Klein, L. R. (1996) 'The internet and international Marketing', *Sloan Management Review* spring: 60–75.

Samiee (1998) 'Exporting and the internet: A conceptual perspective', *International Marketing Review* 15 (5): 413–26.

Schlegelmilch, B. and Sinkovics, R. (1998) 'Viewpoint: marketing in the information age – can we plan for an unpredictable future', *International Marketing Review* 15 (3): 162–70.

The Industry Standard. (1998), www.thestandard.com

USA Today (2000), November 21, p. 2b.

World Trade Organization. (1998), 'The Role of the WTO in Internet Commerce', *World Trade Organization*, Geneva.

Zakon, R. H. (2000) *Hobbes' Internet Timeline v5.2*, http://info.isoc.org/guest/zakon/internet/history/HIT.html.

Case Study 2 *Southcorp Wines: Using e-commerce to enter Taiwan*
Shane Huang and Richard Fletcher

Introduction

Southcorp Wines (www.southcorp.com.au/) is Australia's largest producer of table, fortified and sparkling wines, contributing approximately 30 per cent of Australian domestic and international wine sales by value. It is a global premium wine company operating in five countries and producing wine in three countries. Almost 45 per cent of its revenue comes from international sales. The company ranks as one of the ten largest wine companies in the world.

Southcorp's vision is to be a global premium wine company with a presence in all of the major wine growing regions in Australia and in a select number of strategically important premium wine growing regions overseas. In pursuit of this strategy, in the early 1990s, Southcorp Wines established offices in key international locations including London (to serve Europe), Monterey (to serve the Americas), Auckland (to serve New Zealand) and Singapore (to serve the Asia-Pacific).

Southcorp and Taiwan

The first issue for investigation, is whether a market for wine exists in Taiwan. A broad indication can be obtained from the statistics. In 1998, Taiwan consumed 113.3 million dozen units of alcoholic beverages, and 80 per cent of these came from local producers.[1]

Australia is the third largest source of imported wine in Taiwan wine behind USA and France (Table 2.13).[2]

The tariff rate for imported alcoholic beverages is 50 per cent for Australian

Table 2.13	Country	Value (AU$)
Value of wine imported to Taiwan	France	82m
	USA	15m
	Australia	4.5m
	Whole segment	125m

▶

companies.[3] Taiwan does not produce significant quantities of wine, relying on imports from other countries to meet demand.

At present, Southcorp does not have an office in Taiwan and all business activities are controlled and managed by its office in Singapore. In Taiwan, its products are sold to local importers who are responsible for the marketing the wine to the public. Southcorp does not have any direct contact with the public in this market. Southcorp believes that sales to this market can be improved. However, they are reluctant to commit extensive resources to develop the market. Southcorp is considering use of the Internet as a relatively inexpensive way of increasing their penetration of the market.

Southcorp has commissioned a study of two major international Internet retail operations to see what elements of their success might apply to the marketing of its wines in Taiwan. The operations were Amazon.com and Duck Head. Some of the reasons underlying the success of these companies that attracted the attention of Southcorp include:

- the ability to offer a wider range of items than the traditional retail outlet
- the ability to service a greater number of customers than traditional outlets
- the ability to deliver large volumes of information to customers
- avoidance of major expenses of retailing (i.e. sales persons salaries and store rentals)
- ability to combat situations where profit margins are low or under threat
- convenience of 24-hour shopping, 7 days a week without having to pay overtime or penalty rates.

The second issue to be investigated is whether Southcorp can create an Internet operation in Taiwan and, if so, whether it is likely to provide the same advantages as were enjoyed by Amazon and Duck Head? This involves an assessment of the extent to which e-retailing exists in Taiwan and how widespread is the ownership of the necessary infrastructure for consumers to access the web.

The International Development Corporation (IDC) predicts that e-commerce profits will reach US$325 billion in the Asia-Pacific region by 2003 and e-commerce profits will reach US$28 billion in Taiwan by 2003. The IDC estimates that the number of Internet users would reach 57 million in the Asia-Pacific region by the end of 2003, 4.35 million of whom will be in Taiwan. (This compares with 8 million in Australia, Southcorp's domestic market.)

Currently, 75 per cent of Taiwanese companies use computers and slightly more than half of this use the Internet, giving a company usage of the Internet of around 40 per cent. According to research,[4] 25 per cent of Internet users in Taiwan will use online shopping in 2000. The following reasons were offered as reasons by people not interesting in shopping via the Internet: it is not secure (33.2 per cent); it does not have the same feeling as real world shopping (27.6 per cent); uncertainty as to quality (20.9 per cent); online shopping is not reliable (11.7 per cent); unsatisfied with the delivery schedule (6.6 per cent).

The majority of Taiwanese online shoppers spend around AU$35 per month (under AU$50, 66 per cent; AU$50–250, 30 per cent; AU$250–500, 3 per cent; above AU$500, 1 per cent.[5] Research shows that 40 per cent of online shoppers are female, but their cumulative shopping expense is greater than for males. The reasons for females shopping online are convenience (57 per cent), greater product information (43 per cent) and discount prices (31 per cent).[6] The primary motivations for online shoppers in Taiwan to visit and purchase products online are:

- assurance that the privacy of personal information supplied would be protected and not passed on to third parties
- the web site provides a secure shopping environment

- technical support is available when required
- the web site content is innovative
- there is on-time delivery of the purchased product.

It was found that people that do not shop online might be persuaded to do so if they could be assured of the protection of the personal information (69.4 per cent), if online shopping offered more discounts (65 per cent), and if goods can be changed or refunds obtained in real world shop (28 per cent).[7]

Given the information at hand, Southcorp had to make a decision as to whether their proposed strategy of developing the Taiwan market further using the Internet was feasible.

Questions

1. Identify the crucial elements responsible for the success of Amazon.com. Which of these elements might likely also apply to Southcorp?

2. What are the benefits of online versus real world shopping for wine?

3. What are the likely benefits of e-commerce for Southcorp?

4. Can Southcorp adopt e-commerce as new marketing channel strategy in the Taiwanese market?

5. What segments would be best for Southcorp to target using the Internet?

6. Given Southcorp's range of brands and diversity of operational locations, what strategic approach would you adopt for the Taiwanese market?

Notes

1 Statistical department, Directorate General of customs, Ministry of Finance, ROC.
2 Statistical department, Directorate General of customs, Ministry of Finance, ROC.
3 Customs import tariff, Classification of import–export commodity of ROC.
4 www.chinatimes.com.tw (15/7/1999).
5 www.findorg.tw
6 www.cw.com.tw
7 www.find.org.tw
8 www.find.org.tw

3 The Internet and the e-value chain

Learning objectives

After studying this chapter, you should be able to:

- Appreciate the difference between the physical value chain and the international e-business value chain.

- Identify ways in which the international information chain operates.

- Appreciate how globalization operates in the Internet environment.

- Recognize different ways in which the Internet can be used to reach customer segments.

- Differentiate between e-business as a paradigm shift and e-business as a technology change.

This chapter explores how the physical value chain differs from the virtual value chain in the international business environment as this has consequences for globalization using the medium of electronic business. A discussion about using the Internet to reach customers in international markets follows. The conclusion is that e-business is not a new paradigm, but rather an additional vehicle for the conduct of international marketing.

The virtual value chain in the international environment

In this section, the elements of the value chain are described and the concept of a value chain in an international e-business context is evaluated. The role of information in the international e-business value chain is considered, as is the concept of 'netchising'.

Value chain issues

The value chain describes a series of value adding activities that connect a company's supply side (raw materials, inbound logistics, production processes) with its demand side (outbound logistics, marketing and sales). By analysing the stages of a value chain, managers can redesign their internal and external processes to improve efficiency. Information is the 'life blood' of the business process.

The physical value chain treats information as a supporting element of the value adding process, not as the source of value itself. The physical value chain differs from the virtual value chain, which places more emphasis on the role of information. The virtual value chain is a realm where products and services exist as digital information delivered through information-based channels. Here the value adding steps are 'virtual' in that they are performed through and with information.

Often the physical and virtual value chains exist side by side. An example of this is the use of the voicemail service offered by telephone companies. This involves both hardware and the purchase of an electronic answering service from the phone company. Another example is airlines that now sell tickets in both the marketplace (travel agents and ticket sales at airports) and marketspace (online travel sites). In many cases, the virtual value chain has its origins in the physical value chain. This is the case with the implementation of Just-in-Time (JIT) and Total Quality Management (TQM) business processes, both of which have had the effect of increasing the dependency of client companies on their suppliers.

Physical or virtual value chain?

The goal of the firm is to maximize value to its stakeholders (e.g. clients, shareholders, employees, etc.). To achieve this goal, a firm should only use elements of e-business that suit its objectives. This leads to the question 'Which elements of the value chain should be undertaken online?' Figure 3.1 illustrates the basic differences between the physical and virtual value chains.

In the context of a business-to-consumer (B2C) setting, some activities are more appropriate to be undertaken online than are others. Table 3.1 (p. 53) provides examples. In a business-to-business setting (B2B) there are different considerations. For example, online payments are not as likely to be required and the technical situation is simpler. In a B2B environment, it typically makes sense to undertake the following online: broadcast information, request additional information and solicit replies, take orders, confirm orders, notify shipping arrangements and provide after sales advice and service (Monnier, 1999).

Adoption of value adding activities

Companies tend to adopt value adding information activities in three stages. These are:

1. *Visibility.* This involves the use of large-scale information systems to coordinate activities in the physical value chain.

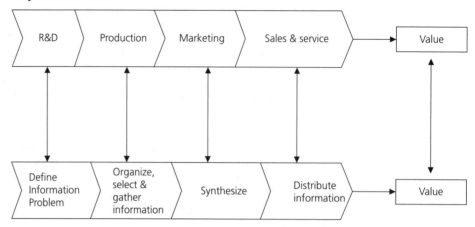

Figure 3.1

The virtual value chain in relation to the physical value chain

Source: Hollensen (2001)

2. *Mirroring capability.* Mirroring is the substitution of virtual activities for physical ones and the creation of a parallel value chain in marketspace. This leads to activities that shift value adding activities from the physical to the virtual value chain (i.e. can something be done more efficiently in 'marketspace' than in 'place'?). This has implications when scale economies do not apply, as is often the case in services marketing.

3. *New customer relationships.* These draw on the flow of information to deliver value to customers in new ways. The operation of parallel physical and virtual value chains enables firms to deliver value to their customers in both 'place' and 'marketspace', and to create marketspace-based relationships with customers.

There are five steps in the virtual value chain: gathering, organizing, selecting, synthesizing and distributing information. These value adding steps allow companies to identify customers' desires more effectively and fulfil them more efficiently. This happens, for example, when a car manufacturer shifts its R&D from the physical to the virtual value chain. In so doing, it can engage customers in the new product development process wherever they are located around the world. Whereas the physical value chain is linear (a sequence of activities with defined inputs and outputs), the virtual value chain is non-linear (a matrix of potential inputs and outputs that can be accessed and distributed by a wide variety of channels).

International value chains

Plumley (2000) created a series of diagrams that illustrate differences between the physical value chain, the e-business value chain and the international e-business value chain (Figures 3.2–3.4). Figure 3.2 shows a physical value chain.

| Table 3.1 | Which part of the value chain should be done online? |

Element of the value chain	Online or offline?	Comments
1. Information broadcast (i.e. electronic catalogue)	Online	Here online has a very low cost. However, traditional means (e.g. print documents) are often necessary to generate some basic confidence.
2. Request for additional information and corresponding replies	Online	E-mail or electronic feedback forms are very effective. In addition, a mailing list of potential clients can easily be built.
3. Act of selling (i.e. convincing people to buy)	Offline	Should mostly occur offline, including by person-to-person contacts.
4. Order taking (i.e. transmission of order taking data except sensitive data)	Online	online order taking is often very efficient, especially if processes are automated and even integrated.
5. Transmission of data regarded as sensitive (i.e. credit card details)	For the time being offline, soon online	Since safety is currently (erroneously) deemed to be insufficient, offline transmissions (i.e. by fax, phone or 'snail' mail) are often more effective.
6. Verification of customers liability limit/solvency ('authorization')	Online or offline	As far as credit cards are concerned, online (in real time) is very efficient for large numbers of orders but it requires a still somewhat uncommon infrastructure, especially in developing countries.
7. Address verification	Online or offline	As far as credit cards are concerned, online (in real time) is very practical (as long as the corresponding banks have this capability) but it requires a still somewhat uncommon infrastructure, especially in developing countries.
8. Identity verification	Online or offline	For the time being, few systems (e.g. SET) allows this much needed identification. However, none of these systems are widely disseminated yet. An alternative solution is to consult (in real time or not) black lists. So far, only a few large e-merchants do it.
9. Order confirmation	Online	Optimal step. Can be done by e-mail (automatically or manually).
10. Shipping notification	Online	Optimal step. Can be done by e-mail (automatically or manually).
11. Payment fulfilment ('capture')	Online or offline	Online (in real time) is very efficient for a large number of orders but it requires a still somewhat uncommon infrastructure, especially in developing countries.
12. Goods delivery	Online (if possible!) or offline	Ideally, goods are delivered through the Internet (e.g. music, text, or images).
13. Verification of the conformity of goods delivered	Small amounts: online; large amounts: offline	Ideally, goods are delivered through the Internet (e.g. music, text, or images).
14. After sales services	Online	In most cases, online systems are handy and low cost.

Source: Monier (1999: 27)

Figure 3.2 The physical value chain

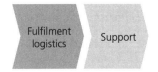

Source: Plumley (2000: 21)

At each step in this chain, the company has an opportunity to add value to the previous input. Firms that execute the key linkages between steps in the chain will tend to enjoy a competitive advantage. Poor linkages or poor execution will remove significant value and hence reduce competitive advantage.

Figure 3.3 shows the basic e-commerce value chain. Here, the supply, manufacturing and inventory elements are integrated, rather than being treated as separate functions. E-commerce platforms add this and secure transaction support. The e-commerce platform and transaction support elements in a single country site is complex, especially when integrated into inventory and logistics systems.

Figure 3.4 shows the international e-business value chain and builds into the e-commerce platform individual country business rules. It also builds into the transaction support system currency clearing and legal requirements. Figure 3.4 assumes single country sourcing and inventory management for the sake of simplicity. However, even with this simplification, there are additional layers of both features and processes involved in the most complex portions of the system, each with varying levels of dependency.

The Gartner Group has identified Internet linkages in terms of their impact on the supply chain (Figure 3.5). Figure 3.5 shows applications based on a specific technology that streamlines the entire supply chain cycle. Consumers can shop, buy and pay for products and services conveniently, and suppliers can communicate directly with customers as well as streamline their own internal communication.

Figure 3.3 The e-business value chain

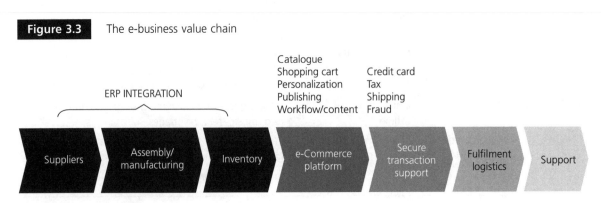

Source: Plumley (2000: 21)

Figure 3.4   International e-business value chain

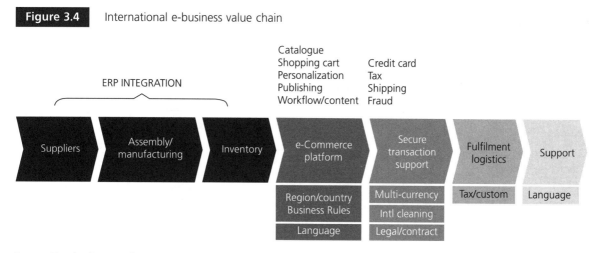

Source: Plumley (2000: 22)

Example   *Boo.com*

An interesting example is Boo.com, the UK based online fashion retailer (Boo.com closed its doors in 2000, but their URL is now home to a revitalized fashion site). Boo.com was the first e-tailer to launch from the ground up in multiple countries from day one. This represented a set of challenges that were previously unaddressed, ranging from technology challenges to the problem of generating a global brand. Boo.com developed a back-end fulfilment system that could handle multiple currencies, multiple languages, on the fly tax calculations, and integration with multiple fulfilment partners. The site allowed the user to select language and currency. Beyond issues of currency and language, Internet sites face local customs, and a host of known and unknown regulatory issues. For example, comparative advertising is not allowed in Germany. Local rivals took Land's End to court over their pledge of 'lifetime guarantee' as being unfair comparative advertising. If you click on a children's item in a catalogue, triggering a banner ad inviting a click through for a free yo-yo, you would be in violation of rules against advertising to children in Denmark. Of course, if the ad were in English, it would be illegal in France.

International information chains

Karmarkar (2000) argues that international information chains link to Internet value chains. The linguistic and cultural features inherent in information have tended to create localization and regionalization of markets. However, where information is in packaged form (as in music, books or software), it is easier to treat the item as having a global market. It is also easier to develop global markets in information areas where linguistic and cultural factors are not as important, for example, technical publishing and industrial services. With the virtual value chain, the widespread use of English is to some extent reducing the linguistic barrier for those whose native language is English.

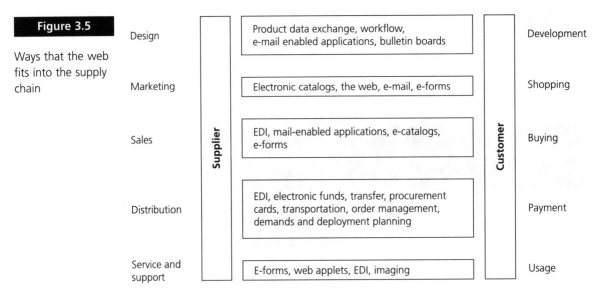

Figure 3.5

Ways that the web fits into the supply chain

Design	Product data exchange, workflow, e-mail enabled applications, bulletin boards	Development
Marketing	Electronic catalogs, the web, e-mail, e-forms	Shopping
Sales	EDI, mail-enabled applications, e-catalogs, e-forms	Buying
Distribution	EDI, electronic funds, transfer, procurement cards, transportation, order management, demands and deployment planning	Payment
Service and support	E-forms, web applets, EDI, imaging	Usage

Source: Gartner Group (2000)

Metrics related to similarity in language, culture and communication determines the topography of information chains more so than is the case for physical supply chains. This will influence the future membership of information supply networks. In the virtual value chain, the cost of transportation, distribution and delivery are lower because of the Internet. New file formats (e.g. MP3 for music) have made it possible to change the distribution of some forms of information from packaged to online formats.

As the relative cost of hardware and software has dropped, labour has become the limiting factor in the production of many information products and services. This has led to a shift in the labour function to low labour cost locations such as India and the development of areas of IT concentration such as Bangalore. As an example, the initial cost of producing first release software is three times more expensive in the USA than it is in India. This trend is not confined to software, as a wide range of information services is outsourced, often to firms in other countries (e.g. call centres). With information chains, physical infrastructure does not play as great a role and there are few physically determined bottlenecks or other physical barriers.

Netchising

Beck and Morrison (2000) argue that globalization involving physical value chain activities (such as manufacturing overseas/joint ventures) have yielded disappointing returns. This is because firms often deploy personnel and resources in overseas activities at the expense of more lucrative opportunities in established core domestic markets. The often heard comment that 'our best people are constantly on planes' reflects this.

Low returns can be due to costs of maintaining 'bricks and mortar' abroad. Other costs include expatriate staff, coordination of physical operations across geographical and cultural distances, communication across t environments where transnational companies (TNCs) are vieweᴑ suspicion, and vulnerability to environmental risks that can damage worldwiᴆ reputation. These factors individually or collectively, can increase managerial information processing demands and result in governance costs outweighing the benefits of globalization.

Beck and Morrison (2000) have come up with the term 'netchising' to describe the process of creating and utilizing the virtual value chain to restore profitability to global operations. It enables companies to achieve many of the advantages of globalization without requiring a physical presence in foreign, culturally distant locations. It replaces far-flung empires of corporate owned operations and relies on the Internet for procurement, sales and customer relationship maintenance.

Netchising involves assigning overseas operations to partners through subcontracting, outsourcing or franchising. This reduces governance problems and environmental uncertainties, while creating greater flexibility. As resources are exchanged or rented, they can be reallocated to meet time pressures or changing market demands (e.g. environmental legislation, exchange rate fluctuation, and political instability). There are three specific advantages of netchising:

1. *Efficiency.* Partner firms specialize in value adding activities supported by their own distinctive competencies.
2. *Convenience.* Information can be sent to customers directly, irrespective of their geographical location, and orders placed direct with the company instead of through a local agent/salesperson.
3. *Achievement of lower transaction costs.* This will reduce the costs of doing business to the benefit of ultimate profitability.

Netchising is likely to result in different modes of operation overseas. Manufacturing operations are likely to be replaced by franchising or licensing – modes that enable control without providing equity. Strategic alliances are also likely to replace equity forms of involvement. On the other hand links with the customer are likely to be improved because they are direct with the firm rather than via a subsidiary or intermediary.

Reaching the customer

This section explores ways of reaching the international customer in the marketspace environment.

Reaching Internet users

The effectiveness of the Internet for globalization relates to the ability to reach international customers using the Internet. As in all marketing, winning a large portion of a well-defined market segment is likely to be more profitable than winning a small share of the whole market. Research by Accenture in the USA shows that despite the enthusiasm of young consumers, people over 35 make up the majority of heavy spenders on the Internet (i.e. more than US$100 per month). This survey of 2000 consumers across 17 industries found that Internet spending was split as follows: 18–24 years = 13 per cent, 25–35 = 36 per cent, 35 years and older = 51 per cent.

New versus repeat customers

Experience in the marketplace shows that in most instances the cost of acquiring new customers is greater than the profit made on the initial transaction and that profitability only occurs with repeat business. One reason why few firms operating on the Internet have made money is that their efforts have been devoted to attracting new customers and few e-businesses make an effort to develop loyal customers. The typical offline business spends three to five times more on customer retention. A major challenge faced by international marketers using the Internet is to convert browsers into buyers and initial buyers into repeat buyers. Two ways of achieving this are:

1. *E-commerce loyalty programs.* Businesses can use data in consumer profiles generated by their web sites to predict customers likely to migrate and launch loyalty programs targetted at consumers who show a tendency to shop around.

2. *Tailoring the Internet offer.* The Internet makes it easy for a firm to profile (rather than to know) its profitable customers. Credit card numbers provide a link to customer data, allowing sites to tailor offers or product recommendations. Companies can also look at surfing patterns, purchasing activities and responses to specific stimuli online. Personalizing transactions with the customer's name and preferences can also increase the 'stickiness' of a site (i.e. increase the time spent viewing the site).

Profiling the global Internet buyer

An increasing percentage of online shoppers now reside outside the USA. However, the resulting global market opportunities have not to date been captured by the web pioneers, most of which are based in the USA. Companies with a web presence in the USA reach less than 5 per cent of the world population and less than 25 per cent of global purchasing power. Considering the costs of establishing and maintaining a 'bricks and mortar' operation, the operational costs of web globalization are minuscule by comparison.

The literature profiles global Internet consumers as typically being relatively young, well educated, middle to upper class, males in professions associated with technology. However, while having a high level of education is still a factor (64 per cent of online shoppers have at least a bachelor's degree), in some countries female shoppers either have or soon will replace male shoppers as the main users of the Internet (Table 3.2).

Cross-cultural research indicates differences in trust towards Internet shopping between relatively collectivist cultures such as Israel and individualistic cultures such as Australia. It also reveals differences in the level of comfort that consumers have about sharing personal information on the web between Europeans on the one hand and Canadians and Australians on the other

(Bellman *et al.* 2000). This suggests that cross-cultural Internet shopping differences vary as to both the amount of time spent surfing the web and the culture to which Internet users belong.

Apart from common demographic profiles, the emergence of a 'world culture' resulting from increased interconnectedness of local cultures and by the development of cultures independent of geographic location drives Internet strategy. Also important are similarities in media and image exposure that give rise to shared scripts between consumers. These drive consumption behaviour to match activities communicated in the media. Therefore, segments of consumers in different countries may have more in common with one another than with consumers in different segments in the same country. However, it should be borne in mind that, although consumers may be the same between countries, their motives for using the product might vary considerably. As an example, the Sony Walkman is a global product developed for global consumers. However, whereas in the West the motive underlying purchase is to enjoy music without being bothered by others, the motive in the East is to enjoy music without bothering others (reflecting individualism as opposed to collectivism).

Macro and micro level variables influence beliefs, attitudes and Internet shopping behaviours around the world (Lynch and Beck 2000). The authors used a global sample that matched the typical demographics associated with the Internet buyer to test for the presence of a global Internet consumer in 20 countries using a scenario-buying task. They found that North Americans expressed the least fear of shopping on the Internet and Asians the greatest. This may be because Asians enjoyed the act of shopping far more than did Americans or Europeans. Overall, Asian countries displayed the lowest degree of favourability towards the Internet and USA the highest. Furthermore, North Americans were significantly more satisfied with the utility and aesthetics of web sites than were respondents in other countries. This may be because many US sites are not tailored to appeal to customers outside the USA. This research illustrates the inappropriateness of adopting US norms and practices as a guide for Internet marketing in other countries.

Table 3.2

Female composition of Internet usage (at-home users, May 2001)

Country	% Female	Country	% Female
United States	52	Norway	43
Canada	51	Singapore	42
Australia	48	Brazil	42
New Zealand	46	Taiwan	41
Finland	46	UK	41
South Korea	45	Netherlands	41
Sweden	45	Spain	40
Denmark	45	France	39
Ireland	45	Germany	37
Hong Kong	44	Italy	37

Source: Nielsen/Net ratings, cited in CyberAtlas

Is e-business a paradigm shift or just a technology change?

This final section of the chapter addresses the ongoing debate as to whether e-business is a paradigm shift or just a technology, in the context of both business-to-consumer (B2C) and business-to-business (B2B) marketing. The relevance of this debate for multinational companies (MNCs) is also considered.

> I don't agree that there are old-economy and new-economy businesses ... the new ways of doing business are breakthroughs like the wheel or the steam engine. ... Old and new will come together. The old will take on technology and the new will have to get customers. Customers are what the old companies have. (Rodney Adler, *BRW*, 20 August 2000)

There is a difference between what we say about a new technology (espoused theories) and how we actually use the new technology (theories in use). This is the case with e-business. The conduct of e-business is quite different to media reports of e-business use. E-business operates in two domains – B2C and B2B. Although treated as two separate business models, both involve demand and supply of goods and services from the value chain. Where the term 'business-to-consumer' is used, the focus is normally on distribution channels and selling products to consumers, whereas when the term 'business-to-business' is used, the focus tends to be on internal costs, especially those involved in procurement.

Example	*Australia New Zealand Bank (ANZ) and Wingspan: Native e-business versus existing structures*

Traditional 'bricks and mortar' banks like ANZ develop, package and sell financial products through proprietary distribution channels (i.e. local branch offices). Regulatory pressures and customer relationship demands create strong incentives for local responsiveness over most components in the value chain. In banking, the traditional mode of competition was scale, market coverage and breadth of product service offerings. Hence, banks ran their operations very much in a multi-domestic fashion. The arrival of virtual banks like Wingspan represented the first foray into banking by contractual players where e-tail delivery was backed up with contracted services rather than ownership.

ANZ's response has been to avoid commodity status. This bank has come down firmly on the side of complementing its traditional operations with an integrated e-business capability, particularly in its alliance with the on-line broking operation, E*trade. E-business provides both an opportunity to reduce costs and add value, enabling customers to review transaction details, transfer funds and pay bills in a secure manner over the Internet. The level of transactional completeness remains relatively low. Local responsiveness is still important and control through vertical value chain integration is still dominant.

Wingspan on the other hand reflects the trend towards a more globally integrated, commodity based approach to banking. Their site offers a confusing array of financial products and services and the firm adopts a strategy that

▶

seeks to expose more of the value chain to market competition. Financial products are sourced via contractual arrangements with Bank One (Wingspan's parent company) and vendor partners. To date however, virtual banking has not had much impact on the global banking industry.

Source: Adapted from Coltman, Devinney, Latukefu and Midgely (2000: 18–19)

Business-to-consumer (B2C)

Most people still lack or choose not to have Internet access. This is not just due to infrastructure, although this is important. It is often due to other factors. For example, Germany, despite its excellent telecommunications infrastructure, has been reluctant to adopt the Internet because of delayed deregulation of the business environment, historical reluctance to use credit cards and conservative business practices.

B2C adoption has been slow and the repeat purchase rate low. Table 3.3 shows Internet retail commerce in Australia. Most B2C commerce in that country is in products that are validated externally (e.g. books, music, etc.), and

Table 3.3 Consumer Internet purchasing behaviour by product category	Growth in consumption %	Repeat purchase rate %
Books	42	7
Non-education software	35	7
Music (CD, MP3)	29	5
Magazine subscriptions	16	5
Shares/financial information	15	NA
Event tickets	15	3
PC hardware	14	4
Games	14	4
Travel tickets	13	3
Online classifieds	11	NA
News articles/subscriptions	11	3
Educational software	10	3
Clothes and shoes	10	2
Adult entertainment	9	3
Food	6	1
Wine	6	1

Source: www.consult (1999); *Computer Industry Alamanac* (1999) as cited in Coltman, Devinney, Latukefu and Midgley (2000: 33)

where little consumer loyalty is involved. Another example is with the ordering of groceries online. Less than 1 per cent of Americans order groceries online. Many products/services are 'experience' goods that have to be seen, felt or touched as part of the purchase process. In many cases with the Internet, consumers use it to find the lowest prices available and then ask 'bricks and mortar' outlets to match prices.

Business-to-business (B2B)

With B2B, exploitation of the Internet lies in upstream rather than downstream activities. This is because most MNEs are less interested in selling online to consumers than in using the Internet to interact with suppliers and large buyers. MNEs are better equipped to communicate electronically, are more cost conscious about procurement and are more open to strategic alliances, which e-business can facilitate. The Boston Consulting Group (BCG) estimates that 25 per cent of all B2B purchasing will be conducted online by 2003, mostly reordering and routine purchases. The BCG claims that this online purchasing will be driven by transaction savings related to product and vendor selection, filling out requisition forms, sending purchasing orders and checking against invoices.

Example — *SMFlive: Sydney Fish Market's online trading system*

Few people would associate the traditional craft of fishmongering with electronic business, but the Sydney Fish Market (Australia) offers a different perspective and a radical change in the selling of this traditional commodity. The SFM live system provides insight into how e-business is used to add value and support transactions between businesses. An intermediary located between the fish processor and the buyer move high quality perishable goods (fish) cheaper and faster than the competition. Distribution logistics, flexibility and local responsiveness are critical in this process. Ensuring operational standards and procedures are followed to maintain high quality increases transaction costs. E-business is a natural adjunct to the business operations by reducing invoicing exchanges, supporting online settlement and providing a level of rigorous management throughout the transaction. Fish quality is a function of time and temperature — the higher the temperature, the less the time before the fish deteriorates. Since most people cannot determine the reliability of the product, low levels of transaction completeness charac-terize the fish industry. In such an industry, a highly trusted fishmonger plays an important role and relationships and trust are extremely important. The Sydney Fish Market model uses technology as a complement to local respon-siveness, providing:

- over 100 different species sold on any one day
- access to approximately 60 tonnes of chilled seafood daily
- speed of auction (more than 1000 crates an hour)
- filleting room which allows buyers to have fish filleted on site before shipping to the store or restaurant
- loading facilities
- promotional activities such as Fish Line (free telephone seafood cookery advisory service), Sydney Seafood School cooking classes and Sydney Fish Market NSW Seafood Awards.

Sources: http://www.sfmlive.com.au/; Coltman, Devinney, Latukfu and Migley (2000: 23–4)

According to Coultman *et al.* (2000), it is unlikely that we will ever be operating in an environment where speed is paramount, scale is irrelevant, intermediaries are bypassed, brands are not important and lower prices prevail. They argue that the degree to which the Internet will have an impact will depend on whether in a particular situation, the change is *competence enhancing* (in which case the benefits of change will accrue to existing firms), or *competence destroying* (in which case the benefits will accrue to new entrants and existing firms willing to jettison their old structures). This may explain why the B2B take-up in Internet use has been so much greater than the B2C take up. Table 3.4 compares predictions regarding the impact of E-business with the state of reality.

E-business evolution in multinational enterprises

A number of factors influence e-business evolution. The most important of these are:

1. *Global integration.* The driver is supply-based pressures. There is no evidence that e-business has removed the underlying environmental, technological, economic and cultural pressures upon business in the global environment. The pressures are still there, but their impact may be different because of e-business. Preferences associated with specific cultures continue to exist (e.g. cash over credit in India and China).

2. *Local responsiveness.* Demand-based pressures drive responsiveness. These will evolve as consumer access to the Internet widens and if the promise that technology changes the nature of the relationship between customer and producer proves true. Extraneous factors may operate. As an example, one reason why online shopping is more successful in Europe than the USA is that retail hours are much shorter.

3. *Transaction completeness.* Pressure to outsource as many non-core activities as possible drives this factor. The Internet facilitates transaction completeness in an outsourced environment. For example, the Internet reduces complications with international commodity trade. Internet auctions replacing global commodity exchanges reflect these benefits.

Conclusion

A more sober and realistic perception of Internet use has replaced the hype associated with the Internet speculative bubble. Arnott and Bridgewater (2002) have made a study of the real impact of the Internet on international marketing, in particular the extent to which managers feel that the Internet delivers benefits and the main barriers to using the Internet in international marketing. Their findings are summarized in Table 3.5 (potential benefits) and Table 3.6 (barriers).

The highest ranking barriers to international marketing via the Internet relate to market structure. Low penetration of the Internet in some international markets is the most significant barrier, while competition via the Internet also

Table 3.4	Prediction	State of current reality
E-predictions and e-reality	**Brands will die!** The Internet represents a major threat to brands making brand strength weaker than ever before (Kalakota and Whinston, 1996).	In an overcommunicated environment, the Internet provides no guarantee of customer attention or lower search cost. It is likely, therefore, that users will continue to gravitate towards brands as a way to simplify choices, reduce search costs and build trust (Barwise, 1997).
	Middlemen will die! 'In every industry – from retailing to insurance – the key impact of the computer-network revolution is to remove the middleman' (Gilder, 1994).	We have still seen few examples of successful disintermediation resulting from e-business investment. This has nothing to do with whether profits are possible. Rather, it has everything to do with the difficulty of working out how to move into a new distribution channel without jeopardizing existing channel relationships.
	Scale is irrelevant! Esther Dyson, has suggested that size will be less important for online firms (Dyson, 1997: 64).	Networks, be they real or virtual, work to a relatively simple logic. The larger the network, the more attractive it is to users. Markets for portal companies (e.g. Yahoo.com), hardware (e.g. Intel) and software (e.g. Microsoft) all provide recent examples of companies deriving increased value from wider reach. Equally standardization of interorganizational systems will require governance mechanisms and large finns will leverage their bargaining power to encourage co-operation among channel members. Such cooperation is often in the best interests of the large firm.
	Being first is the key! In the networked economy, speed is god and first movers will reap the rewards (Downes and Mui, 1999).	There is no guarantee that pioneering firms like Amazon or eBay will be able to maintain their position as the market evolves. Information technologies, by themselves, will not produce sustainable competitive advantage and pioneers must be careful not to develop the 'wrong' resources. Provided high switching costs do not exist, the early follower is often well positioned to exploit their existing resources and core competencies. In many cases, the early follower has complementary assets (e.g. brands) that will be their basis of competition.
	Lower prices! E-business will lead to more efficient markets and lower prices.	Reduced information exchange and coordination costs have enabled finns to capture a larger part of the customer value proposition. Whilst the cost of getting the right item to the right customer has got cheaper, there is no guarantee that this will result in lower prices. Specualtion about whether prices will go up or fall is something of a red herring.

Source: Coltman, Devinney, Latukefu and Midgely (2000: 34)

represents a major barrier. Marketing mix issues, such as price transparency, promoting the existence of the web site and physical distribution are also barriers. Evidence points to the fact that the most successful cases of the international adoption of e-business are likely to occur with firms with a physical presence in the 'marketplace' that supplement their operation with 'marketspace' activities.

Table 3.5	Variables	Mean score[1]	Standard deviation
Potential benefits of international marketing via the Internet	1. Increased profits	4.8	0.42
	2. Increased sales	4.7	0.47
	3. Visibility	4.7	0.47
	4. Corporate image	4.6	0.50
	5. Ease of access to international markets	4.4	0.68
	6. Interaction with customers	4.0	0.82
	7. Speed of business	3.6	1.34
	8. Low resource market entry	3.4	1.26
	9. Global niche strategies	3.0	1.56
	10. Ability to tailor products/services	2.9	1.37

1. Where 5 = extremely important and 1= not at all important

Source: Based on Arnott and Bridgewater (2002)

Table 3.6	Variables	Mean score[1]	Standard deviation
Barriers to international marketing via the Internet	1. Low penetration of Internet	3.8	1.03
	2. Competition	3.4	1.26
	3. Price transparency	3.4	1.17
	4. Need to build awareness of web site	3.4	1.07
	5. Logistics of serving international markets	3.4	1.17
	6. Legal complexity	3.3	1.09
	7. Cultural barriers	3.1	0.74
	8. Need to alter market offering	3.1	1.29
	9. Language barriers	3.0	0.94
	10. Costs of serving international markets	2.9	1.05

1. Where 5 = extremely important and 1= not at all important

Source: Based on Arnott and Bridgewater (2002)

Questions

1. Discuss the ways in which the physical value chain differs from the virtual value chain in international marketing.
2. What does the concept of 'netchising' add to the virtual value chain?
3. Discuss the role of standardization versus localization in international marketing in marketspace.
4. How does globalization in marketspace differ from globalization in the marketplace?
5. Are all firms that restrict their marketing to the Internet from their inception born global firms?
6. Is e-business a paradigm shift or just a technology change?

References

Adler, R. (2000) *BRW* 20 August.

Arnott, D. C. and Bridgewater, S. (2002) 'Internet, interaction and implications', *Market Intelligence and Planning* 20(2): 86–95.

Barwise, P. (1997) 'Brands in a digital world', *Journal of Brand Management* 4 (4): 220–23.

Beck, J. C. and Morrison, A. (2000) 'Netchising: The next global wave', *Proceedings of the eCommerce and Global Business Forum*, 17–19 May Santa Cruz, CA: Accenture Institute for Strategic Change.

BRW (2000) 20 August.

Coltman, T., Devinney, T. M., Latukefu, A. S. and Midgley, D. F. (2000) 'International perspectives on the state of the e-business Revolution', *Proceedings of the eCommerce and Global Business Forum*, 17–19 May, Santa Cruz, CA: Accenture Institute for Strategic Change.

De la Torre, J. and Moxon, R. W. (2001) 'Introduction to the symposium E-Commerce and Global Business: The Impact of the Information and Communication Technology Revolution on the Conduct of International Business', *Journal of International Business Studies*, 32 (4), 617–39.

Downes, L. and Mui, C. (1999) *Unleasing the Killer App: Digital Strategies for Market Dominance*, Boston: Harvard Business School Press.

Dyson, E. (1997) *Release 2.0: A Design for Living in the Digital Age*, New York: Broadway Books.

Gartner Group (2000) www.Gartner.com.

Gilder, G. (1994) *Life After Television: The Coming Transformation of American Life*, New York: Norton.

Hollensen, S. (2001) *Global Marketing – A Market-Responsive Approach*, 2nd edn, Harlow: Prentice Hall.

Kalkota, R. and Whinston, A. B. (1996) *Frontiers of Electronic Commerce*, Boston: Addison-Wesley.

Karmarkar, U. S. (2000) 'Technology and global value chains: Growth, structure and transformation', *Proceedings of the eCommerce and Global Business Forum*, 17–19 May, Santa Cruz, CA: Accenture Institute for Strategic Change.

Knight, G. A. and Cavusgil, S. T. (1996) 'The born global firm. A challenge to traditional internationalisation theory', *Advances in International Marketing*, 8: 11–26.

Kotha, S., Rindova, V. P. and Rothaermal, F. T. (2001) 'Assets and actions: Firm-specific factors in the internationalisation of U.S. internet firms', *Journal of International Business Studies*, 32 (4): 769–91.

Lynch, P., and Beck, J. C. 'Profiles of global internet buyers: Evidence supporting region-specific strategies', *Proceedings of the eCommerce and Global Business Forum*, 17–19 May, Santa Cruz, CA: Accenture Institute for Strategic Change.

Monnier, P. D. (1999) *Cyber Marketing: A Guide for Managers in Developing Countries*, Geneva: International Trade Centre p. 27.

Plumley, D. J. (2000) 'Global eCommerce: The market, challenges and opportunities', *Browne Global Solutions*, January.

Rayport, J. F. and Sviolka, J. J. (1995) 'Exploiting the virtual value chain', *Harvard Business Review* November: 75–85.

Case Study 3 *Marel Iceland: Virtual design and the e-value chain*
Sharon Loane and Jim Bell

Introduction

Founded in Reykjavík in 1983, Marel (www.marel.com) has risen to become one of the world's leading developers and manufacturers of high technology processing equipment for the food industry. Listed on the Icelandic Stock Exchange and owned by around 1800 shareholders, the Marel Group is composed of a core of nine companies bearing the Marel name. Along with Danish-based Carnitech A/S, CP Food Machinery and Arbor Technologies of France, the Marel Group operates ten subsidiary companies in Australia, Europe and North America. Its network of agents and distributors covers some 30 countries on 6 continents giving the group a truly global presence. The company derives 99.2 per cent of its revenues from export activity.

Marel offers a range of weighing units, software, monitoring equipment and intelligent portioning and grading modules as well as integrated systems suitable for use in all major sectors of the food industry. Marel's vision is to be an international leader in developing and marketing high-tech processing equipment for the food processing industries to increase the productivity of their customers. In order to do so Marel engage in ongoing R&D, and have produced significant innovations within the food processing industry.

Virtual design and the e-value chain at Marel

Even as Iceland turns to the global high-tech economy, it is not neglecting the humble fish as Marel sees its technology used around the world. In recent years, the Marel Group has moved increasingly towards the design and installation of ready-to-run turnkey processing plants for fisheries, meat and poultry producers. Although there is most definitely a physical product at the end – a processing plant or weighing equipment – Marel have been able to incorporate new electronic business forms into their business model to produce a form of e-value chain. At the heart of this process lies the Marel flowline software which is custom designed to help processors exploit their raw material to the full. As all Marel modules share a common core, they can be run independently or as part of a wider system, and can be connected to the Internet via a modem for remote access or instant servicing by Marel technicians. Therefore, Marel can incorporate e-value into both ends of the supply chain – the supply side and the demand side.

Figure 3.6

Flexible manufacturing processes

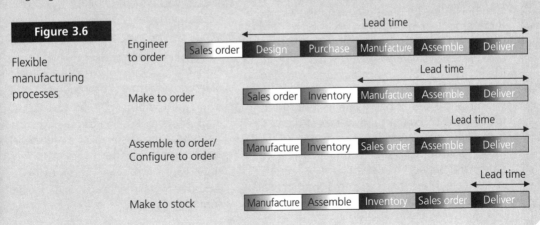

Internally Marel has been streamlining its production, logistics and financial operations. It has had particular success with reducing inventory and lead times and tightening financial control. It now plans to extend the use of software into all other business areas. Marel had rather a rigid workflow that began with sales, continued into production, and ended with delivery. The process lacked all the benefits of materials and resource planning. But these days, production at Marel is far more flexible. Marel now has several different processes that bring dramatic cuts to inventory and lead times.

In addition, Marel can send whole productions or subproductions to its overseas subcontractors at any time. The software keeps track of the materials sent to all subcontractors and the manufacturing processes of each and every one. This supply chain visibility makes quality control far easier.

Meanwhile, in the design centre, AutoCAD users are taking full advantage of the link to this software. They now have direct access to inventory, availability, lead times and prices. AutoCAD now automatically transfers material lists to the software BOM. The integration of the applications eliminates the need for separate interrogation and inputting. Marel also have the ability to divide production projects into as many sales orders, subprojects or activities as needed. The project module can also handle complex customer/invoice/delivery combinations. Therefore the company can communicate with one party, send the invoice for a project or project part to another, and deliver to a third, achieving extremely efficient levels of electronic document exchange (EDI). Marel have greatly improved their ordering process and reduced inventory levels held.

The whole set-up brings great flexibility to the analysis of current and historical data. A subsidiary can view orders, projects or invoices for all its customers, and customers can view orders and projects by department or factory. In addition, Marel have Business Intelligence software which has added functionality to keep track of all aspects of after sales service (spare parts, maintenance, education, software updates, warranties, and so on). The extension means they can meet the highest quality standards. After sales care and technical back-up ensure that all modules and systems continue to run as smoothly as possible, and help and advice are never more than a phone call away. On line monitoring, servicing and even remote operation via the Internet are features now incorporated into most Marel systems. Marel have a sophisticated approach to connectivity, and all subsidiaries, clients and staff away from their desks are connected. All that is required is a modem. Therefore high standards of delivery and customer care can be provided.

Concurrently, Marel's financial procedures have undergone significant change. In invoice approval, for example, managers now have a better overview and can approve invoices via the Internet while travelling. In banking, the majority of customer and vendor payments are now made automatically. Marel generates vendor payment proposals (according to due dates or cash discount dates) and, once approved, sends them to the bank electronically. When the bank receives electronic payments from domestic customers, these are automatically updated with the transaction information.

Questions

1. Would you describe Marel as a new economy business, and why?
2. What are the likely benefits of an e-value chain for Marel?
3. How has this form of virtual supply chain aided quality control procedures?
4. What are the other spin-off business improvements experienced by Marel as a result of using this e-value chain model, and Internet based technology?
5. How would implementing the Marel e-model improve financial management control?

International marketing strategy and e-business

4 The Internet, foreign market entry, internationalization and globalization

Learning objectives

After studying this chapter, you should be able to:

- Recognize Internet related issues that facilitate and restrict entry into foreign markets.

- Identify factors affecting the international diffusion of the Internet.

- Appreciate the role of the Internet as an agent of change in international markets.

- Discuss how the Internet fits with traditional theories of internationalization.

- Describe the patterns of internationalization likely to be adopted by firms using the Internet.

- Appreciate the process of globalization in marketspace.

Internet issues and foreign market entry

It is useful to examine how the existence of the Internet affects decisions about which overseas market a firm should enter. Issues influencing such decisions include competitiveness, government, language, site content and logistics.

International competitiveness issues

Oxley and Yeung (2000) argue that there are three factors determining e-commerce readiness: the rule of law, the transactional integrity of online business, and the availability of infrastructure. These factors constitute the institutional environment in a country, and can either increase or undermine confidence in becoming involved in overseas markets, and the decision to invest in going online. They also improve prospects of doing business internationally.

These three factors determine the attractiveness of an overseas market from an e-business perspective.

Rule of law

For e-business to flourish, potential customers must have confidence that if they purchase goods and services online they will receive the items in a timely manner and that they will be of the advertised quality. Such confidence is less with international online transactions. A 1997 European Union (EU) study revealed that much of the €60 billion that Europeans lost was because of fraud involving online sites that were fronts for criminal activity. Some suppliers now use software to track what country a customer is from in order to reduce the potential for online fraud. A country needs to offer an environment in which property rights are well defined, courts are efficient in resolving disputes and consumer credit and consumer protection regulations are well established and enforced (i.e. a strong tradition of the rule of law).

Transactional integrity of online business

Information is asymmetric between buyer and seller, and this can impede the efficient execution of many transactions. E-business compounds this, as there is often potential uncertainty about the identity of trading partners. This is particularly the case with online auction markets where traders are identified by e-mail addresses, many of which are impossible to trace and very easy to change. Furthermore, the barriers to entry are low. Although claimed to be an advantage of e-business because ease of entry and exit can bring lower prices, it is a disadvantage when firms can effectively change identity. Traditional forms of fraud become easier and new forms of fraud open up. Web technology makes it easy for a business to change the name and appearance of a company in order to shake off a bad reputation and re-enter the market with a different identity and virtually no break in activity. The global reach of e-business can also be a double-edged sword. When a dispute arises, tracking down a dishonest trader and pursuing litigation in a different country can be prohibitively costly, especially if the transaction is of small value.

Adequate physical infrastructure

Without access to personal computers and Internet connections at reasonable cost, consumers in an overseas market are unable to migrate from traditional markets to online markets. However, simply having access to the necessary equipment and infrastructure facilitates international purchasing. As will be discussed later in the chapter, countries vary substantially in terms of Internet related infrastructure and the financial infrastructure necessary for online transactions such as the widespread use of credit cards.

Oxley and Yeung (2000) tested the above factors relating to the global diffusion of the Internet. They obtained positive results using cross-sectional data for 62 countries. They concluded that in countries with a weak rule of law, it is difficult to attract users to e-business, and there will be a slower migration of transactions from traditional to online markets. In addition, as consumers migrate to the web, they are more likely to turn to companies from countries where transactional integrity is greater. As a result less developed countries are likely to become more marginalized in a world driven by e-business. Figure 4.1 shows how e-business develops from a domestic to a global orientation.

Internationalizing a web site properly is expensive. In the USA, Forrester Research claims that companies must sell $US1 million per year to cover costs of internationalizing a site and offering the expected degree of telephone support to customers outside the USA. In 23 per cent of the leading 114 web sites surveyed by Forrester Research, there was minimal or no localization of the site (i.e. local content/another language/registered foreign domain name).

E-business targets marketspace, and is influenced by different factors to those that apply in the marketplace. The most important of these factors are telecommunications infrastructure, PC ownership, available logistics and cultural considerations.

Government involvement issues

The second issue related to foreign market entry concerns the attitude of the government of the overseas country towards the Internet. Traditionally, governments have competed with each other in the areas of trade and investment. In the future governments that hope to attract transnational companies (TNCs) will have to create an attractive e-business environment. This will involve following:

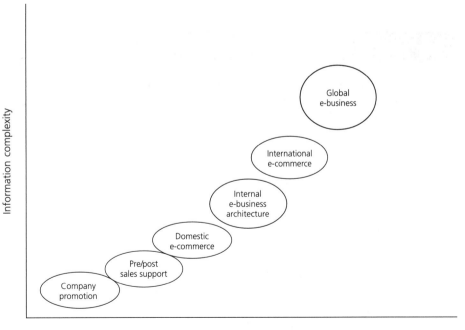

Figure 4.1

E-business development

Source: Plumley (2000: 29)

- *Establishing the environment*: creation of a legal and regulatory framework conducive to e-business and the necessary environment of trust in a climate where paper-based transactions are replaced by digitally-based transactions.
- *Demonstrating the business case*: to encourage the uptake of e-business, governments have to show commercial firms how e-business operates as part of their overall business strategy.
- *Targeting barriers and improving infrastructure*: government must remove system incompatibility barriers and imposts from the infrastructure necessary to operate via the Internet. They should also provide an incentive structure to encourage the creation or acquisition of improved infrastructure to facilitate Internet adoption.

Language issues

The third issue affecting market entry is that of language which was briefly discussed in Chapter 2. In 2000, 80 per cent of Internet content was delivered in English, but over 40 per cent of users did not read English. Furthermore, 78 per cent of web sites and 96 per cent of e-business sites were in English. This restricts the reach of the Internet as far as people who do not speak English are concerned. There are, however, an increasing number of sites in languages other than English, though having sites in multiple languages is costly for small and medium sized exporters. It is estimated that the number of people online who were non-English speakers was 128 million in 2000, and that by 2005, non-English web site users will account for 67 per cent of worldwide Internet users (Hashimi and Dhafamanpour, 2000).

Example	*OBO uses Internet to lead in global market share*

OBO's managing director Simon Barnett was an early believer in the marketing power of the Internet. He guided OBO onto the Internet in the mid-1990s to increase interaction with their customers – cricketers and hockey goalies – and to sell their sportsgear in markets where they did not already have a distributor.

OBO sells a niche product, and the domestic market is small. However, globally there are around 100,000 goalies, and OBO can now reach them directly via its web site. OBO sells via agents in 15 countries, with another 11 handled by the European agent. OBO's web presence helps the company to reach a wider audience than can be served by these agents alone.

OBO has won a number of awards of the years, including Innovative Business of the Year

1993, a TradeNZ Export Commendation in 1997, and Exporter of the Year from the Manawatu Business Awards, 1998. Located in Palmerston North, a small city on the North Island of New Zealand, OBO has secured nearly 60 per cent of the world market for its field hockey equipment.

OBO's web site includes a virtual community for goalies. The objective is to forge a market from an otherwise highly fragmented group of customers. The more OBO gets its customers involved with each other and with the company, the stronger their feelings for the brand. The web site is also used for research and development – ideas come from customer enquiries and comments, and from online focus groups.

OBO was founded in 1964 to import manufacture and distribute table tennis equipment in

▶

◄

NZ. In 1986, it began importing field hockey protective equipment, and in 1990 moved into the design and manufacture of its own line of protective wear. OBO manufactures and distributes closed cell foam protective equipment including leg-guards, kickers, hand protectors, chest guards and helmets, with a range of sizes and quality that covers the needs of children through internationally competitive adult players.

Source: www. obo.co.nz

Until a significant increase in the number of non-English sites happens, the use of English as the web medium will impede use of the Internet as a vehicle for foreign market entry. This is especially the case in countries where the target audience does not speak English. This will disadvantage firms wishing to enter foreign markets where English is not widely spoken, as is the case in many of the developing countries. As an example of this linguistic disadvantage, while 40 per cent of Europeans speak some amount of English (15 per cent as first language, 28 per cent some English), less than 10 per cent of Japanese have any English ability. Many small and medium exporters are also disadvantaged, as they often cannot afford the cost of having sites in multiple languages, and foreign language speakers in their offices to respond to inquiries.

Early adopters who alter their web strategy to accommodate linguistic and cultural differences are most likely to obtain a first mover pay-off from localization of sites. To sustain this advantage, firms will need to localize further in terms of style and all aspects of the buying process (i.e. product selections that combine local taste, original content, local payment methods and accessible customer service). These modifications to the site are necessary to both establish trust and capture overseas online customers.

Marschan-Piekkari, Welch and Welch (1999) argue that e-business may delay or shift the language hurdle to a different part or stage of international activity. Although initial contact with potential customers is facilitated, some parts of the international activity will occur in foreign markets thereby involving a foreign language component. It is therefore likely that for e-business firms, the language learning curve in international operations will start later than in the 'old economy (Table 4.1).

Table 4.1	*Language*	*1998 (In millions)*	*2000 (In millions)*
Comparison of language use on Internet	English	107.2	160
	Japanese	14.4	23
	Spanish	14.2	Not listed
	German	13.9	25
	French	8.3	16
	Chinese (Mandarin)	6.4	Not listed

Source: Korper and Ellis (2000), as cited by Hashimi and Damanpour (2000: 16)

Site content issues

Another related issue affecting market entry is what the content of the site should be. A specific issue in the context of market entry is the extent to which the firm should have a global site as opposed to a separate site for each overseas market. In the first place, the firm must decide how their product or service fits into the global economy. The next decision is whether the product and advertising need customizing for each country. Any firm planning to trade internationally has to conform to international trade laws and regulations regardless of whether they operate in marketspace or marketplace. Many of these laws and regulations have implications for site content. Technical standards differ from country to country and although the Internet is a driving force towards worldwide communication standards, existing differences may influence site content.

Finally, there is the issue of cultural sensitivity. Some products and services are more culturally sensitive than are others. The more culturally sensitive the product, the greater is the need for a localized as opposed to a global web site. The greater the extent to which a site is a vehicle for transactions as opposed to information, the more it must localize. Other advantages of localized sites, especially when non-native English speakers are being targeted, are that visitors linger twice as long as they do at English-only URLs; business users are three times as likely to buy when addressed in their own language; customer service costs drop when instructions are displayed in the user's own language

As a rule, when firms commence Internet operations, they tend to have a fully centralized site. Then as they become more aware of local needs, they tend to have a series of local sites. This can lead to inconsistency between the content of each of their sites and have the effect of obscuring the corporate message and the brand identity. This leads to the third stage of having semi-centralized sites whereby there is consistent look and feel to conform to corporate branding and positioning objectives, but provision for country sites to develop relevant content and information for regional target markets. This is illustrated in Figure 4.2.

Because of the influence of technologists rather than marketing people in site development, often an English language site is translated literally into a foreign language rather than the concepts themselves being translated. This diminishes the effectiveness of many such foreign language sites. Furthermore, e-business requires that the global content management system integrate with a global workflow system. There are significant cost implications in that sites must be monitored 24 hours a day so that in whatever country customers are located, they can get an immediate response. In addition, sites must be updated regularly in all language versions; otherwise, the use of e-business looses its timeliness.

Bandwidth issues

Related to government involvement in e-business facilitation is the ability of national infrastructure to receive web-based communications. This is often a matter of bandwidth and nations vary significantly in the availability of bandwidth. There are places in the world where the Internet cannot be accessed

Figure 4.2

Site architecture
evolution

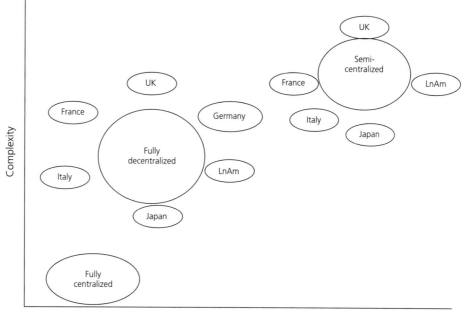

Source: Plumley (2000: 15)

Table 4.2

International
Internet bandwidth
by region,
1999–2001

Nation	2000 (Mbps)	2001 (Mbps)	Percentage growth
Africa	649.2	1,230.8	89.6
Asia	22,965.1	52,661.9	129.3
Europe	232,316.7	675,637.3	190.8
Latin America	2,785.2	16,132.5	479.2
U.S & Canada	112,222.0	274,184.9	144.3

Source: TeleGeography research cited in CyberAtlas (September 2001)

properly because the particular region does not have sufficient infrastructure to support Internet connectivity. Table 4.2 illustrates the availability of bandwidth by country.

Logistics issues

Finally, there are logistics issues to take into account in selecting which markets to enter overseas. Beyond the complexities of language, site architecture and content management, global orders must be fulfilled. Forrester Research found that e-commerce sites regularly get 30 per cent of their traffic and 10 per cent of their orders from overseas. In the USA, business-to-business (B2B) and business-to-consumer (B2C) sites regularly turn away half the international orders they receive. This is because they are unable to handle the complexities of shipping across borders. As an example, the US retail giant 'The Gap' only accepts US-based orders. Increasingly specialist transportation intermediaries such as DHL are undertaking the logistics role in e-business.

These logistics complexities are illustrated by the fact that a customer can be in one country, the supplier in an another, the purchase made through a web site in a third country and delivery made to the customer's holiday home in a fourth country. Which country has legal jurisdiction and where are taxes assessed?

Attitudinal issues

Although many firms appreciate the existence of the Web's global reach, many are either unwilling or ill equipped to handle overseas orders. The obstacles to international involvement in Web mediated commerce range from inability to handle orders, to language and cultural barriers, to different stages of Internet adoption and lack of adequate infrastructure in overseas markets.

Location issues

Zaheer and Manrakhan (2001) categorize motivations to locate internationally as driven by the seeking of resources, the seeking of markets, obtaining increased production efficiencies and acquiring new assets and capabilities. In each case, these motivations will be changed or influenced when electronic access is available. Table 4.3 summarizes these motives and the influence of the Internet.

Zaheer and Manrakhan conclude that firms may need to reconsider their global portfolio of locations due to the remote access possibilities of the new IC technologies, and reassess the relevance of lead markets and clusters as potential locations for their industry. In addition, a networked world economy provides opportunity for firms located in peripheral countries to participate in markets previously closed to them. Finally, more thought, they argue, will need to be given to harmonizing taxation and immigration as 'remote electronic access and lowered coordination costs greatly increase the fluidity with which location of value-added activities can be shifted around the world'.

Other issues

Purchase behaviour is another relevant issue. In Asia, for example, relatively few people use credit cards. This impedes Internet transactions. Purchase behaviour is also influenced by the extent to which an overseas market is known for piracy in items such as computer software and in CDs (items that are often sold via the Internet). A final issue, discussed in more detail in a previous section, is that of the existing infrastructure in the overseas market and its impact on the ability of people there to transact business on the web.

The Internet as a change agent in international markets

It is apparent that the Internet has the potential to change international marketing. In this section, the changes in international marketing caused by the

Table 4.3	Motivations to locate activities internationally		
	Traditional motivations for physical locations in specific countries or markets	*Fundamental assumptions on why physical collocation is necessary*	*How do assumptions change with remote electronic access?*
Resource seekers	To acquire specific resources at lower real costs. Resources could include: • Physical resources • Labour • Technological capability, management skills, knowledge and intellectual capital	• Immobility of resources • Cheaper to engage in FDI than import • Extractive type industries: pre-emptive lock-in • Capability cannot be acquired in market • Knowledge spillover and agglomeration effects are localized	• Resources delivering digitized content can be remotely accessed (e.g. animation or graphic design labour) • Requires new forms of employment contracts and control mechanisms for remote telecommuters
Market seekers	(1) Locate production and/or marketing to supply country or region, to: • Achieve sales growth, scale economies • Service global customers • Facilitate local adaptation, learning • Minimize production and transaction costs (2) Have a physical presence in leading markets served by competitors, for strategic blocking and knowledge spillovers	• For locating downstream activities: Building customer relationships and servicing global customers requires physical co-location with them • For locating upstream activities: Access to markets restricted (e.g. tariff barriers), transport costs, low scale economies.	• Customer relationships for simple products may be better built through digital channels (e.g. Amazon versus bricks and mortar bookstore), as may digitizable service elements, such as help desks • How local are knowledge spillovers? Tactic knowledge spillovers likely to remain localized, codified knowledge less so. Rate of knowledge spillovers likely to be higher in local rather than global arena
Efficiency seekers	• Rationalize structures to take advantage of differences across countries in cost of traditional or created factor endowments • Tend to take place in countries of broadly similar economic levels	• Differential locational advantages (e.g. tax, performance incentives, labor market, living conditions) • Low coordination costs • Optimizing location portfolio • Cross-border markets are well developed and open • Knowledge spillover effects	• Physical and regulatory locational advantages cannot be remotely accessed • Coordination costs lower • More opportunities to optimize location portfolio (e.g. global relay strategies) • Extent of regulation of Internet commerce? • Again, how local are knowledge spillovers?
Strategic asset or capability seekers	• Aims to capitalize on the benefits of common ownership of diversified activities/capabilities	• Arise from market imperfections in asset markets in which the MNE operates	• Information as a strategic asset • Will asset/capability markets become less susceptible to market failure?

Source: Zaheer and Manrakhan (2001: 671)

Internet are discussed, and issues involved in the search for information in marketspace are explored.

Changes in marketspace

Traditionally the country was the unit for planning and executing international marketing strategy. This is not the case with e-business marketing as the Internet has created a cyber marketplace structured around Internet access and commonality of interests and consumption needs. The separation of information search and transaction on the Internet means that information search will no longer parallel the bounds of physical markets. This is likely to result in the following four trends.

1. *Denationalization.* The Internet is rapidly changing the significance of national boundaries in defining market areas. No longer does business have to be structured around political boundaries and this lessens the degree to which national governments can control what happens within their jurisdictions when transactions occur using the Internet.

2. *Tiering.* Markets are more likely to be rated in terms of ease of Internet access, rather than other marketplace variables such as psychic distance (discussed later in the chapter). Tiering is influenced by both infrastructure (PCs and telephone access) and language. Consumers without Internet access will be restricted to information from traditional sources and a more limited range of product offerings. As Internet access is least likely to be available in the developing countries, this will deepen the 'north–south divide'. Figure 4.3 shows the location of both country specific and generic domains per inhabitant.

3. *Connecting isolated markets.* The Internet reduces the influence of geographic proximity in facilitating market integration and the diffusion of ideas. Consumers with Internet access in geographically isolated or distant markets can easily link into the global market structure. This will particularly benefit isolated developed countries. As an example, although geographically isolated, levels of Internet access in Australia and New Zealand are high by world standards.

4. *Global disintermediation.* With the Internet, consumers can directly access information and marketers can target consumers on a direct basis. The Internet establishes direct channels of communication between exporters and importers and reduces the need for intermediaries such as the overseas agent. In some cases, however, reintermediation occurs and cyber intermediaries that perform matching functions replace traditional intermediaries.

When different social and business cultures are considered, as far as e-business is concerned, the main differences are to be found in limitations on access and control of information. Research by Bauer (2000) illustrated this in a comparison of Germany with China. Whereas Germany had sophisticated logistics, strong telecommunications infrastructure and Internet access, and a stable manufacturing capacity, China had limited telecommunications and substantial controls over access to the Internet, a growing logistics capacity and high growth in its manufacturing sector.

Another influence on the conduct of international marketing is ensuring that there is an Internet infrastructure available for use. Infrastructure availability may not be the same in all countries and the existing infrastructure prior to the introduction of the Internet will influence how the Internet develops in that country. However, companies can build their own infrastructures, bypassing inadequate national infrastructures. The existing physical infrastructure of a supplier may also affect global E-business readiness. As an example, if a supplier has already made an investment in prior technology with a five-year life span, they may be reluctant to scrap older infrastructure, which has not yet exhausted its lifespan.

Figure 4.3

Network effect:
Internet hosts per
'000 inhabitants,
July 1999

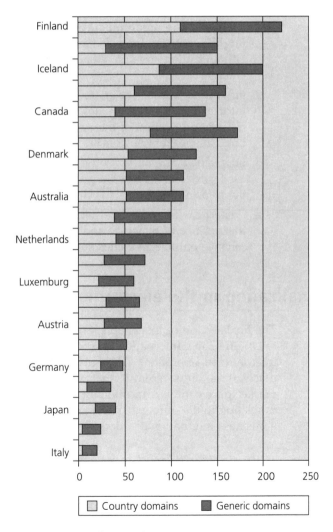

Source: Craig, Douglas and Flaherty (2000: 32)

International information search, perception, use and evaluation

The Internet extends both the depth and the breadth of the search process. It changes the way information is sought, viewed and used in international marketing. In addition to company sites, consumers can also access product category sites, retailer sites and consumer-dominated sites such as bulletin boards and chat rooms. With the Internet, the initiative in the search process shifts to the consumer resulting in topic focused rather than a sequential process oriented search. The search process is also influenced by the fact that information is timelier and the costs of acquiring it are less than via conventional sources. However, the information environment on the Internet differs in that the majority of sites reflect the conventions and symbols of Western culture. Interpretation and retention of information is difficult where communication crosses cultural and linguistic boundaries. This is manifest in four ways.

1. *Language*. The predominance of English on the Internet implies that non-English speakers have access to a more limited range of information, although there are signs that a global Internet vocabulary is starting to emerge.
2. *Information misinterpretation*. Because there are few filters on Internet information, there is greater scope for misinterpretation and miscommunication of messages on the Internet, especially by non-native English speakers or non-Western consumers.
3. *Information credibility*. As 'word of mouse' replaces word of mouth, there are few means of assessing the objectivity or biases of the presenter of the information.
4. *Product cues*. On the Internet, consumers face a truncated set of cues and the absence of olfactory and sensory cues. This leads to a greater reliance on objective cues such as price and product description.

Internationalization in the electronic age

The final section of this chapter discusses the process of internationalization in the Internet age. Internationalization is the process of increasing involvement in international operations. The subject of considerable research in the market-place, it is only recently that internationalization has been studied in a marketspace context. Traditional theories of internationalization are considered in relation to the unique features of the Internet, and then the actual patterns of e-business internationalization are discussed.

How do traditional internationalization theories fit with the Internet?

Many e-business companies emerged rapidly onto the business scene and, unlike traditional companies, they were virtually born global. They ignored national boundaries and jumped into global markets from their commencement or soon after their founding. They exist as a new species of business organization that operate in marketspace, transcending both time and space. As such, they do not fit with traditional theories of internationalization. Traditional approaches to internationalization include:

- *behavioural approaches:* characterize internationalization as an incremental progression as firms increase their understanding of foreign markets and involvement in foreign operations.
- *economic approaches:* these approaches link cost and risk with increasing the extent of firms' international involvement. Firms gradually move from 'low-cost/low-risk' to 'high-cost/high risk' entry strategies.
- *product life cycle approaches:* here firms move from domestic innovation and production, to production by foreign subsidiaries, to production anywhere where costs are lowest. Typically, production commences in developed countries and moves to less developed countries.

Most traditional approaches have the following characteristics:

- *the incremental pace at which firms expand into overseas markets:* firms approach internationalization in an incremental way moving from market to market in terms of perceived difficulty of entry.
- *the sequence of foreign market expansion and entry strategy:* firms move from forms of internationalization which involve the least commitment of resources (such as indirect export) to forms which involve increasing commitment of resources (such as joint ventures), as they gain experience with international marketing.
- *limited coverage of foreign markets in the early stages of internationalization:* when firms first become involved in international marketing, they only focus on one or two overseas markets and with experience, increase the number of overseas markets in which they operate.

Underpinning the above are:

- *the concept of psychic distance:* this concept posits that initially firms target overseas markets that are perceived to be similar in terms of culture, geography, standard of living, and history. The most powerful determinant of psychic distance is culture, which is often used as a surrogate for psychic distance.
- *experiential learning:* this concept posits that firms increase their international involvement because of experience, moving from similar markets to markets that are more distant and from involvement requiring limited resources to involvement requiring substantial resources as they learn the intricacies of doing business in foreign countries.

Internationalization of e-business firms

Figures 4.4 and 4.5 show the contrasting paths followed by e-business firms compared with traditional firms. Figure 4.4 shows the characteristics of traditional business and reveals that:

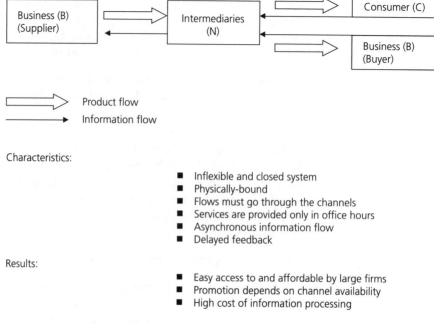

Source: Zhao and Du (2000: 24)

- it is a closed system
- channels of transaction and communication are framed in a physical workplace
- product, services and information flows takes place in bounded spaces erected by intermediaries
- international and external information exchange is unidirectional in that it flows from providers to users, but feedback is delayed due to time zones or layers of intermediaries
- it is constrained both physically and culturally and this usually requires firms to sequentially increase their involvement into foreign markets.

By comparison, Figure 4.5 reflects the characteristics of e-business. It shows that the e-business firm:

- is anchored on increasing integration of telecommunication and computer technology
- operates in dimensionless space where business, customers and consumers interact
- is involved in a multidirectional flow of products and information
- engages in information exchange that occurs in real time allowing rapid responses
- has multidirectional information and business exchanges that facilitates organizational learning

Figure 4.5

Internationalization
of e-business firms

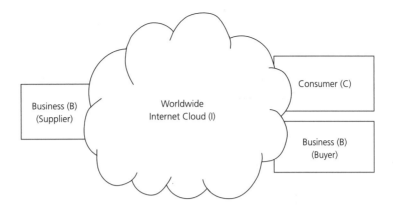

Characteristics:

■ The Internet is flexible, open, and always on
■ Flows can go any directions and anywhere through the Internet
■ Synchronized product and information flow
■ Real-time feedback

Results:

■ High access by small, medium and large firms
■ Close linkage and wider active participation
■ Cost reduction
■ Organizational learning

Source: Zhao and Du (2000: 24)

- varies in size and location but can more easily participate in the learning process via the low-cost gateway to international markets provided by e-business
- seeks to reduce costs by eliminating intermediaries on the one hand and by the optimal scheduling of shipments on the other.

By comparing the above, it is possible to highlight the factors that play a role in the internationalization of e-business firms. The most obvious of these are as follows.

Acquired knowledge

Existing theories of organizational learning that stress the evolution and accumulation of experience within firms do not explain the speed at which e-business firms go international. Such firms often acquire knowledge, even though they are young and lack experience, through outside recruitment of key managers with international experience.

Internetability

E-business firms can only internationalize by dealing with countries that are Internet enabled and use the Internet. A country with a large percentage of the population using the Internet is more attractive as a market for e-business firms to enter.

Technology parity

Global technology parity involves availability of both computers and accessible telecom services in a country. E-business firms cannot implement an internationalization strategy in countries where this parity in technology with the firm is absent. The higher the level of technology parity a country exhibits, the faster the e-business firm is able to move into it.

Legal imperatives

This includes the extent to which there is legal protection of intellectual property rights in a given country. The lack of such protection is detrimental to e-business firms since the core competencies of such firms are centred on the development of technology, expertise, patents and software. The better the legal protection, the more rapidly the e-business firm will move into a country.

Cultural distance

As with the internationalization of traditional firms, cultural distance is significant for determining the speed of internationalization of e-business firms (e.g. language and failure to properly use it, may delay e-business firms in preparing their web sites and portals.)

Zhao and Du (2000) found that in terms of cultural distance, e-business firms were much more inclined to enter overseas markets that were more culturally distant, than was the case with traditional firms (Tables 4.4 and 4.5). In terms of speed, e-business firms began international activities much sooner after establishment (2.71 years) than did traditional firms (30 years) and in terms of scope, e-business firms entered a larger number of new foreign markets a year (3.62) than did traditional firms (1.60). The internationalization of e-business firms differs from that posited by traditional internationalization theory in that it is not incremental and sequential. Second, acquired knowledge is the explanation of the more rapid internationalization of the e-business firm, and finally, high degrees of technological parity and legal protection of intellectual property rights (IPR) are a necessary condition for the internationalization of e-business firms.

Kotha, Rindova and Rothaermel (2000) argue that the major drivers of internationalization in e-business are intangible assets and resources on the one hand and competitive and cooperative activity on the other.

Table 4.4	Key constructs	Traditional firm	E-business firm
Comparison of key constructs of internationalization	Speed	Incremental	Rapid
	Scope	Undirectional	Multidirectional
	Sequence	Distinct	Indistinct

Source: Zhao and Du (2000: 22)

Table 4.5	Traditional company		E-business company
Speed			
Mean	29.98		2.71 (p = .000)
Standard deviation	22.02		1.79
Scope			
Mean	1.601		3.62 (p = .000)
Standard deviation	1.507		3.13
Cultural Distance			
Mean	8.817		21.48 (p = .000)
Standard deviation	7.783		17.78

T-test of mean differences between traditional companies and e-business companies

Source: Zhao and Du (2000: 22)

Intangible assets and resources

These consist of existing R&D (which serves as an important proxy for knowledge assets), reputation (as evidenced in media visibility) and site traffic (as indicated by the volume of Internet hits and responses).

Competitive and cooperative activity

Competitive activity is reflected in propensity to introduce new products and services (as these threaten rivals) and willingness to continually develop new products and services that render existing products obsolete (so as to preserve the relationships with demanding customers). Cooperative activity is illustrated by forming partnerships with others on the Internet. In e-business, cooperative and competitive activity are not necessarily polarized and what is cooperative at one level can become competitive at another and vice versa.

Other aspects of e-business internationalization can be divided into barriers and success factors. According to Hamill (1997), using the Internet overcomes a number of traditional barriers to internationalization. The main barriers and their Internet solutions are:

1. *Psychological* (ethnocentrism, short termism, fear, risk aversion). Psychological barriers are reduced by access to global information, which increases international awareness, confidence and commitment.
2. *Organizational* (resource lack, knowledge deficiency, international experienced personnel, no export training). Organizational barriers are reduced by access to low-cost export market research resources; improved knowledge of international markets and cultural norms; reduced dependence on agents through direct marketing and creation of virtual network of partners.
3. *Operational* (documentation and management of export, language, payment delays and problems). Operational barriers are reduced by

simplified export documentation through electronic data transfers, electronic payments and provision of export assistance online.

4. *Product/market* (need for modification, different business practices, customer identification, barriers to trade). Product/market barriers are reduced by the availability of online research, rapid feedback; savings in communication costs and adoption of global niche as opposed to country centred strategies.

Table 4.6 shows the critical success factors for internationalization and the contribution of Internet use.

Where lack of size or financial resources impedes success, as is often the case with SMEs, the Internet can often overcome or ameliorate the disadvantages from which firms suffer. The impact of the Internet on small and medium sized exporters SMEs is illustrated in Figure 4.6.

Table 4.6	*Critical success factor*	*Contribution of Internet*
Critical success factors in internationalization and Internet contribution	Finding the right 'overseas agent or distributor	Use of online databases and searches to find suitable overseas representation: and/or reduced dependency on agents/distributors through direct selling, etc.
	Effective management of the agency/ distributor relationship	Electronic communications to support more traditional forms of collaboration and contact: creation of virtual communities based on mutual trust
	Strong commitment to exporting	Increased commitment to overseas markets through participating in global electronic networks
	International awareness, knowledge and orientation	Increase in international awareness, confidence and commitment through access to global information sources: participation in global network communities; enquiries and feedback to WWW site from potential global customers
	Selectivity in market selection	Significantly simplified through Internet-based export market research resources
	Respect for and orientation to foreign customers	Closer company/customer relationship through electronic communications, feedback, interactivity, etc.
	Export planning and strategy development	Utilization of the Web's potential in strategic export planning
	Fast communications and documentation procedures	Electronic communications with foreign agents/ distributors; customers; partners governments, etc.
	Effective marketing mix policies, long-term perspective	Target marketing. Internet resources supporting the development of longer term export objectives

Source: Hamill (1997: 314)

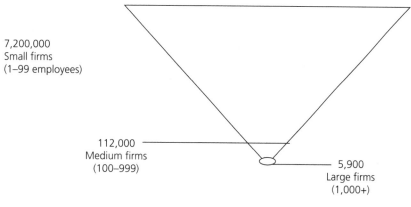

Figure 4.6

Internet adoption by firm size

Source: Plumley (2000: 25)

Summary of internationalization issues in the electronic environment

The factors influencing export success are complex and varied. They include:

- agency/distributor choice
- effective management of the agency/distributor relationship
- strong management commitment to exporting
- international awareness
- knowledge and orientation
- selectivity on market choice
- adopting a strategic long-term perspective.

As far as the process of internationalization is concerned, behavioural approaches fail adequately to explain the realities of internationalization. These realities are a climate characterized by increasing globalization of business and competition, cross-border mergers, acquisitions and strategic alliances, and the need for companies to globalize much earlier and more quickly than in the past. This is a process made easier by improvements in global telecommunications and information technology.

The knowledge creation ability of the Internet may help firms obtain a considerable amount of information about foreign markets. Information is gathered using search engines and by conducting online surveys. The Internet enables firms to communicate with foreign customers, distributors, suppliers and other business related organizations. The innovative nature of both information technologies and communications technologies has enabled the acquiring of information in a manner that is substantially more efficient for firms all around the world. The relevance of the incremental approach to internationalization is called into question by the explosion of international business activity on the WWW. Slow incremental internationalization no longer makes sense when the technology exists to provide SMEs with a low cost instant gateway to global markets.

There is a wide range of information on foreign markets available on the Internet. As such, the Internet operates as a virtual library accessed by users everywhere. However, the level of usefulness of information for internationalization provided by the Internet depends on the ability of the firm to use it effectively. Nguyen (2001) called this ability 'Internet infusion'. Through a process of Internet infusion, firms are able to obtain useful information for their internationalization and the traditional information barriers to internationalization are reduced.

In order for firms to increase their internationalization by using the Internet, Srirojanant and Thirkell (1999) contend that firms need to have an interactive web site, effective communications with their stakeholders, the support of top management for conducting international business electronically, and intensive Internet usage to foster acceptance. These researchers found that the benefits of having an Internet-based export strategy are more efficient product and distribution strategies offshore, improved competencies in market knowledge, international orientation and communications capability, and enhanced ability to overcome perceived barriers to export.

Because of the Internet characteristics of interactivity and speedy access to information, knowledge of overseas markets is acquired more quickly in marketspace than it is in the marketplace. As a result, Internet-driven internationalization is more likely to follow a contingency process of reacting to opportunities as they occur rather than a stages or sequential approach based on learning, experience or resource commitment.

Globalization

De la Torre and Moxon (2001) raise a number of issues regarding the impact of e-business on globalization. They note that national borders, cultures and institutions are traditionally considered critical factors impeding the globalization of markets as they result in nationally responsive strategies. On the other hand, economies of scale and the move towards standardization have permitted the adoption of global policies by multinational firms. All these elements have been affected by information and communications technology and in the process upset the balance between global and local priorities. Issues for consideration include:

- Will information and communications technology cause greater integration of industries and markets?
- Are consumers becoming more homogeneous?
- Will brand and marketing investments spill over into other markets?
- Will MNCs move away from strategies permitting subsidiaries local autonomy towards closer global integration of operations?
- Will small firms achieve a global reach making the expensive global networks of large firms obsolete?

- Will information and communications technology cause greater concentration of industries and global 'winner take all races'.

This section addresses globalization issues arising from the Internet, especially as they influence international competitiveness. The issue of 'e-globalization' and 'e-localization' is discussed as is the role of the 'born global' firm in the electronic age.

Global opportunities

The impact of the Internet on international business has led to new global opportunities. In 1970, US per capita income was 31 per cent higher than that of other large industrialized countries. By 1991, the difference had narrowed to 10 per cent. With the dawn of the Internet age, the gap is widening again, to more than 22 per cent the year 2000 (*BRW*, 2000). These statistics reflect the pulling away of the leading technology country. It also indicates that the Internet should make many more industries open to globalization. The Internet makes it easier to provide services of all types – banking, education, consulting, retailing, gambling. However, as with education, the product must be constantly updated. Although the Internet lets companies and countries play on a large field, the laws of comparative advantage have not been rendered obsolete. In this new environment, the US has two advantages – it was the first and it has the largest domestic market.

The drivers of Internet demand are twofold. In the first place, Internet demand is driven by communications (e-mail and information) and in the second, by commerce. The enablers of such demand are access, security and bandwidth (see Figure 4.7) and these require significant investment. Without being able to access the Internet, there will be unfulfilled demand. Without being

Figure 4.7

Drivers of Internet demand

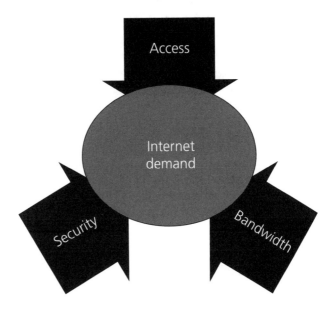

Source: Plumley (2000: 3)

able to feel secure about doing business via the Internet, there will be little fulfilment of demand. Without adequate bandwidth, customers will become tired of waiting and revert to marketplace modes of conducting international business.

The Internet has opened the floodgates to competition. Reduction in the cost of communication removed a major barrier to the benefit of small agile firms. Whether buying paperclips or books, purchasers are more likely to complete the online transaction when they are confident that they understand what is presented to them. In such an environment, it is essential that the site designer consider an architecture that accommodates global e-business including multicurrency and multilanguage flexibility.

Consequences for global competitiveness

Internet adoption has consequences for the ability of firms to compete on a global basis. Some of the more important consequences in this connection are:

1. *Digital assets.* Unlike physical assets, these are not depleted by consumption. Once created, they can be applied to other activities with little extra cost, as the variable cost of creating value using digital assets is virtually zero. This facilitates aggressive pricing to gain market share in a new market when competition is with firms reliant on physical assets.

2. *Economies of scale.* These are redefined and no longer as important. This change allows small firms to compete with large firms as they also enjoy low unit costs.

3. *Economies of scope.* These occur because in marketspace firms can draw on a single set of digital assets to provide value across many different and disparate markets.

4. *Transaction costs.* In the virtual value chain these are lower than in the physical value chain and continue to decline as the processing capacity unit cost for microprocessors doubles every 18 months.

5. *Changes in thinking.* The above stimulates a shift from supply side to demand side thinking as firms are better able to sense and respond to customers' desires.

Process of globalization

According to Plumley (2000), the phases of globalization in e-business are:

- global brand abdication – like most US-based sites
- brand defence – involves redirection of a flagship.com site
- market presence – such as translated brochure ware
- market penetration – aggressive attempt to pursue foreign market share and build a global brand.

The pursuit of a market penetration strategy reflects a process of evolution such as that depicted in Figure 4.8.

Figure 4.8

E-business evolution

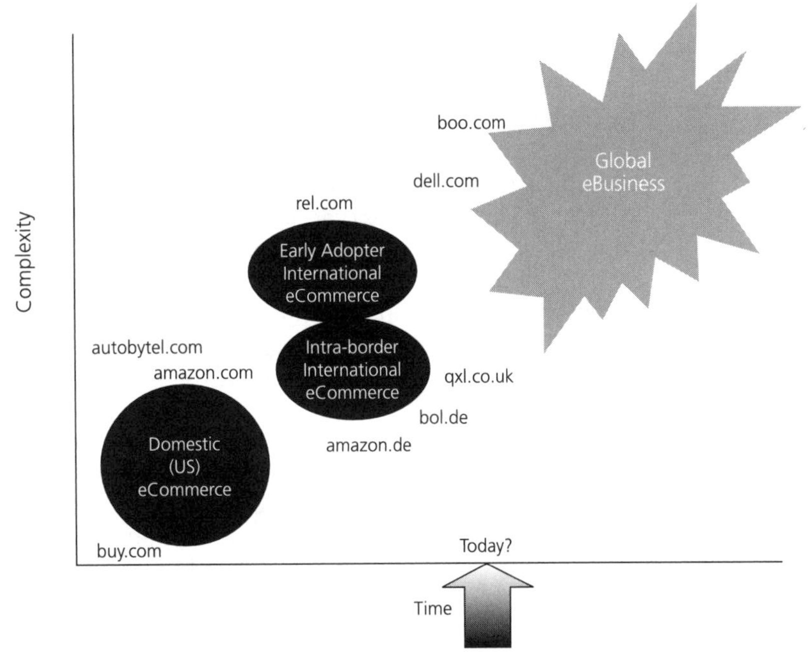

Source: Plumley (2000: 19)

The strategy changes from a domestic e-commerce focus to e-commerce that crosses national borders to a full-scale global e-business strategy. To accomplish this requires the integration of interrelated elements in the production value chain combined with a deep understanding of the cultural dimensions of global business.

Localization imperative

Although the Internet stimulates globalization, it is increasingly necessary to have a local web site. Early adopters are doing this and seeing a pay-off. Plumley (2000) reports the case of an IT firm that created a Korean web site and its revenues rose by 8 per cent.

European and Asian businesses are likely to have an advantage in creating multilingual web sites as historically they have had considerable experience in selling in transborder, transcultural environments.

It is necessary for sellers to adopt a buyer's perspective when competing in foreign markets as language, content and interface are necessary to establish trust and engage the attention of the online customer. This is illustrated in Figure 4.9. Forrester Research argues that the further the site enters into actual transactions, the more it must localize as localization turns visitors into prospects and prospects into customers.

The born global firm in the electronic age

The Internet offers an opportunity for young SMEs to establish a global sales operation by developing e-commerce web sites. Many small firms are born global in that they are 'start-ups' on the Internet and sell to a global audience from their web site. Such firms do not suffer from the problem of diminishing returns as their share of market increases. Unlike marketplace firms, for most Internet start-ups, variable costs are not high in relation to fixed costs and the law of diminishing returns does not always apply (Hollensen, 2001). This is especially true for products delivered in digital form where a single copy (e.g. software) can satisfy market needs or for products with a very high investment in intellectual content as with pharmaceuticals.

Born global firms are firms that commence international activities either from inception or shortly after founding. Knight and Cavusgil (1996) found a number of factors resulted in a growth in the number of born global firms. These include: demand among customers in mature economies for specialized or customized products; recent advances in process technology; decrease in telecommunications charges and increase in level of available telecommunications technology; ability to offer quick response times to changes in demand from their markets, and falls in cost of acquiring new technology.

Given the nature of the Internet, all Internet start-ups are potentially born global firms. Notionally all born global firms should be advantaged in the new electronic environment. This is because firms operating in marketspace:

- tend to rely on cutting edge technology
- have the ability to operate internationally almost from inception
- often have unique products or process methods
- are often managed by entrepreneurial visionaries

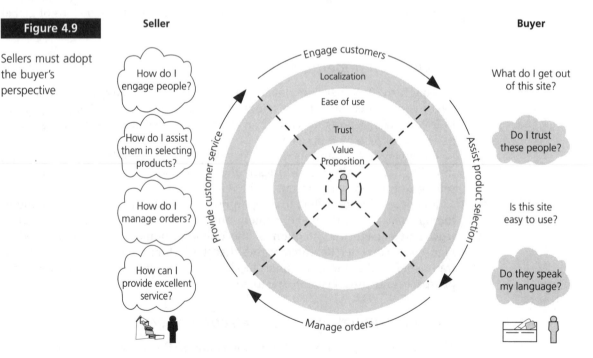

Figure 4.9

Sellers must adopt the buyer's perspective

Source: Plumley (2000: 13)

- tend to view the world as one market
- are successful in niche market strategies
- mostly avoid direct competition with larger, more efficient operators
- emphasize value and quality rather than price.

Although firms that start selling products and services online may be classified as born global, they are affected by different factors. In marketspace, the barriers to entry are much lower, the marketspace firm has the opportunity to offer (and customers are demanding) a better level of service than provided in marketplace and competition emerges from firms that traditionally have not been in the industry. As a case in point, competition for BHP-Billeton Australia now comes from a group of small start-up born global firms that trade in steel and other commodities and recently listed on the Toronto Stock Exchange.

Research by Kotha, Rindova and Rothaermel (2000) into the internationalization activities of US-based Internet firms contradicts the commonly held assumption that Internet-based firms are necessarily born global. They found that global involvement of such firms in fact varies according to the level of their intangible assets and strategic activity. Two types of intangible assets, reputation and web site traffic, were found to be positively related to the degree of internationalization. The same was true of levels of competitive and cooperative activity.

Questions

1. What are the issues affecting the readiness of firms to conduct business via the Internet?
2. What are the environmental factors and practical issues influencing e-business marketing?
3. How does the Internet operate as a change agent in international markets?
4. How do traditional theories of internationalization fit with e-business marketing?
5. How does globalization in marketspace differ from globalization in the marketplace?

References

Bauer, M. J. (2000) 'The effect of the internet on the supply chain and logistics', *World Trade* September: 72–80.

Bennett, R. (1997) 'Export marketing and the internet', *International Marketing Review* 14 (5): 324–43.

Craig, C. S. Douglas, S. P. and Flaherty, T. B. (2000) 'Information access and internationalization – the internet and consumer behavior in international markets', *Proceedings of the eCommerce and Global Business Forum*, 17–19 May, Santa Cruz, CA: Accenture Institute for Strategic Change.

Cyber Atlas (2001) www.cyberatlas.com

De la Torre, J. and Moxon, R. W. (2001) 'Introduction to the Symposium E-Commerce and Global Business: The Impact of the Information and Communication Technology Revolution on the Conduct of International Business', *Journal of International Business Studies*, 32 (4): 617–39.

Donovan, K. and Rossson, P. 'The internet and iternationalization', *Proceedings of the 17th Annual IMP Conference*, 9–11 September, Oslo: Norwegian School of Management.

Hamill, J. (1997) 'The internet and international marketing', *International Marketing Review* 14 (5): 300–18.

Hashimi, M. A. and Dharmanpour, F. (2000) 'The role of the internet in globalization of business operation', *Journal of Current Research in Global Business* fall: 111–18.

Hollensen, S. (2001) *International Marketing*, 2nd edn, Harlow: Prentice Hall.

Knight, G. A. and Cavusgil, S. T. (1996) 'The born global firm. A challenge to traditional internationalization theory', *Advances in International Marketing*, 8: 11–26.

Korper, S. and Ellis, J. (2000) *The E-Commerce Book, Building the E-Empire*, San Diego: Academic Press.

Kotha, S. Rindova, V. and Rothaermel, F. T. (2000) 'Firm specific factors that influence internationalization among US internet firms', *Proceedings of the eCommerce and Global Business Forum*, 17–19 May, Santa Cruz, CA: Accenture Institute for Strategic Change.

Marschan-Pickkari, R., Welch, D. and Welch, L. (1999) 'In the shadow: The impact of language on structure, power and communication in the multinational', *International Business Review*, 8: 421–40.

National Office of the Information Economy, Australia (1999) *Australia's e-Commerce Report Card*, www.dca.gov.au/nsapi_gra.

Nguyen, T. (2001) 'A Study of the internet and the internationalization of firms in transitional markets', unpublished PhD Thesis, University of Technology, Sydney.

Oxley, J. and Yeung, Y. (2000) 'E-commerce readiness – institutional environment and international competitiveness', *Proceedings of the eCommerce and Global Business Forum*, 17–19 May, Santa Cruz, CA: *Accenture Institute for Strategic Change*.

Plumley, D. J. (2000) 'Global eCommerce – The market, challenges and opportunities', *Browne Global Solutions* January.

Quelch, J. A., and Klein, L. R. (1996) 'The internet and international marketing', *Sloan Management Review* spring: 60–75.

Srirojanant, S. and Thirkell, P. (1999) 'Driving international business performance through use of internet technologies: A survey of Australian and New Zealand exporters', *Proceedings of the 1999 Annual Conference of the Australia – New Zealand International Business Academy*, University of New South Wales, 30 September–2 October, pp. 250–75.

Stafford, E. R. (1994) 'Using Co-operative Strategies to Make Alliances Work', *Long Range Planning*, June, Figure 1 and pp. 65–7.

Zaheer, S. and Manrakhan, S. (2001) 'Concentration and dispersion in global industries: Remote electronic access and the location of economic activities', *Journal of International Business Studies* 32 (4): 667–86.

Zhao, J. H. and Du, J. (2000) 'Electronic commerce and international business: A new test of internationalization theory', *Proceedings of the eCommerce and Global Business Forum*, 17–19 May, Santa Cruz, CA: *Accenture Institute for Strategic Change*.

Case Study 4 *Replicating Internet marketing strategies in another country*
Sean Sparks and Richard Fletcher

Introduction

Australia presents significant opportunities for the astute Internet company embarking on a program of internationalization. It is a stepping-stone into the Asia Pacific for Western economies, while also having the potential to be a key market in its own right. Online advertising in particular is one area where there is significant potential.

Current state of play

Online usage and spending internationally continues to outstrip growth in more traditional mediums. In 2000, 3 per cent of all advertising spent in the USA was online, while in Australia this figure hovered around the 1 per cent mark (or $85,386,000). Internet use worldwide has also grown from 44 million in 1995 to over 350 million today, a figure

▶

that is forecast to grow to over 750 million by 2005.[1]

North America dominates current Internet usage worldwide, with over 40 per cent of the world's online community. Europe accounts for just over 25 per cent, while the Asia Pacific region accounts for 20 per cent of online users.[2] However, when these figures are analysed with regard to the percentage of total population online, the Asia Pacific region is an area of great potential. As a region, its online population sits at around 1 per cent of total population, thanks mainly to the presence of China. Of all the countries in the region, Australia has by far the highest percentage of online companies looking to develop a presence in the Asia Pacific.

As the Internet grows, it will become less US centric. It is predicted that the Asia Pacific will account for upwards of 25 per cent of the worldwide Internet community by 2005.[3] For US-based companies that have been responsible for the growth in online revenue, this scenario presents a double-edged sword. While their own domestic market is not necessarily shrinking, if they are to survive and prosper they must react to the fact overseas markets will present significant revenue opportunities. As online activity becomes more of a global phenomenon and less US centric, companies must look at the benefits an international network can offer.

Realmedia USA

Realmedia was born out of the trend that saw an increasing percentage of advertising revenue finding its way onto the Internet. As well as using traditional mediums, advertisers looked to utilize the one-to-one communication benefits of the Internet. Not only did this provide a targeted environment, but such advertising also provided the main revenue stream for many web sites. Realmedia looked to function as a 'content aggregator', in that it provided clients with targeted Internet advertising campaigns from a selection of 500 web sites. As well, Realmedia also developed a proprietary ad serving technology, called 'openadstream'. This technology allowed banner ads to be served to web sites according to specific time and day specifications. The benefit of having both an online sales and adserving arm for Realmedia, was the creation of two distinct revenue streams.

Just as companies have become increasingly global in their focus, so too are advertising agencies that are looking to build international networks in response to globalization. A study by Kitchen and Shultz[4] found that the amount of time and resources devoted by advertising agencies to cross-border integrated marketing communications was increasing rapidly. The study also found that this trend is very much client driven. As well, numerous common elements were identified among advertising agencies in the USA and Australia. It follows that media brokers selling advertising space to agencies should also move to accommodate the move by advertising agencies towards globalization.

Australia: market overview and analysis

From a theoretical perspective, the Australian market makes a great deal of sense for Realmedia USA. If they are to stay ahead of their competitors, it is a market that presents opportunities from both a strategic and a revenue perspective. It has the potential to provide a stepping-stone to the Asia Pacific region, while at the same time being a valuable market in its own right. In looking to develop overseas markets, Kotler[5] identified six key factors that firms must take into account. These included demographic features, the economic situation, natural resources, technology, and both political and cultural issues. At first glance the Australian market appears to offer RealMedia USA genuine potential relative to these features.

By way of demographics, the key issue for Realmedia is the percentage of the population that will access the internet. This effectively provides the reach figure for online as a media. In late 1999 when Realmedia began its operations in Australia, 35.8 per cent of the population was online[6] (this figure now sits at 46 per cent). This represents the fourth highest percentage of online penetration across all countries. From this it can be inferred that there is significant potential within the Australian marketplace. This is particularly the case when as a medium online only continues to grow. As well as this, it is important to note that people in higher income groups have the greatest propensity to use the Internet. This is a key issue for advertisers who are looking to reach those with the greatest spending power.

When Realmedia entered the Australian marketplace, the dot.com boom was still very much in play. The finance markets as a whole could not get enough of online companies and the boom was showing little sign of relenting. For an online media sales company this meant the continuation for advertising campaigns by existing dot.coms and advertising launch campaigns of new ones. As well the Australian market as a whole was about to embark on one of the most buoyant years ever in terms of advertising growth and spend. On the back of the Olympics, 2000 represented the culmination of many long-term marketing and advertising campaigns. (The building blocks of which were put in place when Sydney first was awarded the right to host the Olympics.) In terms of the online marketplace, it was the general belief that Australia was around 12–18 months behind events in the USA. Based on this it was expected online revenue as a share of overall advertising spending would grow from $40 million in 1999 to over $100 million in 2000. The Australian economic arena appeared to be one of significant potential for an online company in the field.

By way of national resources, the key issue for any online company is that of the telecommunications industry. For the Internet to grow, there must be an appropriate delivery platform in place. Although Australia is technically competent in this field, many potential internet users are struggling to be connected because of internet service provider (ISP) issues. The problem is that Telstra (and many other telecommunications companies) is not able to keep pace with demand. As well as this Telstra, is not always cooperative in helping to provide lines for competitive ISP companies. However despite this, while the current infrastructure may create some delays in providing internet access, it is technically sound. As well, for Realmedia such platform issues are unlikely to affect the nature of their core business because they have already achieved a significant Internet penetration rate.

Paralleling the natural resource infrastructure is Australia's ability to take advantage of, and grow with technological changes. In terms of the shape of online and interactive media in the future, there still seems to be a great deal of uncertainty within the Australian marketplace. Although 2001 has seen the first steps by the free to air networks in moving to digital television, there is very little if any movement towards taking advantage of the interactive elements associated with such technology. Given that ultimately there will be some degree of convergence between traditional and online media, Australia is lacking in this respect relative to the rest of the world. Additionally clients in the Australian marketplace have been slow to embrace many of the opportunities that have grown out of the internet. Technology developments in online database management are an obvious extension of the benefits provided by the internet. However, despite these advances, very few clients are able to facilitate and implement the customer relationship marketing opportunities the Internet provides. The key for Realmedia is to understand that they are dealing with a young market. As well, one is in the process of coming to grips with the benefits online marketing can provide.

Another issue for Realmedia is the legal and political landscape of the market into which they are hoping to expand. Both Australia and the USA have a relatively stable political environment and freedom of speech is a feature of both countries. The similar landscapes will go some way to minimizing expansion difficulties. Further to this the USA is seen as very much a 'traditional friend, ally, and important trading partner'.[7] This increases the appeal of Australia as a marketplace.

The final point Kotler makes is that of social and cultural differences. While there are several small differences between Australians and Americans in terms of psychic distance, Australia is very close to the USA. Australian society is closely tied to events in the USA, and many of the trends in Australia are inherited from the USA. Language and attitudes to business are also relatively similar. These result in a market that is likely to operate according to many of the basic tenets and ideals in place in the USA.

Based on Kotler's key market factors, Australia as a market appears to make sense both strategically and financially for Realmedia. However, in looking to measure the viability of such an expansion, the business model and strategies used in the USA must be assessed. Simply replicating what has succeeded in one country does not ensure success in another. When starting operations in the USA, Realmedia, in building up its core base of sites to represent looked to discount in terms of commission. Where existing online site representation companies were charging 50 per cent commission of all revenue written onto the site, Realmedia pitched for and secured business based on a 20–30 per cent commission rate. This enabled the company to build up a strong inventory level of sites. In addition, when Realmedia successfully pitched for the *New York Times*, they obtained instant recognition among the online advertising community due to involvement with a 'marquis' site. While this side of the business was built, revenue was sourced through the proprietary adserving technology that had been developed. This ensured a consistent cash flow while the volume of advertising dollars required to make site representation profitable was established. The openadstream

adserving technology then provided the initial revenue source, while online advertising revenue was allowed to build gradually as the advertising industry moved towards spending dollars online.

The Australian online industry

When Realmedia looked to enter the Australian market, there were already several established players. Of the content aggregators similar to Realmedia, BMC Media that began operations in January 1998 was the biggest online sales company. They relied solely on advertising revenue spent on sites for income, with no adserving arm. When Realmedia entered the Australian market, BMC represented over 400 web sites, including Telstra.com.

In terms of adserving Doubleclick (who recently shut down their site representation arm) was the dominant player in Australia. With only one competitor, Sabela, in the adserving field, and with a superior product, Doubleclick all but monopolized this section of the market.

The other key player in Australia was the Ninemsn portal. Ninemsn represented a joint venture that drew on Microsoft technology and PBL content. It was launched in March 1998, incorporating over 50 sites and associated services. Currently, Ninemsn reaches more than 53 per cent of Australia's online population.

It was within this environment then that Realmedia looked to become a key player. BMC has the advantage of being a local player, as well as being first to market. Doubleclick had quickly established a dominant position in adserving, while Ninemsn was able to take advantage of the already strong PBL presence in the Australian advertising industry. As well as this, where the online spend in the USA was moving up to around 3 per cent of overall adspend, in Australia this figure was struggling to reach 1 per cent. In addition, there was in 2000 the Sydney Olympics, which was the biggest advertising revenue event ever in Australia history.

Realmedia: expansion into the Australian market

The Realmedia office in Australia was opened in January 2000. As with their approach in the USA, Realmedia Australia looked immediately to build its site representation base (replicating the cut-price commission structure used previously to secure business). Although successful, unlike the US operation the Australian office was unable to secure a 'marquis' site. Additionally there was a significant delay in bringing the Openadstream technology to the Australian market. Due to technical issues, it could not be offered to the marketplace for the first nine months of Realmedia Australia's operations. To compensate for this, a far greater emphasis was placed on revenue sourced from web site advertising. Staff levels were ramped up significantly, and a Melbourne office was established. By March, Realmedia Australia had over 30 staff. It was also at this point that the dot.com crash hit. Realmedia Australia closed its doors in February 2001, just a little over a year after it first began operations. Although in principle Australia as a marketplace made sense for Realmedia, it proved to be a very difficult environment for a variety of reasons.

The Sydney Olympics ensured that 2000 would be a year like no other in the Australian advertising industry. With literally billions of dollars being spent on the greatest audience reaching event ever, it dominated all advertising and marketing strategies (as well as absorbing huge amounts of dollars). As a result, most companies' focus across the year revolved around this one event. For the online advertising industry looking to establish itself, this meant taking very much a back seat. While marketing directors were interested in online opportunities, it was not an area many were prepared to start working on during the year 2000 as they were in the final stages of implementing four years' worth of marketing strategy.

Another blow to the industry was the dot.com crash. With this section being a major spender online, the drying up of advertising funds had an immediate impact on internet sales companies. Budgets were cut overnight, while the crash as a whole created an air of cynicism in the industry.

Despite these external issues, Realmedia would still be operating today had more foresight been shown in their entry into the Australia. Like many dot.com related businesses, too little emphasis was placed on costs relative to revenue sourced. The Australian online advertising industry, although growing, was developing at a much slower rate than the US market, where volume is not such an issue. In Australia a cut-price commission approach created incredibly tight margins. This was compounded by the difficulties associated with sourcing revenue in an Olympic year. Additionally, going from 3 to 30 staff in a short period of time did not guarantee that revenue secured would be relative to staff numbers. Far more insight into staff levels was required, particularly in an uncertain marketplace.

Another issue was the failure to secure a 'marquis' site. Where BMC became known to the market as a result of Testra.com, Realmedia was unable to gain such recognition. They were forced to rely on numerous 'medium sized' sites not necessarily known and recognized by the advertising industry.

Exacerbating the cash flow issue associated with the commission structure was the failure to source revenue through the Openadstream adserving technology. Where this provided the initial revenue stream for the US office, in Australia it proved to be little more than a white elephant as technical issues delayed its sale and made it very difficult to transfer the technology from the USA. The result was almost total reliance on online advertising revenue sales in a difficult market.

Conclusion

Realmedia had the potential to succeed in the Australian market but made a variety of fundamental errors. While external forces combined to make Australia a relatively difficult marketplace to enter, it was lack of foresight internally that ultimately led to Realmedia's downfall. Being unable to utilize one of two revenue sources for nine months will place unnecessary strain on any start-up operation. This is particularly so when this revenue source has been the catalyst for success in other markets. Additionally, operating on tight margins in a market that is more responsive to yield as opposed to volume-based deals creates further pressure.

Because of companies such as Realmedia failing, the Australia online sales scene is currently going through a period of immense change. Smaller companies with increasing focus on costs relative to revenue are succeeding; while sites no longer have the option of securing 20 per cent commission deals. The learning from failed companies such as Realmedia is being applied to creating better business plans. All of this augurs well for an industry that, despite ongoing teething, can only continue to grow.

Questions

1. What is the key learning that should be taken from the Realmedia experience?

2. In what way does the Realmedia experience replicate the problems encountered by so many failed dotcoms?

3. How does Porter's theory of competitive advantage provide insight into the Realmedia experience?

4. What was the key problem from a promotional mix perspective that saw Realmedia disadvantaged in the marketplace?

Notes

1 Computer Industry Almanac www.bmcmedia.com
2 Computer Industry Almanac www.doubleclick.net
3 Computer Industry Almanac www.ninemsn.com.au
4 Kitchen and Shultz (1999) 'A multi-country comparison of the drive for integrated communications', *Journal of Advertising Research*, Jan/Feb. www.yahoo.com.au
5 P. Kotler, *Marketing Management*, 9th edition, Upper Saddle River, New Jersey: Prentice Hall International, p. 167.
6 *The Current State of Play: Australia and the Information Economy* (2000) National Office for the Information Economy, November.
7 M. Byrnes (1994) *Australia and the Asian Game*, NSW: Allen and Unwin, p. 99

5 International competitive strategy in the electronic environment

Learning objectives

After studying this chapter, you should be able to:

- Recognize the main factors that influence international competitive strategy in the e-business environment.

- Appreciate the effects of e-business on international competitiveness.

- Differentiate between the operation of marketing models in marketspace as opposed to marketplace.

- Identify ways in which e-business improves the international competitive advantage of SMEs.

- Appreciate how the influence of the Internet on marketing enhances international competitiveness.

Introduction

At the height of the Internet boom, business commentators argued that the international competitive environment would change fundamentally because of the Internet. De la Torre and Moxon (2001: 617) list some of the changes that global e-business could bring about:

- Infinitely responsive and elastic supply chains that could be simultaneously constructed or deconstructed for each product as conditions warranted.
- International distribution of value added activities so that the relative competitive advantage of each geographic location ensures diffusion of the benefits of globalization.
- Orders delivered immediately to customers in any part of the world.
- Speedy and accurate product development due to the availability of extensive data bases on customer preferences.

- Mass customization of products and services tailored to different cultures or national idiosyncrasies.
- Change in corporate boundaries due to outsourcing all but the most central processes to specialized firms leading to virtual corporations and networks of alliances.
- Self-regulated markets subject to constant competitive pressure requiring no intervention by government.

The crash of the dot.coms in the second half of 2000 brought realism to the euphoric predictions about the influence of e-business. A more sober evaluation of the effects of e-business on international competitiveness follows, especially in terms of some of the constraints.

Effects of e-business on international competitiveness

In this section, a number of general issues affecting competitiveness in the international e-business environment are considered. A discussion of factors in the environment that directly influence international competitiveness follows. An examination of the impact of the Internet on SME competitiveness concludes the section.

General issues

There are a number of factors in e-business that impact on the application of traditional marketing concepts in the global electronic environment. The most important of these are as follows.

Culture

In traditional marketing models, culture is a key variable explaining geographic variations in consumer behaviour. Culture plays a smaller role in virtual markets where a cyber culture dominates and local culture acts as a contingency variable that mediates behaviour. Compounding the situation is that in e-business information can be acquired in one cultural sphere, and the associated transaction can take place in a different cultural sphere.

Opinion leaders

Models focusing on the role of personal influence no longer apply to the same extent. With the proliferation of chat rooms and bulletin boards, the role of such influence becomes more diffuse and depersonalized.

Diffusion of innovation

Geographic proximity will no longer be as important, as the Internet provides a vehicle both rapidly to communicate the latest developments and to deliver digital products.

Complexity of evaluations

In an e-business environment consumers have to evaluate stimuli and make choices based on heterogeneous and often unfamiliar cues (e.g. does the hotel stars rating system mean the same in all countries?).

Country of origin effect

The role of national culture in the formation of values and behavioural norms is likely to decline in importance. This will occur as the Internet increasingly exposes consumers to stimuli from other countries. As this occurs, consumers will become more global in outlook and treat country of origin cues as less salient.

Self-selection bias

The degree of consumer involvement in the purchase process is likely to become less, and the distinction between high and low involvement goods not as meaningful.

Buyer stereotype

A final factor is that the consumer who uses the Internet is different from the consumer who does not (in terms of demographics, education and innovation adoption). Are we therefore positing global trends, or trends for a particular global segment when discussing e-business?

Electronic business and international competitiveness

The Internet affects international competitiveness. Some of the major effects of e-business on international competitiveness are as follows.

Shifts in important strategic dimensions

With e-business, price and quality are no longer the only determinants of competitiveness. Fast delivery and customization are also important factors, for which customers are willing to pay a premium. E-business combined with flexible production systems such as computer integrated manufacturing, flexible manufacturing system and just in time, make mass customization possible by compressing the time it takes firms to deliver products/services to customers.

Compressed value chain

Not only do some of the traditional elements in the chain disappear with e-business, but also sharing information about demand throughout the value chain helps to plan and control upstream activities. This process reduces excessive inventory and back orders. Online ordering and the real-time transfer of ordering information to the manufacturer significantly shortens lead times to meet customer demands.

Globalization of markets

No longer is producing the best product or service in a country a guarantee of success, as the market is also accessible by foreign competitors. To be competitive it is necessary to create a product or service that is attractive to global customers, while at the same time customized to specific needs in a country. No longer is it feasible for country specific units of multinational firms to act independently from each other. To do so means that they are unable to coordinate operations between different countries, carry separate stocks for different countries and may end up with a poor match between customer demand and warehouse inventory.

Outsourcing as a strategic weapon

E-business makes it convenient and efficient to share information among different firms in the value chain, using electronic data interchange (EDI) and the Internet. This facilitates firms outsourcing activities. Outsourcing can take the form of activities that provide little added value if done internally (e.g. bookkeeping, maintenance, etc.), cannot be done due to lack of resources (e.g. R&D, logistics), and can be done better by other firms (e.g. advertising).

Globalization of the supply network

International business has traditionally been inefficient and time consuming because of wide areas to cover and long lead times. E-business has compressed time and distance, making it easier for firms to overcome national boundaries. Many multinational activities can be executed with the efficiencies of domestic operations. As an example, Dell Computers have built a worldwide network of suppliers and customers into a virtual corporation, providing what customers want in a fast and efficient manner. With e-business, firms no longer have to confine sources of supply to domestic suppliers. A supply network on a global scale can be an important source of a firm's competitiveness. This is shown in Figure 5.1 (p. 106).

Competitiveness for small and medium enterprises (SMEs)

A central concept in international marketing is that size matters. Smaller firms are likely to be competitively disadvantaged in terms of factors such as access to information, supply of small shipments on a competitive basis, ability to visit overseas markets and in targeting and promoting to profitable niches in overseas markets.

E-business reduces these disadvantages in a number of ways. It provides inexpensive access to information, enables direct interaction with customers, is a relatively cheap promotional medium, stimulates unsolicited trade inquiries and facilitates alliances involving risk sharing, outsourcing and information sharing. In addition, the Internet enables firms to bypass many of the constraints of the marketplace networks in which they are embedded. Figure 5.2 (p. 107) illustrates the direct connections that result between customer and supplier, customer and competitor, supplier and business partner, and competitor and business partner.

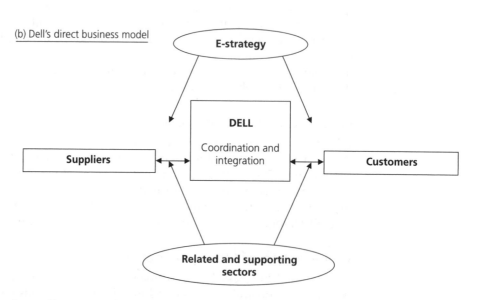

Figure 5.1

The traditional model vs. Dell's direct business model in the personal computer industry

(a) Traditional model

Suppliers → Manufacturing → Distribution channels → Customers

(b) Dell's direct business model

E-strategy

DELL
Coordination and integration

Suppliers ↔ DELL ↔ Customers

Related and supporting sectors

Source: Cho, Moon and Park (2000: 23)

Poon and Jevons (1997) suggest that SMEs in the Internet age can further overcome the disadvantages of size by banding together or taking advantage of the associations to which they belong. Table 5.1 (p. 108) lists ways of doing this.

Example	*Global opportunity for SMEs through the Internet*

The Web will reduce the competitive advantage of economies of scale, making it easier for small companies to compete internationally. Advertising costs, formerly a barrier to overseas marketing will almost disappear as the web makes it possible to reach a global audience at low cost.

Traditional intermediaries will be less important as the Internet connects producers directly with end users. Price differentials between customers and between countries will narrow, as consumers become more price aware. The web will act as an efficient low-cost medium for continuing worldwide market research, gaining customer feedback, tracking customer behaviour, and establishing virtual communities. The Internet will provide SMEs with low-cost access to global markets by reducing the barriers to internationalization commonly experienced by small companies (Hamill, 1997).

Things are moving fast! As banks, telecoms and computer firms increase the security, speed and infrastructure for e-business, we can expect to see the most entrepreneurial SMEs rapidly taking up international market opportunities accessible via the Internet.

Figure 5.2

Internet enabled
bypasses in the
context of a small
business network

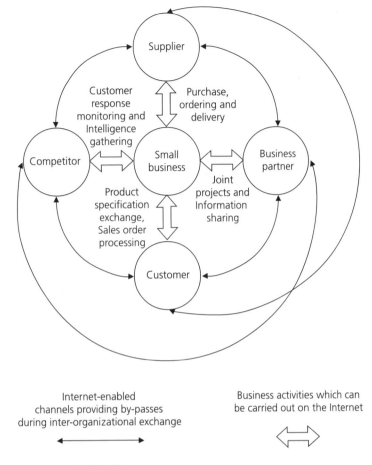

Internet-enabled
channels providing by-passes
during inter-organizational exchange

Business activities which can
be carried out on the Internet

Source: Poon and Jevons (1997: 35)

Applicability of traditional competitive models to the Internet environment

This section of the chapter discusses Dunning's eclectic paradigm (1993), the integration–responsiveness framework, and Porter's (1990) model of national competitive advantage in the context of the e-business environment.

Dunning's eclectic paradigm

This paradigm has three elements – ownership, location and internalization (OLI) – that determine the most appropriate form of market entry. Incorrect application of the paradigm can lead to market failure. In e-business there is little need to internalize intermediaries. However, while traditional intermediaries are disappearing, new types of intermediaries are emerging such as content providers, search engines, portals, and Internet service providers (Cho,

Table 5.1	Inter-organizational relationship	Internet marketing strategy
Comparison of inter-organizational relationship types with Internet marketing strategies	Confederations (e.g. small business groups sharing resources through contractual agreements)	Central management provide resources for network members to market their products and services on the Internet (e.g. a virtual agency service) Include in the agreements arrangements to provide reciprocal home page links between members included in the contract
	Conjugate collectives (e.g. closed group agreements between supplier and customer)	Allow reciprocal links on members' home pages. Make available market intelligence on the closed group's intranet (if available) with log-in control Share market intelligence in order to improve supplier–buyer relationship
	Agglomerate collectives (e.g. trade associations)	Trade association provide market intelligence data (local and international) on its home page or member use Mutual agreement between (international) trade associations to market the member's products and services
	Organic collectives (e.g. community services groups)	Advertise products and provide low-cost/free services for charity members of community networks on the Internet (e.g. www.link.net.au). Link community calendar of events to one's home page

Source: Poon and Jevons (1997: 37)

Moon and Park, 2000: 4). This is termed 'hyper mediation' (Carr 2000) and is the opposite of 'disintermediation'. Even with these new forms of intermediary, firms do not have to internalize market processes to the same extent because the e-business market is relatively efficient.

Integration–responsiveness framework

The integration–responsiveness (I–R) framework considers the cost advantages of globally integrating certain tasks compared with the benefits of responding to national differences in tastes and business practices. Levitt (1983) argues for integration. Douglas and Wind (1987) argue for local responsiveness. Bartlett and Ghoshal (1989) argue for a transnational solution combining global integration and local responsiveness.

An essential element of e-business is 'navigation' (a distinctive competence that is frequently associated with Amazon.com). There are three dimensions of navigation (Evans and Wurster, 1999): *reach* (i.e. how many customers can a business access or how many products can it offer); *richness* – the depth and detail of the information the business gives to or collects about the customer; *affiliation* – whose interests the business represents. In marketspace, these dimensions of navigation can replace the concepts of integration and responsiveness in marketplace.

Porter's diamond of national competitive advantage

Porter (1990) modelled the factors causing nations to gain competitive advantage in certain industries and drew conclusions as to the implications for company strategies and national economies. His model had four determinants: factor conditions, demand conditions, related and supporting industries, and firm strategy, structure and rivalry. In addition, he included two variables external to the firm, those of government and chance.

He emphasized domestic rivalry and geographic concentration. With e-business, however, firms cannot restrict rivalry to the domestic scene and geographic concentration in the home country is less important. In the case of factor conditions and demand conditions, there are a number of upstream and downstream activities in the value chain to take into account, as well as the existence of intermediaries. The possibilities in e-business to deconstruct the value chain and of disintermediation of agents will change the businesses in the chain that relate to factor conditions and demand conditions.

In addition, the elements of domestic rivalry and the geographic concentration of related and supporting industries are less important in e-business. This is because geographic constraints are not as important in an increasingly digital environment. Porter largely ignored the role of human factors. These are very important in e-business as the competitiveness of an organization can be a function of the computerized capabilities of its members.

Porter focuses on the home base and does not incorporate the effects of multinational activities in his model. Moon, Rugman and Verbeke (1998), who have created a 'double diamond' as illustrated in Figure 5.3, have subsequently addressed this shortcoming in the context of the international marketplace.

The internal diamond represents the operation of conditions in the domestic market, the dotted diamond conditions in the international market for the country and the outer diamond combined domestic and international conditions. The shape of the outer diamond will vary from country to country

Figure 5.3

The generalized double diamond

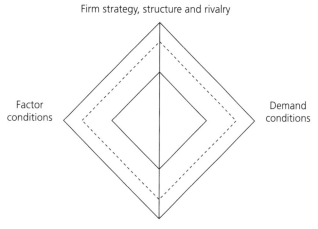

Source: Moon, Rugman and Verbeke (1998: 135–50)

according to the relative importance of each of the four determinants of competitive advantage in both the domestic and international markets.

Cho, Moon and Park (2000) suggest that the factors in Porter's original diamond need modification to account for e-business:

1. *Factor conditions.* Porter's focus on domestic resources is not applicable in the Internet age. The Internet, combined with an international logistics infrastructure and trade related deregulation, enables companies to produce goods in foreign countries (i.e. countries where it is cost efficient) and then distributes them to the global market, or to source low-cost, high-quality parts from foreign countries for incorporation into domestic production.

2. *Related and supporting conditions.* Firms no longer have to rely on domestic related and supporting industries as globalization offers the opportunity to use foreign related and supporting industries such as international logistics or communication services.

3. *Demand conditions.* With e-business, firms can sell their products/services to customers in the global market, and can customize their goods/services.

4. *Structure, strategy and rivalry.* A firm can get closer to both suppliers and customers to maximize its value to both parties through the integration of online ordering, real-time transfer of order information throughout the value chain and an efficient logistics system.

Figure 5.4 incorporates both the e-business aspects of competitive advantage with Porter's determinants of national competitive advantage.

Impact of e-business marketing models on international competitiveness

This section reviews two recent models of the impact of the Internet on international marketing. These are the Rayport and Sviokla's (1995) model, which contrasts marketplace with marketspace, and the Dutta and Segev's (1998) model of interactivity and connectivity in marketspace.

Rayport and Sviokla (1995) model

Rayport and Sviokla (1995) argue that the information revolution has changed the nature of buyer–seller transactions. Information systems make both physical location of inventory and the actual site of the buying largely irrelevant. Marketspace transactions eliminate the traditional physical marketplace interaction between seller and buyer. Figure 5.5 illustrates this process.

Rayport and Sviolka argue that brand equity is created in the traditional marketplace through:

- *content* – the product offering
- *context* – the communications programmes
- *infrastructure* – pricing and channel activities related to distribution.

Figure 5.4

An extended
diamond model in
the age of electronic
business

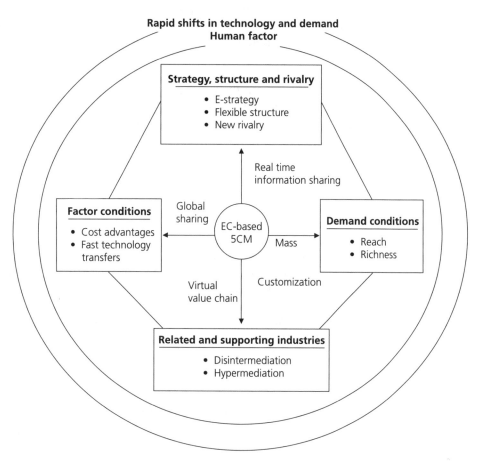

Source: Cho, Moon and Park (2000: 9)

Figure 5.5

Marketspace
compared with
marketplace

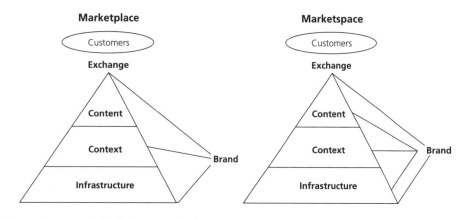

Source: Rayport and Sviolka (1994: 142)

In Internet (marketspace) marketing on the other hand, they argue that content, context and infrastructure are disaggregated to create new ways of creating value (e.g. using e-mail to distribute a newsletter). The Internet changes the way these factors operate:

- *content* – this involves provision of information, services and where possible, having the product delivered electronically. Product delivery is changed through a transformation of time (speed) and place.
- *context* – this involves accessing information in a new way via mobile phones or computers.
- *infrastructure* – the Internet provides the backbone for connection and delivery of value.

These three components pose new questions for international marketing (Fletcher and Brown, 1999: 575). Regarding content: What information and service can and should be provided? How much information should be provided on products, pricing and availability? How much access should be given to customers to interrogate the firm's database? Regarding context: Who and where are prospective customers connected electronically? Is there compatibility between computers and other access modes? Finally, regarding infrastructure: What is the reach, capability and value creation potential of the Internet and other electronic networks? What communication potential exists via the television medium, the electric power grid and mobile telephone networks?

Dutta and Segev (1998) model

Dutta and Segev (1998) studied 100 major US corporations, and found that marketspace has two dimensions: technological capability and business strategy. The dimension of technological capability divides into two components, interactivity and connectivity:

1. *Interactivity.* Because of the real time nature of the Internet, relationships between organizations and customers are becoming more interactive. Dutta and Segev argue that this makes for richer and more intense relationships and creates new paradigms for customer service and product design.
2. *Connectivity.* The global nature of the Internet is fostering the creation of a shared marketspace. The growth of connectivity gives rise to new communication and co-ordination mechanisms linking organizations to their customers, as well as stimulating greater communication between customers themselves.

Together these aspects are transforming business models of organizations, especially when applied to the 'Four Ps' of product, price, promotion and placement. To these, Dutta and Segev add a fifth element – customer relationships – as indicated in Figure 5.6.

Dutta and Segev (1998) also explored the following aspects of marketspace:

1. *Technological sophistication.* This relates to ease of navigation of the site; degree of customization possible of the web interface; speed and ease of access to site features and advanced technological capabilities such as video.
2. *Transformation of products.* This relates to availability of product-related information online; customization of products for individuals or groups of customers; and participation of customers in the specification and design of products.
3. *Transformation of promotion.* This relates to the use of online advertising; the use of online promotions such as sales and discounts; customization of online promotions; participation of customers in online promotions; and links with other organizations in organizing online promotions.
4. *Transformation of pricing.* This relates to the availability of pricing information online; dynamic customization of prices; availability of online price negotiation; and possibility of charging customers for only proportions of products consumed.
5. *Transformation of placement.* This relates to the availability of online ordering; availability of secured online payment; real time processing of orders; distribution of products online; and involvement of partner organizations in online distribution.
6. *Transformation of customer relationships.* This relates to the provision of online customer service; provision of online customized services; provision of online communications to customers; and solicitation of online feedback from customers.

Dutta and Segev found that the Internet transforms the marketing mix variables to differing degrees. Their research revealed that companies scored highest on using the Internet to support customer relationships, especially when they used their web sites to provide better customer service. This took the form of supplying product guides online, providing online chat services, and encouraging the formation of online clubs or groupings as happens with airlines promoting and operating their frequent flyer programs via the Internet.

Technology was the second most important factor. There is a move towards simpler sites, which download quickly as most Web users are not willing to wait more than 30 seconds for a page to download. This has resulted in the use of

Figure 5.6	The marketspace model

The marketspace model

Source: Dutta and Segev (1998: 5)

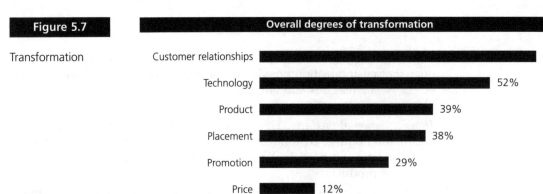

Source: Dutta and Sergev (1998)

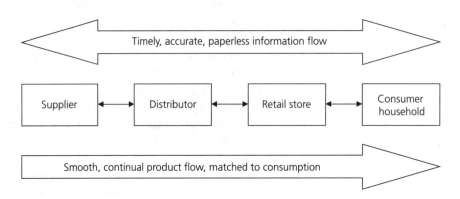

Source: Johnston (1999)

technology to replace graphics and video (which delay downloading), with more use of animation, site maps and search engines so that the site is both interesting and user friendly. The degree to which the Internet affects various factors is shown in Figure 5.7.

In general, a timely accurate paperless information flow, a smooth continual product flow matched to consumption, and a delayering of the distribution channel characterizes the new buyer–seller relationships in marketspace. Figure 5.8 summarizes the relationship between buyers and sellers on the Internet.

Summary

This chapter discussed the impact of e-business attributes on international competitiveness, and examined a number on international marketing models in terms of their applicability in the international e-business environment. Several specific e-business models were reviewed in terms of their likely impact on international competitiveness. De la Torre and Moxon (2001) have created a comprehensive summary of the impact of e-business on the various traditional theories of international business. This summary is provided in Table 5.2

| Table 5.2 | Potential impacts of information and communications technology on IB theory |

Theoretical construct	Selected elements of the construct	Elements sensitive to ICT-driven transformation	Potential direction of change
International theory	• Market failure resulting in transaction costs which exceed coordination costs.	• Search costs diminished. • Alternative sources of resources enlarged. • Increased value of intangible assets. • Lower coordination costs within network.	Indeterminate since forces acting in different direction; drop in coordination costs may result in greater internalization and concentration simultaneous with more outsourcing.
	• Risk and uncertainty favours internationalization.	• Market information easier to access and of higher quality.	Favours increases in outsourcing and market-based transactions.
	• Externalities, scope economies, etc.	• Increased availability of alternative channels. • Greater resource availability and sources.	Favours disintegration and market-based transactions
Locational advantages	• Differences in factor endowment and costs.	• Information content of tasks more transferable.	Favours greater dispersion of economic activities.
	• Transport costs and distance (physical and cultural).	• Logistics, coordination and communication facilitated by ICTs.	Fewer changes with respect to physical products; larger changes for intangibles.
	• Artificial barriers and market impediments.	• Border controls increasingly difficult for digital products.	Little change for physical products: large impact on digital products and content.
	• Infrastructure and incentives.	• Critical role of infrastructure and protection of intellectual property.	The digital divide will favour locations with good infrastructure and IP protection.
Ownership advantages	• Structural or asset-based, e.g. technology, trademarks and other monopolistic advantage.	• Digital piracy and greater availability of technical information shortens life cycles. • Increased permeability of borders to information. • Greater returns to scale.	These effects would seem to enhance the relative power of MNEs and lead to greater concentration and integration in global industries.
	• Knowledge and organizational capabilities.	• Virtual and internal communication networks expand capabilities.	Increases the value of intangible assets and internal capabilities.
	• Political connections.	• Increased transparency and availability of political information.	Should lead to a reduced advantage from 'insider' positions or knowledge.
The liability of foreignness	• Foreign firm faces higher operating costs due to lack of knowledge.	• Increased availability of public and private information reduces liability of foreignness.	Market integration and lower foreignness costs will lead to higher competitive advantage for MMEs.

Theoretical construct	Selected elements of the construct	Elements sensitive to ICT-driven transformation	Potential direction of change
Drivers of global integration or local responsiveness	• Economies of scale.	• Greater coordination of production and demand. • Sharing of best practices.	Increases opportunities to extract value from centralization.
	• R&D complexity and rising product development costs.	• Increase in information content of new products and services.	Potential for disaggregating R&D and product development within corporate system.
	• Homogeneity of consumer demand.	• Rapid and efficient sharing of information. • Leveraging brand values.	Increases value of multimarket positions.
	• Multinational customers.	• Demand for similar product and services across operations.	Drives out local suppliers and enhances competitiveness of global players.
	• Common market agreements.	• Growing uniformity of product standards.	Increases value of multimarket positions.
	• Political pressures.	• National governments under increasing pressure to invest in ICTs.	Weakens national pressure for local responsiveness.
The obsolescing bargain	• Pre-investment risk and uncertainty.	• Information available on local conditions, previous deals and behavior, etc.	Reduces risk of entry and enhances ability to divide and assign risks to those best able to carry it.
	• Hostage effect.	• High value to reputation.	Convergence of political behaviour and incentives.
	• Growth in host country capabilities.	• Codification of industry information anticipates learning.	Better pre-investment bargaining reduces need for post-contractual negotiations.
The role of culture and management	• Differences in consumer behaviour and values.	• Information sharing and global media affect consumers everywhere.	More scope for global market segments.
	• Management policies, employee needs and incentives.	• Growth in cross-national teaming and virtual teams.	Difficulty in differential compensation in global teams.
	• Need for elaborate HR practices.	• Ability to manage from a distance.	Reduction in personnel transfers and foreign assignments.
Financial arbitrage	• Foreign investment driven by differences in the cost of capital.	• Information on market rates and opportunities widely available. • Better knowledge of market financial risks and positions.	Convergence and integration of the world's financial markets reduce the scope for arbitrage; intermediaries have better information to absorb risks.

Source: De la Torre and Moxon (2001: 620–22)

Questions

1. Analyse how e-business influences international competitiveness.
2. How does its impact differ between SMEs and MNCs when they undertake international marketing?
3. Discuss the shortcomings of Porter's theory of competitive advantage when applied in marketspace.
4. Do Rayport and Sviokla's and Dutta and Sergev's approaches convincingly explain the differences when conducting international marketing in marketspace?

References

Bartlett, C. A. and Ghoshal. S. (1989) *Managing Across Borders: The Transnational Solution*, Boston: Harvard Business School Press.

Carr, N. G. (2000) 'Hypermediation: Commerce as clickstream', *Harvard Business Review* Jan–Feb: 46–7.

Cho, D. S. Moon, H. C. and Park, S. (2000) 'Competitiveness impacts of electronic commerce: Supply chain management perspective', *Proceedings of the eCommerce and Global Business Forum*, 17–19 May, Santa Cruz, CA: *Accenture Institute for Strategic Change*.

De la Torre, J. and Moxon, R. W. (2001) 'Introduction to the Symposium E-Commerce and Global Business: The impact of information and communication technology revolution on the conduct of international business', *Journal of International Business Studies*, 32 (4): 617–39.

Douglas, S. and Wind, Y. (1987) 'The myth of globalization', *Columbia Journal of World Business* 24 (4): 19–25.

Dunning, J. H. (1993) *Multinational Enterprises in the Global Economy.* Wokingham, Addison-Wesley.

Dutta, S. and Segev, A. (1998) *The Global Internet 100 Survey 1998*, www.info-strategy.com/G1100.

Evans, P. and Wurster, T. S. (1999) 'Getting real about virtual commerce', *Harvard Business Review* Nov–Dec: 85–94.

Fletcher, R. and Brown, L. (1999) *International Marketing: An Asia-Pacific Perspective*, Sydney: Prentice Hall.

Hamill, J. (1997) 'The Internet and International Marketing', *International Marketing Review*, Vol 14, No 5, pp. 300–318.

Johnston, W. (1999). 'Electronically Wiring the Network: The Case of Electronic Data Interchange' Presentation by Professor Johnston at Georgia State University.

Levitt, T. (1983) 'The globalization of markets', *Harvard Business Review* May–June: 92–102.

Moon, H. C., Rugman, A. M. and Verbeke, A. (1998) 'A generalized double diamond approach to the global competitiveness of Korea and Singapore', *International Business Review*, 7 (2): 135–50.

Poon, S. and Jevons, C. (1997) 'Internet enabled international marketing: A small business network perspective', *Journal of Marketing Management* 13: 29–41.

Porter, M. E. (1990) *The Competitive Advantage of Nations*, New York: Free Press.

Rayport, J. and Sviolka, J. (1995) 'Exploiting the virtual value chain', *Harvard Business Review* Nov–Dec: 75–85.

Case Study 5 *Austel Consortium Pty Ltd: Entering an Islamic market*
Michelle Lim and Richard Fletcher

Michael Mathan, Director of AusTel Consortium Pty. Ltd., an Australian provider of global telecommunications and Internet-based services, was puzzled over the fallout of his

▶

company from a Joint Venture with the Iranian Government. The negotiations had run smoothly and everything had gone to plan. What did the Majlis have in mind when they intervened? Michael Mathan knew he had to develop a response to stay in there but what should his next actions be?

Iran: background business climate

Since the revolution of 1979, the subsequent war with Iraq, US sanctions, and the slowly rising record low crude oil prices, the Iranian economy operating in isolation has moved at a very slow pace. The establishment of the Islamic Republic, governed by strong revolutionary sentiment, widespread nationalism and confiscation of private enterprises, resulted in a virtual cessation of foreign investment. As self-reliance became a main theme of economic policy, the country has increasingly disregarded the importance of foreign investment. Until the mid-1980s relatively high oil prices enabled Iran to earn substantial foreign exchange revenues, thereby making the Law of Attraction and Protection of Foreign Investments in Iran practically dormant. However, after the end of the war, policy sentiment gradually changed and Iran began to adopt a more open approach towards foreign participation. There is a now growing demand for foreign services and various sectors of the economy are opening up.

Iran has a population of 65 million people. Over one-third are under the age of 14 and two-thirds are under the age of 25. Most of the population is located in the major cities of Tehran (15 million) and Isfahan (5 million), and cities such as Tabriz, Shiraz and Mashad (around 2–3 million altogether). While the Iranian GDP in 1999 was less than US$5000 per head of population, external debt is below US$22 billion. Iran has also weathered the recent downturn in crude oil prices while placing particular emphasis on the development of non-petroleum exports in the imminent Third Five Year Development Plan beginning in 2000.

The August 1997 inauguration of Mohammad Khatami as the new president of Iran, with large-scale national support, tilted the balance in favour of the moderate wing. Policies involving economic liberalization for foreign trade, easing of social restrictions and better relations with Western countries were likely to change. Mr Khatami's election victory has prompted many Iranians to express openly their opinions about the state. It is no longer a taboo to discuss relations with the USA, social reform or even criticize the judiciary. Some areas are still off-limits, but momentum appears to be in favour of change.

On the other hand, the right wing remains highly influential. The parliament, although freely elected, is appointed by the Majlis, an Islamic screening committee, an organization of strictly religious clerics. Ayatollah Sayyid Ali Khamenei holds the constitutional position of the rahbar (leader)/Head of Judiciary. This underlying control has been known to influence the process and period with which major reforms are enacted. Also the relaxation of strict cultural and religious beliefs has recently led to a spate of riots and violence.

Shi'a Muslim (89 per cent), Sunni Muslim (10 per cent) and Zoroastrian, Jewish, Christian, and Baa'l (1 per cent) make up the religious composition of Iran. The four goals of the Islamic Republic are the establishment of Islamic divine rule and democracy, the restoration of justice and specifically Islamic economic justice, the creation of a true Islamic person and Islamic society (and economics) over time, and the restoration of the independence of Iran, and other Muslim nations, through export of revolution if necessary. However despite these revolutionary proclamations, private enterprise is encouraged.

The Iranian telecommunications market

The past few years has seen development in the telecommunications network of Iran. In urban areas, the number of telephones has increased from 1.8 million in 1989 to approximately 7.4 million in 1999. In 1989, at the beginning of the First Five Year Development Plan (FFYDP), only 3200 villages had access to telephones. This number by 1999 increased to 17,400.

The national Iranian communications infra-structure has 18 major components, with the three most significant being the dial-up market, infrastructure capacity and standard computer and private networks. Between 1996 and 1998, these segments showed a compound annual growth of 8.5 per cent, 11 per cent and 11 per cent respectively. The number of Internet users is currently estimated to be between 30,000 and 130,000, that is, 0.2 per cent of the population. This is forecasted to grow to approximately 5 million in 2004 or 7 per cent of the total population. This level of demand is parallel with that of highly developed countries when at a similar stage of development. In Australia and the USA, the Internet is used by around 36 per cent and 34 per cent of the population respectively. This kind of demand can be met with sufficient bandwidth and appropriate infrastructure. Bandwidth requirements in 1999 were 180 Mbps, which are expected to be 450 Mbps by 2004.

Currently, the Telecommunications Company of Iran (TCI) has a total of 4 Mbit/s capacity which is connected to the US Internet via a Canadian and a French satellite supplier on the Intelsat satellite (2 Mbit/s each). This amount is equivalent to what a company with an AU$5 million turnover per annum might use.

This limited capacity is supplied to a small number of approved Internet service providers (ISPs), and is delivered only as a clear channel access to the US Internet. All traffic between ISPs passes through the satellite links – including traffic such as email from one Iranian user to another.

There are a larger number of ISPs that obtain capacity from international satellite operators and distribute this to their users with the 'backhaul' traffic often provided via dial-up links over the international direct dialling network of the TCI. Most of the 150 ISPs that operate in this way are unapproved by the government.

Until now, these illicit ISP activities have been tolerated by the Post, Telegraph and Telephone Ministry of the Government (PTT). Recently, however, the PTT have warned international satellite operators that allocation of bandwidth to these entities is illegal and that Iran may launch prosecution against any providers of satellite downlinks or uplinks.

In Iran, the infancy stage of Internet development is marked by the inaccessibility of the market for foreign companies. The economic sanctions placed on Iran by the USA have contributed significantly to this slow development, the Internet largely being derived from the USA. Furthermore, no large professional Internet company, particularly those that are American such as AAPT, Ozemail, etc., are operating there. Since much of ISP involvement in Iran is illegal, professional companies investing in an operation there would be taking extenuating financial and legal risks. Furthermore, the Internet Access supply situation in Iran is a 'greenfields' area in respect to the charging and tariff regimes that can apply in a situation of full supply.

The Iranian telecommunications infrastruc-ture is run as a government monopoly. There have been numerous accounts of leading foreign telecommunications companies en-quiring for licences but being met with government wariness. Politically, the economy is very sensitive and in the past companies such as MCI Worldcom, Optus Communications, Telstra and Ozemail were seen as potential threats.

The players

The Telecommunications Company of Iran (TCI) is a fully owned government subsidiary of PTT and the principal provider of national and international telecommunications services in Iran. Subsidiaries and affiliates of TCI include:

- The Remote Sensing Centre of Iran
- Telecommunications Research Centre

- Iran Telephone Design and Development Company
- Shahid Ghandi Cable Company
- Solar Power and Fiber Optics Production Company
- Iran Telecommunications Factories
- Long-distance Telecom Industries Factory.

AusTel Consortium began in March 1998. AusTel Consortium Pty Ltd is an Australian provider of global telecommunications and Internet services and has its head office in Sydney. It was a start-up company specifically designed to meet the needs of the government of the Islamic Republic of Iran for the purpose of seeking licences (see Appendix I), relevant rights and/or concessions to cover international, national and domestic telecommunications traffic in Iran. The directors of the company, Mr M. Mathan, an Australian citizen, and Mr M. Rasajf, an Iranian national, have had extensive experience in start-up Internet projects.

The consortium group developed by pulling together resources and outsourcing. Members of the consortium included KPMG Consulting of which 20 per cent is owned by Cisco, the biggest provider of hardware in the world which would participate in building the infrastructure in Iran. Other experience among consortium members includes ten years experience with Telstra, ten years of Internet management and Internet engineering, in addition to military, Monash University and ex-government employees. Together this extensive expertise and relevant experience was presented to the government under one umbrella, AusTel Consortium Pty, Ltd.

Australia–Iran relations in the context of the aims of the consortium

Michael Mathan, Director of AusTel Consortium Pty Ltd, claimed Australians are well favoured in Iran. Despite the US sanctions, the Australian embassy is well established there. Michael Mathan partnered with an Iranian-born associate who has worked on offshore projects for large international telecommunications companies. He is also the Managing Director of Global Technology Systems, an Iranian company. Mr M. Rasajf has developed strong personal and business relationships with senior business, government and religious leaders. Parallel forces and institutions exist within the Islamic regime of Iran. Due to this, the actual power and influence of a person or organization can be judged less on the sole basis of his formal position, but rather on his contacts and position in the complex network of informal organizations.

Iranian authorities insist on physical presence in the Iranian market. The stronger the local presence, the better the chances of finding the right contacts in the Iranian hierarchy and determining ways that could facilitate the awarding of projects or purchases. In June 1998, AusTel Consortium Pty Ltd set up a company office in Tehran, the capital of Iran.

The company name, AusTel Consortium Pty Ltd, was specifically formed to create an impression of impartiality both politically and to any particular provider. In other words, AusTel Consortium Pty Ltd was able to source the best Internet from various sources. They were not a particular company selling a particular product. Their services could be provided to over 200 foreign countries through a combination of its own international network facilities, various international termination relationships and resale arrangements with other international long distance service providers. AusTel's products and services are particularly suited to telecommunications development for new housing areas in urban and suburban environments where copper infrastructure is non-existent (such as in remote or saturated areas, or where old infrastructure needs to be rehabilitated).

The joint venture and subsequent developments

In 1998 an opportunity arose to establish a unique joint venture with the Iranian carrier,

TCI for exclusive Internet access, distribution and billing facility. This joint venture proposed that specialized Internet project management, design and technical capabilities, marketing skills, equipment supply, management recruitment, staff training, financing and Australian government support would be combined with the existing resources of TCI to develop the proposed Iranian Internet infrastructure. AusTel Consortium will use its international Internet broadband capacity, ISP infrastructure experience and the telecommunications network infrastructure of TCI in Iran to develop optimum ISP establishment infrastructure capable of delivering a satisfactory quality of service to the joint venture's customers.

By 1999 AusTel Consortium Pty Ltd had invested over 12 months of planning, negotiation, feasibility studies and resources into the proposed joint venture. Already, AusTel Consortium had speculated over AU$2 million towards the capital expenditure of infrastructure which, for the small company, was a lot of money. Furthermore, as part of the joint venture with TCI, the contribution of state-of-the-art access and distribution infrastructure was to be underwritten by AusTel. This would be prior to any dividends being paid by the joint venture.

After long and protracted negotiations with TCI, it appeared that the joint venture arrangement was finally coming through. AusTel Consortium seemed to have convinced the government of their technical and management capability, and moreover that they were a politically impartial company. When TCI were due to provide the licence for exclusive Internet access, distribution and billing facility, AusTel Consortium was met with an unexpected intervention. The Majlis overrode the negotiations and claimed the arrangement was not for the benefit of teachings of and incongruent with the teachings of religious and cultural values of Islam. In short, they would not pursue the arrangement. AusTel Consortium had lost the deal at the flick of the Majlis' switch.

The Majlis claimed they were concerned about how the speed of Internet advancement and increased accessibility might impact culturally on the Iranian population, especially in light of Iran's isolation from the outside world. Negative aspects of the Internet about which concerns were held were malicious propaganda, pornography and dangerous material. There was talk of legislation handing down heavy penalties for organizations deliberately producing and disseminating this material. Therefore, there was an overriding need to provide content filtering of Internet accessed material to accord with the governmental, cultural and religious sensitivities of the Islamic Republic of Iran.

In a translated letter sent to the Iranian Minister for the PTT, Mr Abdul-Hadi Al-Mousawi, Managing Director of the Danafajr Foundation, wrote:

> No person or organisation can ignore the importance of Internet and its role in the lives of people and countries, the vast advancement of this technology and the speed at which it can reach any point in the globe. ... However, this has also brought many negative aspects which contradict with Islamic teaching and Muslim norms and traditions. In addition, the genuine Mohammed's Islam and the specific teachings of Ahlul-Bayt supersede all previous religions and are a vast source of information on all aspects of life.

Furthermore he wrote:

> In Islamic Iran in general, its Hawza (Traditional University) provides the main source of Islamic information. In this regard, it is important that we should all unite and join to raise Islam and the integrity of the Islamic Republic by providing an Internet Service that is strong and free from all negative aspects ... according to the high Islamic teaching, the rules of the Islamic Republic and which contains true Islamic information and thoughts from its main source.

Quo vadis?

The joint venture with TCI recognized the need to ensure that appropriate filtering removed this undesirable content and almost immediately AusTel's managers looked to their technical staff. Consequently, to stand a chance the managers knew they would have to provide a network with the facilities to remove this content while still retaining as much of the useful Internet content as possible.

AusTel Consortium had organized sourcing arrangements with European suppliers as an insurance against any US imposed restrictions. However, access to the US-Internet backbone and the provision of satellite links were not affected by the US embargo.

In any case, an option for AusTel was to establish its own national Internet backbone (ir.com) that ensures the traffic originated in Iran for other Iranian web sites or users is switched in Iran, not the USA.

If a central clearing facility site was installed in Tehran for primary filtering of all Internet traffic to wholesalers and downstream ISPs, this would include the most powerful servers and firewalls that are connected to a high capacity LAN within the site. A telehousing facility could be built where network access, e-mail, proxy and radius servers belonging to other ISPs can be located in a common peering facility at the site to enable intra-Iran traffic to be switched at that site.

Traffic destined for the US Internet from points of presence (POP) all over Iran could then be transmitted and received through the central clearing site in Tehran – thus ensuring control over the content through the central firewall system. If traffic increases, additional satellite downlinks and additional firewall/proxy servers at major regional sites could be installed. This would reduce the terrestrial data links load – retaining them for backhauling purposes to Tehran only. This would help ensure the continuing control of Internet traffic through the central clearing facility and that the Tehran earth station remained the primary gateway for Internet in Iran.

Austel came up with a revised mission statement that sought to improve the access to and quality of Internet-based information services and associated value added services for government departments, private companies and citizens of Iran in accordance with the laws and regulations of the Islamic Republic of Iran, together with worldwide adherents of the Islamic faith.

Mr Rasajf, from the office in Tehran, made use of his established contacts to discuss the lead-up of events. As an Iranian, he knew that the government consisted of tightly knit networks, all working within the framework if Islamic culture and religion, which would either make or break the future of the joint venture. After many long and drawn out discussions, certain issues came clear. In response to the Majlis' intervention, Mr Rasajf took action by proposing joint venture agreements with other parties in order to lead the company down a strategic path.

One was with the Danafajr Organization, which is a government body that provides the framework for the teachings of Islam. The objectives of this joint venture would be to provide an international Internet service with safe content. This would be achieved by use through filters in compressed form that would prevent the user reaching sites that are contradictory to the teaching and manners of Islam and the rules of the Islamic Republic. A second objective would be to monitor and control the Internet network to ensure that it can be defended against hackers and other security attacks. A third objective was to provide content for universities, both Islamic and Western, on activities of the Donafajr Foundation. The fourth objective was to provide remote learning facilities for all Islamic countries with a view to eventually establishing cultural learning centres in these countries. The final objective was to improve access and speed of access, Internet training services and linkage to the main Internet backbone for the benefit of the Iranian public.

A second joint venture was with the Scientific Information Services Centre which was part of the Department of the Ministry of Jihad in Iran. The objectives of this joint venture were to establish and operate a downstream ISP operation for use by their internal staff and/or external persons wishing to access Internet and Internet-related services in regards to the laws and regulations of the Islamic Republic of Iran. This would promote both public and private sector downstream access to the Internet by establishing intranet/extranet and virtual private network facilities.

The third joint venture was with the Islamic Foundation for Research and Information (IFRI). This body seeks to offer and serve through information technology, historical and modern dimensions of Islamic thoughts focusing on the Ahlul-Buayt school. This is through scientific and cultural activities generated in the traditional, conceptual and Hawza (Traditional Islamic University) areas. Specifically:

1. Defining the Shi'Ite thoughts, beliefs, characters and their scientific and literary heritage to the world through implementing these and offering educational services in scientific and educational institutions in Australia and overseas.

2. Preserve and restore Islamic heritage in Australia and overseas by converting information into digital form.

3. To make the Islamic and in particular, the Shi'Ite thoughts, available worldwide through modern means and languages suitable for use in high technology and scientific applications.

These three joint ventures were entered into with a five month period of exclusivity. While AusTel Consortium has made all efforts to promote and support Islamic values, Australian precedents have been used which AusTel management believes will be accepted by TCI during the proposed establishment of its formal joint venture company in Iran. As yet there is no formal acceptance of the model by the Iranian authorities.

Were the latter joint ventures of interest to AusTel Consortium? In January 2000, nearly two years after negotiations began, informal discussions with TCI and the Majlis have shown positive developments. Michael Mathan is confident of the future. AusTel Consortium has no doubt taken large risks, but trust and a good relationship have developed between both parties. In any case, Michael Mathan claims, 'It'll take at least the same time for any other company to compete . . . now we are two years ahead.'

There has been talk of establishing Iran as the Internet hub for the Middle East and CIS countries using Iran's content, expertise and technology. Furthermore, the Chairman of the Expediency Council, Mr Rafsanjani, when recently addressing a group of Islamic missionaries, called for 'a sound and complete planning, making use of the world's communications facilities including the Internet and satellite for propagation of the Islamic Faith globally'.

Questions

1. From this case study, what issues make Iran a complex environment for foreign business?

2. Why was the director of AusTel Consortium Pty Ltd confident and positive about what lies ahead in the future? Do you think his feelings are justifiable?

3. Were the joint venture agreements with Danafajr Foundation, Islamic Foundation and Scientific Information Services Centre in the interests of AusTel Consortium? Why?

4. Recommend alternative strategic steps AusTel Consortium Pty Ltd should have taken to minimize risk and increase chance of success?

6

Relationships, networks and strategic alliances in an Internet world

Introduction

Dennis Malamatinas, the CEO of Burger King, makes the following observation:

> While electronic connections will be invaluable to our efforts to enhance relationships, they cannot replace or replicate the 'animal spirits' and shared learning that happens when people come together.

This view reflects the fact that underlying relationships, networks and alliances in the international electronic environment is the concept of the rational rather than biological man. Because the biological man acts on his feelings, it is the biological man that underlies relationships and networks. On the other hand, the Internet is based on rationality. This raises the question as to whether there is a future for relationships in the Internet age. Although the Internet is based on rationality, does it entirely do away with both memory and affect? While there may appear to be an apparent inconsistency between e-business and relationships, it will be argued that relationships, networks and alliances have a definite role in international e-business. Figure 6.1 illustrates the difference between the concepts of the rational and the biological man. An alternative view is that:

> Customers go to the Internet to save time through a hassle-free experience, so any bump in the road – slow response times, poor navigation, inaccurate information, unresponsive customer service, difficulty in returning items – can seriously weaken the brand. (Almquist and Pierce, 2000: 70)

Efforts must be made to compensate for the relationship creation differences occasioned by the Internet. The Internet may eliminate or make difficult interaction with employees. Even when such interaction does occur, the Internet may create a functional relationship with customers, but it tends to displace the social aspect of customer interaction. Barnes and Cumby (2002) suggest the limitations of the Internet in relationship creation can be addressed in ten ways:

- deliver great service
- gain the trust of customers
- understand the needs of each customer
- engage in two-way communication with the customer

Figure 6.1

Rational vs.
biological man

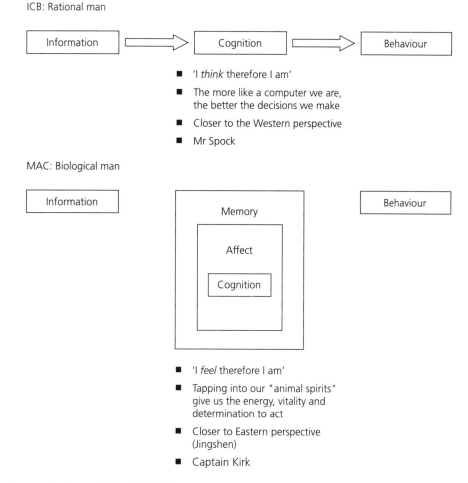

ICB: Rational man

| Information | ⟹ | Cognition | ⟹ | Behaviour |

- 'I *think* therefore I am'
- The more like a computer we are, the better the decisions we make
- Closer to the Western perspective
- Mr Spock

MAC: Biological man

| Information | | Behaviour |

Memory

Affect

Cognition

- 'I *feel* therefore I am'
- Tapping into our "animal spirits" give us the energy, vitality and determination to act
- Closer to Eastern perspective (Jingshen)
- Captain Kirk

Source: Ambler and Styles (2000: 58)

- customize and personalize the contact (e.g. customize the web page)
- be responsive and both acknowledge and follow through inquiries
- create a sense of community by getting customers to communicate with each other
- integrate the traditional offline presence with an effective online offering
- create involvement by offering distinctive experiences that stand out in a crowded landscape
- offer a marketplace option along with the marketspace one.

In short, the key to customer relationship creation via the Internet is to preserve the relationships they have enjoyed in the offline setting while achieving the benefits associated with dealing online.

Management of relationships and trust

In this section of the chapter, relationships in marketspace are discussed in terms of how marketing relationships might be managed, how relationship models in the virtual global organization are considered, and how the issue of trust in the Internet age applies.

Managing marketing relationships in marketspace

Information technology (IT) has altered social exchange in the interaction process. This has led to relationships becoming more impersonal and more formalized as relationship atmosphere has changed. However, businesses still need to interact, albeit in different ways. This is because interactions remain at the heart of successful relationships, which in turn are fundamental to successful business. In the physical value chain 'things are done to goods and services' to add value, whereas in the virtual value chain value is added via intellectual and organizing activity that results in the creation of value as far as the total offering is concerned. Figure 6.2 shows typical applications of IT, and how they have replaced situations where face-to-face activities were formerly involved.

Figure 6.2	
The physical vs. the virtual value chain	

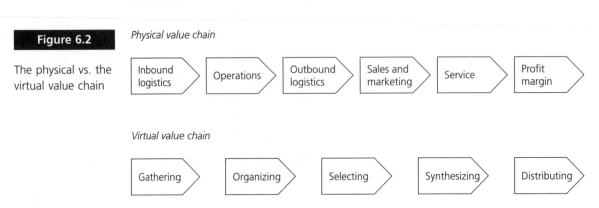

Physical value chain

Inbound logistics ⟩ Operations ⟩ Outbound logistics ⟩ Sales and marketing ⟩ Service ⟩ Profit margin

Virtual value chain

Gathering ⟩ Organizing ⟩ Selecting ⟩ Synthesizing ⟩ Distributing

Source: Speier, Harvey and Palmer (1998: 266)

The virtual organization is a collection of business units in which both people and work processes from such units interact intensively in order to perform work that benefits all. They enable organizational and/or personal competencies to be brought together when needed and disbanded when no longer required. They mirror the fluidity of the global marketplace. The virtual corporation assesses all marketing activities across the entire global value chain in order to 'virtually vertically integrate' across a 'web of companies'. Creating the efficient virtual organization can involve removing inefficient transaction costs from the value chain, such as reducing time to the market, as well as adding value to existing activities in the value chain, thus enhancing the overall value of the product or service.

Virtual global organizational models

These can be based on existing relationships among firms and often reflect prior competitive or cooperative interactions. In addition, firms must have an economic incentive to participate in virtual organizations. Five models have been proposed as illustrated in Table 6.1. The models are as follows.

Shared partnership

Each partner brings nearly equal amounts of commitment to the virtual organization. This requires compatibility of partner goals and values. It usually evolves from strong existing relationships among partnering organizations. A shared global partnership is likely to occur when several organizations wish to undertake a global marketing project requiring their disparate skills and resources. The inter-organizational relationships in the virtual model can provide additional value to participating firms.

Core/satellite

A core global organization maintains relationships with satellite marketing organizations. These satellites, such as advertising agencies, wholesalers, retailers, etc. are able to respond more effectively to market opportunities. They do not need to be co-located and are often located in different countries. The core firm plays a dominant role in establishing the culture of the relationship and in coordinating activities. Transfer pricing and risk/cost sharing are often dominant motivations for this type of relationship, as exemplified in sale of consumer products through a loose coupling of manufacturers, distributors and retailers in various countries.

Virtual value chain

This involves a coordinated set of transactions among companies serving an end customer in different countries, with information technology supporting the product or service. This model can be used for construction projects in developing countries and for managing relationships with international suppliers, as happens with US retailer Wal-Mart. With construction projects, the general contractor often drives the culture of the relationship and the virtual model provides additional support for relationships between subcontractors

| Table 6.1 | Virtual organization model characteristics |

	Location	Work cycle	Culture	Organizational relationships	Virtual management issues
Shared partnership (model 1)	Often co-located, a spin-off approach	Often highly synchronized activities	Typically homogeneous cultures, although distinctive	Typically strong pre-existing relationships	Challenges of adapting existing relationships into virtual management
Core satellite (model 2)	Typically not co-located unless performing physical job functions	Often highly synchronized activities	Less emphasis on culture, more use of contracting relationship	Existing relationships have been established	Ongoing assessment of old/ new partners in constellation
Virtual value chain (model 3)	Typically not co-located	Highly synchronized across adjoining members of the value chain	Some emphasis on culture across adjoining members, but more contractual	Often existing relationships limited to adjoining members only	Identifying alternative partners for expanding value chain globally
Integrated firm (model 4)	Often co-located or located in close proximity	Often highly synchronized with coordinated scheduling	Higher emphasis on culture as a competitive advantage	Strong existing relationships among at the least some members	Initiating offensive, defensive, and existing strategies
Electronic market (model 5)	Rarely co-located	Highly responsive, but not necessarily highly coordinated	Similar service orientated cultures, but not necessary	In many cases few existing relationships	Auditing and exit strategies; competitive response

Source: Speier, Harvey and Palmer (1998: 267)

from different countries who do not have a common board of directors or a joint working relationship

Integrated firm

In this case, vertical integration results in autonomous units utilizing technology to coordinate efforts between functions and countries at the same time. In this type of global virtual relationship, the companies agree to function as a single vertically integrated entity throughout the world. This network of companies is frequently located in different countries participating across a marketing value chain to deliver a product or service to an ultimate customer. A common feature is the sharing of market information, design specifications, and the coordination of manufacturing to maintain a competitive advantage in the global market.

Electronic market

Here, the technology itself serves as a key component in creating the market among the virtual global marketing organizational partners. Individual firms operate within the electronic market using the technology as an intermediary to interact with end customers. This enables firms to compete in global markets while allowing customers to select from a variety of global providers

According to Poon and Jevons (1997), the Internet provides small business with the opportunity to share information and experiences. This can lead to collaboration, such as the sharing of customer orders, or a number of small firms jointly bidding on a large project. Because the Internet is a virtual borderless platform on which suppliers, customers, competitors and network partners can interact, the Internet enables the formation and maintenance of business network links that would otherwise be curtailed by barriers such as distance, time and limited resources. It is desirable for small and medium size exporters (SMEs) to match inter-organizational relationships with Internet marketing strategies. This is illustrated in Table 6.2, which outlines various Internet marketing strategies for different organizational groupings, many of which cross national boundaries.

Virtual management of global relationships

Marketing relationships can be characterized as virtual when a significant amount of activity between relationship partners occurs outside their

Table 6.2	Inter-organizational relationship	Internet marketing strategy
Mapping inter-organizational relationship types to Internet marketing strategies	Confederations (e.g. small business groups sharing resources through contractual agreements)	Central management provides resources for network members to market their products and services on the Internet (e.g. a virtual agency service). Include in the agreements to provide reciprocal home page links between members included in the contract.
	Conjugate collectives (e.g. closed group agreements between supplier and customer)	Allow reciprocal links on members' home pages. Make available market intelligence on the closed group's intranet (if available) with log-in control. Share market intelligence in order to improve supplier–buyer relationship.
	Agglomerate collectives (e.g. trade associations)	Trade association provides market intelligence data (local and international) on its home page for member use. Mutual agreement between (international) trade associations to market the members' products and services.
	Organic collectives (e.g. community services groups)	Advertising products and provide low-cost/free services for charity members of community networks on the Internet (e.g. LinkNet). Link community calendar of events to one's home page.

Source: LinkNet (www.link.net.au)

organizational domains and therefore in a non-face-to-face context. The management orientation will need to go beyond the command and control model and focus on cooperation as a basis for the interaction. These virtual relationships/organizations will develop a culture and identity of their own. This will be apart from and distinct from that of the two parent organizations. Speier, Harvey and Palmer (1998) present seven steps for addressing virtual management of global marketing relationships:

1. *Development of relational criteria.* This involves identifying the domain of the potential relationships. As the domain changes, the degree of virtualness between partners can also change, based on the extent of geographical distance, work cycle synchronicity and differences in culture between the focal organization and the relational partner.

2. *Identification of alternative relational partners.* The organization may choose to focus on one set of marketing relational opportunities over others, i.e. on those that are deemed to be most important to gain a global competitive advantage. This may lead to one domain only being examined to identify key marketing partners.

3. *Comparative assessment of relational partners.* In this case, the goal is to develop a discriminant analysis among potential relationship partners to determine whether there is a significant difference between them.

4. *Initiating relationship strategies.* Here the task is to identify the motivation for forming the relationship. While offensive motivations for forming a relationship dominate, there are often good defensive reasons.

5. *Managing relationships over time.* This involves a relationship auditing process that should include assessing the initial goals of the relationship and commitments made. Other dimensions include analysing changes in the external environment, evaluating the value of the relationship in terms of future competitive positioning, determining the explicit cost of maintaining the relationship, and deciding on an appropriate set of exit strategies as a contingency.

6. *Response to reaction from potential relational partners and competitors.* Existing market relationships have a potential opportunity cost. Hence, an analysis of the constraints of the existing relationship should be undertaken.

7. *Exit strategies from relationships.* These can either have a proactive orientation (such as termination by acquisition, substitution by a new member or selling intangible rights of the relationship to a third party); or a negative orientation (such as unplanned, unfriendly dissolution).

Trust and the Internet

The importance of trust in e-business is high. Trust is first initiated and then enhanced over the period of the relationship (Phan, Styles and Patterson, 1998). The marketplace buying process of problem recognition, information search, information evaluation, reaching a decision and post-purchase evaluation can apply in marketspace, but it will be directly influenced by the degree of trust that the consumer has in the online medium. The physical separation of buyer and seller, the physical separation of the buyers and the merchandise, and the perceived insecurity of the Internet, all challenge marketers to find new ways to initiate and develop trusting relationships with their customers. When there is no personal face-to-face contact between seller and customer, building and maintaining trust is more difficult to achieve.

Needham (2000) argues that there are four areas of trust that online marketers need to take into account. These include trust concerning the quality of the product: with an Internet purchase the goods cannot be examined in advance. Then there is trust concerning the authenticity of the information provided: sensitive information provided by consumers when purchasing over the Internet could end up in the wrong hands. Another area is trust concerning the true identity of the person or business: it is difficult with Internet transactions for consumers to know exactly whom they are dealing with. Finally, there is trust concerning the integrity of a person or business: the consumers need reassurance that they will receive the item as ordered and have recourse if something goes wrong.

Example	*Dingo Blue*

Dingo blue (www.dingoblue.com.au) has positioned itself on a global basis via the Internet, as a rock-bottom price leader with pricing and services that have no surprises. While this provides a current competitive point of difference, Dingo blue realized that it needed to develop an effective customer relationship strategy as a core part of the value proposition and not as an afterthought. The introduction of the customer loyalty programme was a key component of the Dingo blue customer relationship management (CRM) strategy.

The key to producing a programme that ultimately worked, minimized development cost and kept to the project timeline was spending the required time upfront to clearly define the required business outcome. The solution design was the result of close working between the Emagine International team (www.emagine-int.com) that included marketing, information technology and project management, working with Dingo blue and their billing platform providers to build a solution and integrate it into the customers live environment.

The project was a success due to its personalization and interactivity, the level of customer involvement, the ability for customers to select attainable rewards as well as aim for aspirational rewards. It is easy to understand and use, has simple and logical web screen navigation providing a good balance between providing the customer the required information and ensuring the web site was not cluttered or confusing. Dingo blue's customer retention programme is fully customizable and web based, each customer creates his 'personal' loyalty programme enabling true one-to-one marketing via the web.

The launch of the Dingo blue loyalty programme in mid-July 2000 involved direct communications to existing customers via e-mail, or direct mail depending on their selected communications preference. New customers were proactively enrolled into the programme at the time of sign up. The programme was also promoted where possible as a secondary message as part of other Dingo blue advertising and promotion campaigns. Attitudinal research among active customers shows that they are 30 per cent less likely to defect to another competitor than customers who are not enrolled in the programme.

Source: Emagine International

This issue of trust is particularly relevant when doing business in Asia where it is an important element of a relationship. With the continued growth of Internet commerce, there has been a corresponding growth in marketing goods and services under conditions where no face-to-face contact between seller and customer takes place. Building trust in Internet users means ensuring that the ingredients of trust as they relate to the target groups in the overseas market are catered for in the e-marketing approach.

Indicators of trust are twofold – experience-based and cue-based (Beatty *et al.*, 1996). Experience-based indicators are the result of an exchange that has taken place, whereas cue-based indicators occur prior to the exchange and create trust on the part of the customer in advance of the purchase being made. E-business marketers therefore should focus on providing cues to potential customers or business partners so that they trust the company sufficiently to engage in the initial transaction.

In cue-based trust, the cues, which may serve as indicators of trustworthiness, often take the form of return policies, name recognition, the professional look of the web site, the privacy and security policy, the availability of company address and phone number for alternative ordering procedures, and references and testimonials from existing customers. Trust-based web sites should also provide accurate, up-to-date and completely unbiased information. A list of factors that should be applied to build trust in international e-business marketing include the following:

- Use the local language or the most acceptable language for business in that country.
- Provide on the web site interactive entertainment that projects positive feelings towards and encourages repeat visits to the site.
- Have an online club that provides 'give-aways' for frequent use of the product or service being featured.
- Provide information about the offer and invite potential customers to use e-mail, chat rooms and call centres for further information.
- Use cultural symbols and concepts that engender trust.
- Provide endorsements from respected local leaders or well-known figures.
- Link the Internet with other forms of promotion and advertising in print to provide an impression of a substantial presence in the target overseas market.
- Undertake co-branding with established trusted brands.
- Reduce purchase uncertainty by money-back offers and free no obligation samples.
- Provide adequate security and confidentiality for transactions and all communications.

Internet networks and physical networks

In this section of the chapter, the issue of networks in marketspace versus networks in marketplace is considered, as is whether Internet networking will replace physical networking. This is followed by a discussion of the operation of strategic alliances in the electronic environment.

Networking in marketplace vs. networking in marketspace

According to Leek, Turnbull and Naude (2000), there are four basic elements that underpin interaction, which is the basic element of networks. These are the environment, the participants or actors, the relationship atmosphere and the process of interaction itself. Information technology, as reflected in the Internet, impacts on each of these elements to varying degrees. Networks involve establishing upstream and downstream linkages with networks in other countries to facilitate efficiencies in the transnational value chain. This requires efficient and continually evolving communication between the various members of the network. The Internet can facilitate this because of the instantaneous way it communicates over both geographical and psychic distances. However, although the Internet does allow freer and easier flow of communication, it does not replace the need for personal relationship building, especially in cultures that are high context in character such as Thailand or Japan.

The situational dimensions of networking in the marketplace involve behaviour (both communicative and cooperative), attitudes (which are dependent on satisfaction and maintenance of trust), and outcomes (which are the result of commitment and dependence). These need to be reconfigured when marketspace is involved. Although long-term relationships in networking help lower transaction costs, an issue is whether these will disappear and relationships become less stable when relationships are formed in marketspace. Many marketplace networks have been driven by the emergence of new industries. By contrast, marketspace networks tend to be driven by the emergence of new technologies and new competitive environments in which partnering becomes unavoidable.

Marketplace networks are often of the 'starburst type' (Quinn, Anderson and Finkelstein, 1996), with a central core competence and a flow of knowledge from the centre to the outer nodes. In marketplace networks competence is rarely traded from one node to another. In marketspace networks, however, knowledge will flow from the centre to the nodes, from one node to another and from the nodes back to the centre. As a result, Internet-based networks are characterized by higher degrees of uncertainty. When this happens, trust becomes more important, speed of decision making assumes greater relevance and trust will be called upon when agreements must be 'made on the run' in response to competitive pressures.

However, trust cannot quickly be created in marketspace – only after firms begin working together and relationships solidify. In the Internet world, is there time for 'conventional' trust to develop? Research on IT alliances found that the quality of communications between partners and the existence of shared values is positively related to trust. Inkpen and Currall (2000) propose that reputation will play a key role for trust development in marketspace. This places young firms at a disadvantage, as they often have no experience on which to base a reputation. To compensate for this, they may form networks with more established firms.

Will Internet networking replace physical networking?

Axelsson, Johanson and Sundberg (1992) conducted a study of why Scandinavian businesspersons travel in the age of improved communications. The continuing importance of business travel is highlighted by the fact that expenditure on international travel is 50 per cent greater than expenditure on advertising and in real terms is equivalent to 5 per cent of net sales value (NSV). Physical networking will continue to be required in the Internet age, as improved communications do not replace personal face-to-face contacts. Thus, an issue in the Internet age is when should relationship development be via the Internet and when must it be face to face. They found that the answer depended on the specific situation as follows:

- *Local purchaser visits overseas supplier* – personal touch needed when buying new product or dealing with a new supplier.
- *Local researcher meets overseas customer* – personal touch needed when a new customer and/or a new project is involved.
- *Local marketing manager discusses reorganization with overseas business partner* – personal touch needed when information exchange and relationship maintenance is required.
- *Local general manager visits overseas subsidiary* – personal touch needed for general PR and relationship maintenance.

It was found that the percentage of executives taking business trips was highest among marketing and general managers. This indicates that their activities have higher relationship and trust components than those of others in the firm whose functions are capable of being dealt with in a less personal way. This is illustrated in Table 6.3.

The overall aims of business trips in order of importance were: to take action 38 per cent; to exchange information 32 per cent; to cultivate networks 27 per cent. In terms of visits to non-internal units of the firm, network cultivation came first, followed by information exchange and lastly the taking of action. The same pattern also applies early in a relationship, but reverses when the relationship is long term (see Table 6.4). Hence, the ability to substitute Internet relationship formation for physical relationship formation in the international domain may be a function of internal versus external activities; new versus established relationships, and new versus ongoing business activity.

Research by Leek, Turnbull and Naude (2000) found that the interaction model is still valid in the international electronic environment. What have changed in the interaction process are the methods of information exchange and the dynamics of social exchange. These have impacted on the relationship atmosphere and altered the nature of relationships. In the past, a good relationship was one that is long term, cooperative and built on face-to-face meetings to increase trust and reduce uncertainty.

In the IT-driven environment, relationships are based less on face-to-face contact and rely more on electronic forms of communication, especially at the follow-up and maintenance stages.

Table 6.3	Function	Respondents no.	%
Business functions of the travelling manager	General management	57	22
	Marketing	61	23
	Manufacturing	3	1
	R&D	21	8
	Design	5	2
	Technical service	24	9
	Purchasing	17	7
	Data processing	8	3
	Personnel	2	1
	Controller/finance	14	5
	Education	9	3
	Others	21	9
	No answer	18	7
	Total	260	100

Source: Axelsson, Johanson and Sundberg (1992: 97)

Table 6.4	Primary aim orientation	Early %	Relationship stage development %	Long-term %
Aim orientation of visits during different relationship stages	Action	22	44	49
	Information	35	33	27
	Network cultivation	43	23	24
	Sum	100	100	100

Source: Axelsson Johanson and Sundberg (1992: 105)

Strategic alliances in marketspace

The emergence of an information-based business infrastructure has made it more necessary for companies to form strategic alliances. Because no firm has all the capabilities or resources it needs, alliances can help to cater for this shortcoming. Strategic alliance strategies according to Stafford (Table 6.5) (1994) can be categorized as follows:

To illustrate the above, the example of an online advertising agency is used, based on the research of Fausboll (2000).

Handover strategic alliance

Between a mainstream MNC advertising agency and an online advertising agency: here the MNC would hand over only the online media planning and

	Strategic alliance strategy	Definitions
Table 6.5 Forms of strategic alliance	Handover	Integration of business resources, where one partner hands over the relevant resources or value chain activity to the other partner for mutual gain.
	Trade	Exchange of business resources, where the partners trade complementary resources or value chain activities with each other.
	Pool	Pooling of business resources, where the partners share the same value chain activity or resources.

Source: Adapted from Brown (1997: 464)

buying elements of their business so that the MNC would be the supplier of integrated online and mainstream advertising campaigns.

Trade strategic alliance

Between an online advertising agency and non-advertising related firms such as web site developers and/or Internet service providers: in this case, the online advertising agency is able via the alliance to draw on the partner's local contacts to establish a customer base.

Pool strategic alliance

Between an online agency and a mainstream MNC agency that wants to set up an online operation but lacks the technical expertise: in this case both parties pool their funds and resources such as client contacts and form a new business, which they would manage jointly.

Inkpen and Currall (2000) argue that alliances driven by the Internet will operate under different assumptions and create substantially different management challenges than traditional global alliances. Traditional alliances, because of their coordination and competitive costs, tend to be transitional. Many smaller firms shy away from alliances because of the complexities associated with both forming and terminating alliances.

By comparison, the Internet will dissolve many of the constraints of time and geography and make it possible for organizations to connect and collaborate across borders. In the Internet economy, alliances will become easier to create or terminate and location and size will become less critical variables. The classic market entry form of a bricks and mortar joint venture will decline in relevance as firms discover that relationships can be easily and efficiently established electronically. Personal interactions, which are expensive and time consuming, may largely be replaced by electronic interchanges. However, during the alliance formation stage, face to face interaction is still likely to be critical. As the alliance develops and matures, electronic interactions between the partners may be sufficient to maintain the alliance. Relevant factors include the following:

1. *Alliance formation* objectives. Although foreign market entry alliances will still be formed, the Internet is likely to shift the focus of the objective in alliance formation away from market entry towards the achievement of strategic efficiency. In addition, firms will be able to access overseas markets that were previously beyond their reach. Via the Internet, small firms will be able to leapfrog traditional stages of internationalization. The Internet creates opportunities for small firms to collaborate across borders and achieve scale advantages formerly only possible for firms that actually had internal scale.

2. *Need and uncertainty.* The alliance formation motive of the need to acquire new technologies and develop new skills is likely to be more closely aligned to the resource-based view of the firm and an emphasis on uniqueness. The Internet is creating an environment where firms collaborate under conditions of high uncertainty and where the potential hazards of opportunism are often discounted in the interest of creating opportunities for discovery and learning. The need for adaptability and speed creates conditions where rival firms have little time to engage in contentious conflicts that delay decision making and result in lost market opportunities.

3. *Competitors and information.* Obtaining information from only one source creates significant cost efficiencies. The new emphasis on collaboration between competitors, as now happens in the automotive industry, leads to business rivals sharing information to service common customers more effectively. In turn, these mutual customers may have to share information so as to standardize commercial processes. In consequence, firms outside the alliance are likely to be at a disadvantage.

4. *Performances of alliances in marketspace.* International alliances in the marketplace (mainly joint ventures) have been prone to failure. Empirical studies suggest the failure rate exceeds 50 per cent (Inkpen and Currall, 2000). Alliances in marketspace are also driven by the desire to reduce uncertainty. However, such alliances often take the form of non-equity ventures where the criterion for success is not profit but facilitation and network improvement.

As Inkpen and Currall (2000) observe, fully to understand international alliances in the Internet economy the focus must extend beyond equity joint ventures. Such alliances also need to be distinguished from established network concepts. Multi-partner alliances increased by an average of 54 per cent between 1990 and 1996 and have accounted for 20 per cent of alliance activity during the last decade. Some industries such as automotive, airlines and telecommunications compete almost entirely on a group vs group basis. In this type of international alliance, strategic initiatives by the lead firm provide the impetus for multiple interfirm relationships (Lorenzoni and Lipparini, 1999). E-business alliances are not driven by the emergence of new industries, but by new technologies and new environments in which partnering becomes essential for survival. The e-business environment is increasing the number of operating alliance arrangements that the firm must manage in order to create additional value.

Summary

In this chapter the need for relationships in an Internet world is discussed, as are the circumstances that stimulate the formation of international networks and strategic alliances. The different ways in which Internet buyers behave are explored so as to assist in the development of an effective international marketing strategy.

Questions

1. How does relationship formation in marketspace differ from relationship formation in the marketplace?
2. What are the issues involved in managing virtual relationships?
3. Why is trust important when conducting e-business transactions across national borders?
4. What drives the formation of strategic alliances in marketspace?
5. Why is trust so important in Internet-based transactions?

References

Almquist, E. and Pierce, A. (2000) 'Retool your brand for the web', *Mercer Management Journal*, 12: 7.

Ambler, T. and Styles, C. (2000) *The Silk Road to International Marketing: Profit and Passion in Global Business*, London: Pearson.

Axelsson, B. Johanson, J. and Sundberg, J. (1992) 'Managing by international travelling', in M. Fosgren and J. Johanson (eds) *Managing Networks in International Business*, Philadelphia: Gordon Breach.

Barnes, J. G. and Cumby, J. A. (2002) 'Establishing customer relationships on the internet requires more than technology', *Australasian Marketing Journal* 10 (1): 36–46.

Beatty, S. E., Mayer, M., Coleman, J., Reynolds, K. E. and Lee, J. (1996) 'Customer sales associate retail relationships', *Journal of Retailing* 72 (3): 223–47.

Brown, L. B. (1997) *Competitive Marketing Strategy – Dynamic Manoeuvring for Competitive Position*, 2nd edn, South Melbourne: Nelson ITP.

Craig, C. S., Douglas, S. P. and Flaherty, T. B. (2000) 'Information access and internationalisation – the internet and consumer behaviour in international markets', *Proceedings of the eCommerce and Global Business Forum*, 17–19 May, Santa Cruz, CA: Accenture Institute for Strategic Change.

Emagrne International, www.emagine-int.com

Fausboll, A. V. (2000) 'Strategic alliances and small companies', unpublished research project, University of Technology, Sydney.

Inkpen, A. C. and Currall, S. C. (2000) 'Electronic commerce and alliances', *Proceedings of the eCommerce and Global Business Forum*, 17–19 May, Santa Cruz, CA: Accenture Institute for Strategic Change.

Leek, S., Turnbull, P. W. and Naude, P. (2000) 'Is the interaction approach of any relevance in an IT/e-commerce driven world?', Proceedings of the 16th Annual IMP Conference, 8–9 September, Bath: University of Birmingham and University of Bath School of Management.

Link Net, www.link.net.au

Lorenzoni, G. and Lipparini, A. (1999) 'The leveraging of interfirm relationships as a distinctive organizational capability: A longitudinal study', *Strategic Management Journal* 20: 317–38.

Needham, K. (2000) *Building Trust: Building Business* www.paperdots.com/284.html.

Phan, M. C. T., Styles, C. W. and Patterson, P. G. (1998) *An Empirical Examination of the Trust Development Process Linking Firm and Personal Characteristics in an International Setting*, School of Marketing, University of New South Wales.

Poon, S. and Jevons, C. (1997) 'Internet-enabled small business marketing: A small business network perspective', *Journal of Marketing Management* 13: 29–41.

Quinn, J. B., Anderson, P. and Finkelstein, S. (1996) 'Leveraging Intellect', *Academy of Management Executive* 10: 7–27.

Speier, C., Harvey, M. G. and Palmer, J. (1998) 'Virtual management of global marketing relationships', *Journal of World Business* 33 (3): 263–76.

Stafford, E. R. (1994) 'Using cooperative strategies to make alliances work', *Long Range Planning* June: Fig. 1, 65–7.

Case Study 6 *Strategic alliances and small companies*
Annette Valeur Fausboll and Richard Fletcher

Introduction

Strategic alliances are partnerships between companies that have realized that they don't have the full capabilities and resources needed to run their business at optimal efficiency. In ideal strategic alliances, each company focuses on its core competencies for comparative advantage and they rely on the relationships to give them insights into the areas they don't have experience in or are not so good at.

The case study focuses on an online Internet advertising agency called X-Net Communications. The firm is a small company that has defined its core competencies as being online media planning and buying services, although it is also engage in creative development, supervision and production of banner ads and promotions.

X-Net has a corporate goal to increase its presence in the Asian market and aims one day to become the market leader. It could use three strategic alliance forms when entering into this very competitive market. The three alliances are grouped as handover, trade and pooling alliances.

Modern business has a strong emphasis on creating strategic relationships outside the organization, and it is possible for a company to build their business overseas on a set of relationships. This could be a very relevant approach for smaller online advertising agencies such as X-Net.

The company

X-Net is an Internet advertising agency based in Sydney. The agency specializes in creative development and media placement of online interactive advertising. In other words, it creates and places banner advertising and online promotions. X-Net is small and boasts 23 staff. It opened its doors in April 1999 and is now supplying services to clients such as Fairfax Group's F2, Yahoo, Disney and Westpac in Australia (www.netx.com.au, 2000).

In a simplified structure, the company can be broken into three components: the campaign planning and supervision component, the media placement component and finally the production component (Figure 6.3).

The planning and supervising component is self-explanatory. The creative component is the production of banner ads and grabs and the media component is about buying online space for the produced ads. They are likely to be influenced by the forms of strategic alliances X-Net would consider.

X-Net is currently offering its services in Australia, New Zealand and Singapore. The presence in New Zealand and Singapore is due to alliances with existing companies in both markets. In New Zealand, X-Net shares a shopfront with a local and rather basic web site production company. This company specializes in web site production, but through the alliance they are also able to

▶

supply clients with online advertising services of their sites by passing them on to X-Net. This is a trading strategy where both parties exchange value chain activities in the form of web site production and online advertising so they can offer their clients both, and it enables X-Net to have a low-risk presence in New Zealand.

In Singapore, X-Net has entered into an exclusive online media agreement with a multinational advertising agency with offices there. This agreement restricts X-Net from producing creative content as it will be produced and managed through the MNC's mainstream advertising agency. It only allows them to supply the media component of their business, but on the other side the agreement gives X-Net access to an enormous customer base of blue-chip clients. The strategy in Singapore is a handover strategy, where the MNC handed over part of their online advertising business; e.g. media planning and buying only, because they can get the business

from their clients, but didn't have the expertise on the media front, so they outsourced it to X-Net. Figure 6.4 is an illustration of the above alliances, as well as an empty box for Hong Kong.

Following its initial international involvement, X-Net plans to establish an increasing level of presence in the Asian market through its existing and potential connections. Hong Kong is one such step on the way.

Hong Kong

Hong Kong has grown as a British colony since China ceded it in 1845. On 1 July 1997, Hong Kong became the Hong Kong SAR (Special Administrative Region) of China following an agreement with the UK. Following this event: 'China has promised that, under its "one country, two systems" formula, China's socialist economic system will not be practiced in Hong Kong. Moreover, that Hong Kong will enjoy a high degree of autonomy in all matters except

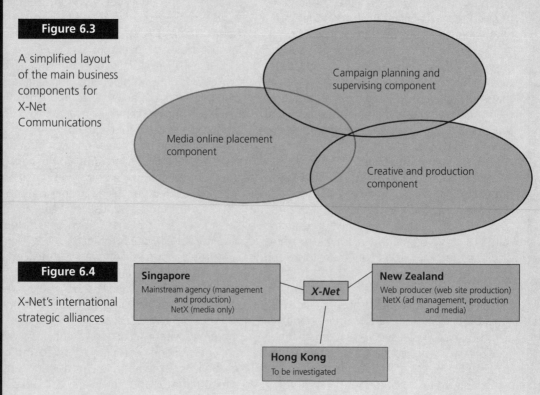

Figure 6.3

A simplified layout of the main business components for X-Net Communications

Campaign planning and supervising component

Media online placement component

Creative and production component

Figure 6.4

X-Net's international strategic alliances

Singapore
Mainstream agency (management and production)
NetX (media only)

X-Net

New Zealand
Web producer (web site production)
NetX (ad management, production and media)

Hong Kong
To be investigated

foreign and defence affairs for the next 50 years' (*The World Factbook*, 2000).

According to Austrade (2000), Hong Kong has one of the most developed IT markets in the Asian region. Hong Kong's spend on IT only falls behind Japan and Singapore in Asia. This, as well as experience with sophisticated designs and multi-media, has made Hong Kong a leader for the rest of the world in the integration of Internet services (www.austrade. gov.au, 2000).

Business is unregulated and the 'government involvement in the IT industry is also minimal in Hong Kong, in the absence of a well-defined, top-down, government-driven IT industrial policy such as that imposed in Singapore of Malaysia' (US Department of Commerce, 1997). The free economy in Hong Kong is driven by supply and demand without (government) intervention.

Further, Hong Kong can also be viewed as an entry point to China. Many ventures are targetting the Chinese masses on the other side of Hong Kong's borders. Hong Kong is one of the busiest financial centres in the world, and foreign investors and business speculants often consider Hong Kong as the gateway to China.

Austrade (2000) suggests that the fierce competition for Australian IT and Internet companies such as X-Net comes not just from the local companies, but also from a wealth of North American and European companies, who have generous resources at their disposition to infiltrate the market.

In 1999, there were at least 49 established Internet service providers (ISPs) in Hong Kong. This translates into numerous content and media space suppliers for the Internet advertising companies (*The World Factbook*, 2000). The clients are the marketers who market their products or services for sale through the online medium. According to IAB figures for the first quarter of 2000, consumer-related services and financial/computing services were amongst the most popular products advertised via the Internet (Ginsburg Bender, 2000).

So, what is the competition in Hong Kong doing? How do they set up to reach the clients? According to Robbie Bempasciuto, creative director of X-Net (2000), the big multinational advertising agencies either set up their own online advertising shop or outsource one or more of the components.

The smaller companies are likely to work with an agent or distributor or even set up their own offices. The local agent, distributor or partnering approach is recommended by the US Department of Commerce (1999) as the best way to minimize the initial investment and risk. It is also said to be very similar to working with agents in Western countries. These can all be classified as strategic alliances.

Strategic alliance alternatives

There are three possibilities for X-Net to pursue. These are by no means the only worthwhile combinations to consider as there can be many more only limited by imagination. They are the handover, the trade and the pool strategies.

Handover strategic alliances To extend a media-only agreement with a MNC mainstream advertising agency that would hand over the online media planning and buying part of their business:then the MNC would still be the supplier of integrated online and mainstream advertising campaigns. X-Net would take on their online media planning and buying function for established clients (Figure 6.5).

Trade strategic alliance To go in with a local partner such as an ISP, web site developer or both, which specializes in something else but actually Internet advertising: this way X-Net could help provide the advertising service whilst also drawing on the partner's local contacts to establish a customer base (Figure 6.6).

Pool strategic alliance To enter into a joint venture with a local mainstream advertising agency that also wants to set up an online shop but does not have the technical expertise: both parties would pool their funds and resources such as client contacts and technical expertise into the new business, which they would both jointly manage (Figure 6.7).

Alternative courses of action

The X-Net business objectives and considerations for the specific Hong Kong market include the establishment of a business base in Hong Kong for potential entry into mainland China. Until that happens, the aim is to increase revenues by just entering the new market, to keep the capital investment and risk down whilst still maintaining as much control as possible over the business' activities in that market.

The X-Net overall corporate goals are to increase its presence in the Asian market in a consistent way and thereby become a market

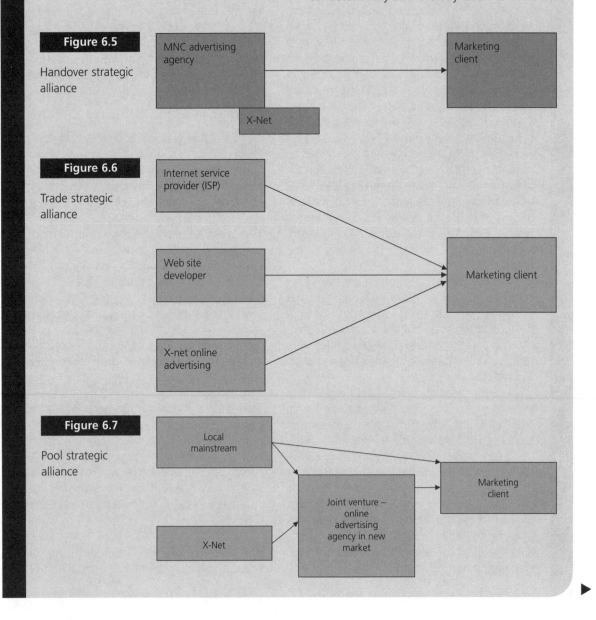

Figure 6.5

Handover strategic alliance

Figure 6.6

Trade strategic alliance

Figure 6.7

Pool strategic alliance

leader in the Asian market by targetting strategic zones.

1. The handover strategic alliance with MNC mainstream agency

Advantages

- the potential to establish connections with high-profile clients
- the ability to focus on the one core competence – online media
- low capital investment restraint and risk
- potential to increase awareness of X-Net due to endorsement from MNC
- consistency with the Singapore alliance
- getting the foot in the door through a solid structure.

Disadvantages

- restrictions of current and future business activities
- limited involvement and input into the total online advertising campaign, because of the media-only agreement
- the possible loss of presence by being a small entity within a large MNC
- loss of control.

2. The trade strategic alliance to supplement local ISP and/or web developer

Advantages

- the business and derived sales will come from all three components of the business
- maintenance of a high level of control and power over business activities
- the limited resources needed for the set-up (staff, capital investment, etc.)
- consistency with the New Zealand alliance.

Disadvantages

- endorsement may be from lower profile companies
- more extensive resources will be needed for the set-up of the business

- more investment restraint and risk
- less support from business partners.

3. The pool strategic alliance as a joint venture with a local advertising agency

Advantages

- the potential to establish connections with clients of the local advertising agency
- lowering the establishment cost by sharing with a local partner
- the business and derived sales will come from all three components of the business
- strong support from partner as the business depend on the success of both parties.

Disadvantages

- profits will be shared with joint-venture partner
- decisions and control will be shared with local partner
- this form is a whole new alliance structure and might create inconsistency.

When reviewing Table 6.6, it becomes apparent that the alliance with an MNC is only marginally superior to the trade alliance, and it also has no absolute negatives in regards to the management criteria. The other strategies are greatly restricted by the limited funds of X-Net. The management of X-Net would consider the first option as the preferred one.

Conclusion

There would appear to be a number of opportunities available to X-Net, however, the facts that it is a small company with limited time, limited strategic corporate expertise and limited funds greatly influence anything they do. They just react to the environment and to changes rather than being proactive themselves. This could possibly be a shared characteristic with other small companies.

A small company planning to enter the Hong Kong market or any other non-regulated international market has a wealth of different combinations of strategic alliances to consider. In reality however, the limited resources of a small company may significantly limit the options.

Questions

1. How can the size and age of a company affect the decision to enter into strategic alliances?

2. Why don't real-life companies always follow the objective strategies that might strategically be best for them?

3. X-Net has the idea that one day it will be able to do all production out of Sydney,

because banner ads and other electronic forms of advertising can be e-mailed to clients for approval. How do you think this would work?

References

Anonymous (1997–1999) *STAT-USA on the Internet, US Department of Commerce*: http://strategis.ic.gc.ca/SSG/dd73359e.html

Austrade Internet site (2000): www.austrade.gov.au

Bempasciuto, R. (2000) X-Net's Creative Planning Director, Conversations.

Ginsburg Bender, S. (2000) *First Quarter 2000 Internet Advertising Revenues close in on $2 billion* (26.8): www.iab.net/news/content/first_qu_iab_revs.html.

The World Factbook (2000): www.cia.gov/cia/publications/factbook/geos/hk.html.

X-Nets Internet site (2000): www.netx.com.au/

Table 6.6 Characteristics of different types of strategic alliances Criteria	Handover strategic alliance with MNC advertising agency	Trade strategic alliance to supplement local ISP or web developer	Pool strategic alliance with local mainstream advertising agency
Business objectives and considerations			
Establish a base in Hong Kong for potential entry into China.	+	+	+
Increased sales and revenues from work for new clients.	++ (media only)	++	++
Capital investment restraint and risk.	+++	–	–
Control and power of own business activities.	+	+++	++
Corporate goals			
Increase X-Net's presence in Asia.	+	+	+
Consistency with existing overseas strategic alliances.	++	++	+
Work to become a market leader in the Asia Pacific online advertising industry.	+ (limited to media only)	+	+

The international environment of e-business

7

Legal and tax issues in the global electronic environment

Introduction

The Internet poses a major challenge to the concept of legal jurisdiction. This is because cyberspace is not localized, but rather international. There is a lack of congruence between cyberspace's global, transnational character and the national geographic limitations adopted by courts. This leads to some important challenges in controlling cyberspace through law. Now it is not uncommon for persons to evade national laws restricting Internet content by establishing Internet-based operations offshore. This creates international havens for material considered indecent by some countries, for consumer-fraud scams and for terrorist or subversive activities. The same techniques for creating havens in cyberspace can be used to avoid legal responsibilities for intellectual property infringement, for defamation and invasion of privacy.

Global computer-based communications cut across territorial boundaries undermining the feasibility and legitimacy of applying laws based on geographic borders. New boundaries have arisen based on screens and passwords that separate the virtual world from the real world. These define a distinct cyberspace that some would argue needs its own laws and legal institutions to cater for new phenomena that have no clear parallel in the real world. Such laws will need to define legal personhood and property rights, resolve disputes and establish a convention as to value in the global virtual marketplace. Furthermore, because of the speed and borderless nature of the Internet, such laws will have to cater for multiple jurisdictions, often simultaneously. They must accommodate persons who exist in cyberspace only in the form of an e-mail address and not a physical presence (Johnson, 2000).

Increasingly, Internet businesses will be scrutinized by legal authorities in many different countries and not just in terms of those operating in their own country. With the exponential growth in international e-business, the volume of international disputes is likely to escalate rapidly. Recent examples include:

- copyright infringement
- trademark infringement
- buyer and seller being located in different legal jurisdictions (Who is liable for taxes? Where has value been added and by whom?)
- intellectual property (web site design, site ownership)
- violation of privacy
- breach of regulations on promotion (What laws govern sweepstakes?)
- cybersquatting (Who owns the site domain name?).

Legal issues in the electronic environment

Some of the more notable legal issues in the electronic environment are as follows:

- The Internet was created 32 years ago with the caveat that it could not be regulated (due to its military application).
- The Internet creates business models that transcend specific areas of business.
- The Internet threatens 'old economy firms' that get government to dust off old regulations to control it in their interests.
- Jurisdictionally, it may be that the best place to regulate the Internet is in the country where the funds are bought to account.
- For how much longer can nations tax 'bricks and mortar' firms while e-commerce firms escape?

- Effective governance of the Internet will require a transnational solution as it transcends national domains.
- Will national governments be willing to cede increasing authority to world organizations in pursuit of effective regulation of e-commerce?
- At the multinational level, does the UN have the muscle to create and enforce a model law of e-commerce? If so, what is the model, e.g. the Law of the Sea?
- Given the nature of e-commerce, are the international certification standards applicable to marketplace relevant for marketspace, or is there a need to develop a new 'trust' standard?

Solving the above issues is complicated because the laws that govern the Internet are still ill defined and in some cases non-existent. In reality, Internet development moves faster than any traditional model that traditional lawmakers are used to. It is debatable whether the laws that apply in the international domain to bricks and mortar business will work for online commerce. Many of the former laws were enacted at a time of slow-moving trains, not high-speed computers.

As an example of the confusion that now exists, US companies doing business in Europe are caught between a 'rock and a hard place'. Since 31 October 2000, firms that transfer customer information collected in Europe to their operations in the USA are likely to be prosecuted under the US Department of Commerce's Safe Harbour principles that the EU has accepted. Even firms with wholly owned subsidiaries in Europe are at risk if they exchange data between Europe and the US via email. While the USA permits wider exchange of information than most other countries, European countries take a much stricter view of privacy, especially as far as the Internet is concerned. They have passed laws to impede the exchange of customer information, the most sensitive being the EU's comprehensive privacy legislation, the Directive on Data Protection.

Law in marketplace vs. law in marketspace

There have been attempts to create new laws to advance, protect, monitor and control e-commerce. Examples of US laws in this connection (either enacted or proposed) include:

- assignment of domain name registration
- web page content (Communications Decency Act)
- consumer privacy
- infrastructure security
- taxation
- intellectual property.

All of these are issues that other countries will need to address if international trade on the Internet is to proceed smoothly.

However, while much of the 'old economy' regulation is being discarded by governments in the interests of promoting e-commerce, according to Jarvenpaa,

Tiller and Beck (2000), some 'old economy' regulation is being used by regulators in a way that constrains 'new economy' companies. They support this argument by reference to Public Choice Theory. This argues that regulation of business is a deal between regulators on the one hand and industry incumbents on the other to provide regulatory advantages over new entrants. They point out that companies can deliver content and products over the Internet in environments where traditional channels would not be permitted. As an example, a Singaporean start-up called Third Voice enabled graffiti to be written over others' web sites. This took place in a country where Michael Fay (an American teenager) was given a caning for a similar 'bricks and mortar' offence. Soon after the company began doing business, the founders decided to move themselves and their company to Silicon Valley, in part to avoid prosecution should the Singapore government decide to take action.

Contracts

One issue is whether contracts entered into via the Internet are valid. In general, they are, if written or notarized documents are not required. It is necessary that the site makes it clear that a binding offer is involved and not merely a promotional message. Another issue is proving that a binding contract has, in fact, been agreed upon. This can only be the case where digital signatures are involved as without them the contract can be repudiated.

Jurisdiction

In the international marketplace, the country of jurisdiction in a transaction is usually the country in which the transaction took place. Not so in marketspace as there is no 'place'. In marketspace, it is unclear whether the transaction is subject to the laws of the country of the seller, those of the country of the buyer, or the laws of the country where the telecom networks or Internet providers involved in the transaction are based. This issue is being addressed by the Hague Convention on Jurisdiction and Foreign Judgments who are endeavouring to arrive at a treaty to harmonize the rules for cross-border litigation between private parties. Such an agreement would require signatories to enforce legal judgments handed down in other countries. The problem is that courts in countries such as Australia, for example, could end up having to enforce judgments against people whose actions were entirely legal under Australian law. The potential problems that this might cause were highlighted when in 2000 a French court ruled that Yahoo! could not sell Nazi memorabilia through any of its international auction sites to users in France. Rather than filter its sites for users in different countries, Yahoo! banned such material from all its sites. The French ruling has in effect been imposed on citizens of other countries (*Economist*, 9 June 2001: 71).

International law and the Internet

E-business adds an increased level of complexity to international business law, and raises issues such as what constitutes a contract in cyberspace, the need for international tax harmonization and tax collection enforcement for online transactions, regulations on disparagement and defamation and finally, consumer protection for international e-business customers. It is argued also in many developed countries that because the Internet is new and is the frontier of international marketing, it is too early for government to become involved in regulating it lest in the process they stifle its growth. Consequently, international e-business faces a chaotic situation in which multiple and contradictory national laws may apply to the same transaction. This creates the potential for the international marketer unwittingly to breach the law of a foreign country and become subject to a lawsuit in a foreign jurisdiction.

The law covering the dissemination of information, advertising, contracting and ownership of intellectual property is mostly nationally based with little international case law to serve as precedent. In the USA a distinction has been drawn between passive and active web sites as far as establishing jurisdiction is concerned. There, the purely passive or largely 'information only' web sites do not give jurisdiction to a court in the litigant's country as it does not exceed the 'minimum contact' criterion. However, if the site is active in that it contains interactive response features such as 1–800 numbers, takes orders, involves targetted solicitation, then a court in the litigant's country may be entitled to jurisdiction in the matter. Likewise, there are cases where foreign courts have exercised jurisdiction over web sites operated outside their country (e.g. the German parliament passed law in 1997 making any web site that is accessible from Germany subject to German law (Zugelder, Flaherty and Johnson 2000).

E-business security

Two different elements must be protected. The first is the web site and the second is the data that is transmitted.

Web sites need to be protected against those that attempt to alter the content of a web site (i.e. hackers). These hackers may also attempt to access a confidential database or penetrate an organization's computer system. Although 100 per cent protection is almost impossible, the objective is to make hacking as difficult as possible by using devices such as a firewall. In order to ensure the security of transmitted data, it is often necessary to encrypt the data so unauthorized parties cannot decipher it. Encryption is easy to install on a site and when this is in place a lock that appears at the bottom of the screen can recognize it. The above elements however do not ensure complete security because they do not allow reciprocal identification of the parties involved.

Example	Computer security

The 1999 Computer Security Survey conducted by various US authorities reported that incidents related to Internet intrusion increased from 37 per cent in 1996 to 55 per cent in 1999. Fifty-five per cent of intrusion was by unauthorized internal access and 26 per cent by cyber attack. Financial losses due to security breaches were over US$100 million. The most serious losses were from theft of proprietary information (US$42.5 million) and financial fraud (US$39.7 million). The National Fraud Information Centre reported that the main Internet scams are in online auctions, bogus business opportunities, work at home schemes, illegal sweepstakes and fraudulent book sales or subscriptions.

Doubt about the security of e-business transactions is a major reason why use of the Internet for procurement has lagged behind use of the Internet for market research and communications. Two technologies underlie the security of the Internet. First, the Internet is a packet switching network that makes it difficult for any party to block information flows from a large number of senders. In the second place, users have access to military grade cryptography that can make messages unreadable to any but the intended recipient. Notwithstanding the new technologies, e-business security is still causing concern.

The above provides some indication of the magnitude of the problem of security, but does not state whether the fraud is initiated from within the country or from overseas. However, it is generally conceded that commerce concluded in marketspace is more vulnerable to fraud than commerce concluded in the marketplace due to both its transaction speed and the current dearth of adequate safeguard mechanisms. The most common computer crimes include:

1. *Program alteration* – these can take the form of:
   - Virus: implanted into a program that is likely to be copied by many users.
   - Trojan horse: insertion into the computer program of incorrect or misleading instructions.
   - Logic bomb: triggers an unauthorized act in the computer system.
   - Trap doors: used for unauthorized acts, preventing debugging of the computer and allowing unauthorized access to the system.
2. *Data manipulation* – This consists of unauthorized modification or alteration of data. It has the effect of triggering a loss of confidence in the system.
3. *Malicious access* – This involves impersonation of an individual's identity.
4. *Hardware/software destruction* – This includes vandalism, sabotage and malicious acts. These acts are often achieved through implanting a destruction device into components of a computer.

Example   *Amazon is not immune*

Hackers humiliated Amazon.com when they successfully obtained access to the credit details of thousands of a subsidiary's customers over a period of four months. Bibliofind, which connects buyers and sellers of rare books, has had to notify the 98,000 on its database to inform them of the security breach, temporarily close its site and remove all customer general and credit information from its server.

Source: *The Guardian* 8 March 2001: 2

Privacy issues

Privacy is difficult to protect when using the Internet. Not appreciated by many is the fact that every site visited leaves a footprint that reveals who is visiting the site and the path they are following when they work their way through it. This enables sites to serve visitors with more targeted advertisements via cookies, personalization and web bugs. Cookies are small text files that a site places on a hard drive to tell it that a person has been there before. They can be teamed up with opt-in personalization to increase the effectiveness of the advertising approach.

There is increasing concern about the volume of personal information being gathered via the web. By analysing the IP/DNS addresses, it is possible for the Internet access provider (IAP) to deduce the probable and approximate place of residence but not the exact identity of the user. Although there are moves to regulate what sites can do with personal data, breaches of privacy are still likely to occur. Web bugs accelerate the problem. These are images served to a web page that relay back the computer's IP address as well as information stored in the cookie file. The Internet user does not know that the bugs are there. As discussed in the next chapter, governments are becoming increasingly concerned at the threat cookies pose to the privacy of the individual.

Intellectual property issues and other problems in marketspace

Patents in marketspace

One aspect of e-commerce is that almost anyone can copy what a person is doing and set up a business virtually next door. Low barriers to entry where the Internet is involved bring about an ultra competitive market environment. If an Internet business builds up significant share of market, there is little to stop someone else replicating the web site, offering lower prices and eradicating profits. In the USA, firms have attempted to address the problem by applying to patent web site features and e-commerce business methods with the objective of forcing competitors to pay licence fees if they want to copy the business methods.

The nature of the Internet also raises problems in the area of patent protection as to specifically what is it that is to be protected in the interests of rewarding innovation on the one hand without diminishing competition on the other. In the marketplace, abstract ideas and theories have never been patentable. You cannot register a general idea – there must be a concrete mechanism for putting it into effect. This traditional approach does not fit with e-commerce and is resulting in a redefinition as to what a new invention actually is. This has led to calls to change patent laws to treat business method and software patents as being fundamentally different from other kinds of patents. It is proposed to create a new patent category to cover these in marketspace with a life span of 3 to 5 years, instead of the normal 17 years in the marketplace.

Several years ago, the US Patent and Trademarks Office granted patents to 'business methods software' to allow firms to arrogate e-marketing processes embodied in software and in effect give monopoly rights to business models.

Such patents are becoming common and in 1998–9, the above office issued 12,779 computer-related and data-processing patents, up 48 per cent over the previous year. The type of protection sought is epitomized in the case where Barnes and Noble copied Amazon.com's patent of one-click shopping. In court it was deemed that this was an infringement and Barnes and Noble had to remove the feature that allowed clients to buy books with one click of the mouse. Now their clients need to click twice to purchase.

The Commissioner for Patents in Australia reports receiving many applications for Internet-related patents, but nothing like the volume reported in the USA. In essence, patent flooding strategies create entry barriers and this impacts on e-commerce as the new economy has legitimized monopoly rights over ideas. Some of the patents granted in this area are so broad that they may be thrown out of court or could be invalidated by production of proof of 'prior art'. This is due to a shortage of patent examiners with backgrounds in information technology and an ability to assess what is patentable in this field. However, the costs of challenge will deter many from disputing e-commerce related patents where little substance is involved. As a result, patenting 'broad business processes' continues to operate as an entry barrier.

The following can generally be patented in the USA and in many other developed countries: most types of computer programs and algorithms relating to electronic commerce: Internet applications; e-commerce products; data-processing systems; hardware devices such as ATMs and card readers.

Patents are territorial and when the firm ventures offshore it operates in a different legal jurisdiction and it may be much more difficult to patent in other countries 'broad business processes'. This is likely to be especially the case where such processes relate to the Internet in countries where adoption of e-commerce has been limited to date.

Copyright

There are a limited number of treaties that may provide copyright protection for material on the Internet. One is the Berne Convention for the Protection of Literary and Artistic Work (which, for example, provided copyright protection for various types of sound recordings). Another is the World Intellectual Property Organization (WIPO), which updated the content of the Berne Convention to protect performers and producers of sound recordings. Approximately 80 countries have ratified the Berne Convention that requires all member countries to open their courts for enforcement of all other members' copyrights so that a copyright established in one country can be enforced in another. However, half the nations in the world do not belong to or recognize the Berne Convention and may not recognize the validity of the webmaster's copyright. This latter group include China, India, Brazil and Taiwan where copyright protection ranges from minimal to non-existent. Yet it is these very countries that represent huge online markets in the coming decade. With the new treaty promulgated by WIPO, a similar situation exists, as although 160 nations are members, it is likely that many will not ratify the treaty.

However, neither of these treaties addresses the issue of online server liability. Despite the major deficiency of lack of any universal copyright law or copyright protection, international marketers can rely on the basic principle that applies in all countries where copyright is recognized – the use of copyright material without permission (including Internet sources such as web sites, text, graphics, etc.), constitutes infringement. The presumption that material taken from a web site does not constitute infringement because the site is in the public domain, is not valid in law. This is particularly the case with common practices like linking and framing.

Linking

The Internet is able to access information linked together through 'hypertext links', whereby the user is directed from one web site to another. While mostly this does not constitute copyright infringement because a site on the Internet gives an 'implied' licence for others wishing to link to the sites, it does constitute infringement when 'deep linking' occurs'. This involves bypassing the home page and linking direct to the interior pages of the site.

Framing

Framing takes place when a user links to another site and views that site's contents framed by the logo and advertising of the first site. This is dubious as the practice can be used to provide a comparison between one's own products and those of a rival, especially if the rival sues for copyright infringement in their own country.

Trademarks

In some developed countries, there has recently been a more liberal and broader definition of what constitutes a trademark. For example, the Australian 1995 Trademark Act introduced a broader range of trademark categories including trademarks for colours, shapes, aspects of packaging, scents and sounds (Hansen 2000). Trademark violation is of great concern to Internet marketers. The majority of international lawsuits against web marketers appear to involve trademark infringement (Abel, 1998). On the Internet, the infringement is mainly caused by registration and use of domain names that use established trademarks of other companies, either intentionally to extort a settlement (cybersquatting) or unintentionally due to failure to check before registering the name. At present there is no universal register of domain names allowing an agency in one country to check whether the trademark has been registered in another country before registering the mark, leaving the applicant liable to litigation. WIPO is in the process of developing a voluntary dispute resolution mechanism for domain name and trademark owners (see Zugelder, Flaherty and Johnson 2000: 262–3).

Domain name issues

Recently, domain names have involved considerable litigation. Cybersquatting is the act of registering domain names with no intention of using them but rather to sell them to companies who have the name registered elsewhere. This has now been ruled as a violation of trademark law. A domain name is a critical element of e-commerce strategy and is both the 'real estate' and the brand image of an e-business. Of the active domain names (359 as at January 2000), 154 were unrestricted (meaning a local presence is not required) and 205 were restricted (e.g. where 'au' appears, the firm must be Australian or a resident of Australia). In some countries, a party can register as many domain names as it wants whereas in others such as Japan only one domain name can be registered, and this can only be registered by a corporation. In the former case, parties are buying and reselling domain names for commercial advantage. For example, Moldova sold its rights to the country code 'md' to a Florida entrepreneur who now sells the 'md' domain names to members of the US medical profession (Jarvenpaa, Tiller and Beck, 2000). One form of protection in B2B marketing via the Internet is the use of a 'secure' web server. Secure servers are used primarily in business and contain encryption software that is registered to the actual country where the server is located. This differs from country domain names (e.g. au, i.e. uk), which do not necessarily match the location of the server. On this basis, Asia now has two-thirds of the number of secure servers in the EU.

Consumer protection laws

Consumer protection covers a number of issues and includes the following.

Unfair and deceptive trade practices

Due to the reach of the Internet, information and advertising claims fall under the laws of in many countries. Those that address unfair and deceptive trade practices, such as false endorsements, apply to Internet advertising.

Consumer privacy

Most consumers do not realize that when they go browsing on the Internet, they leave behind digital footprints in the form of cookies. Some online marketing firms can combine data from a number of cookies and in conjunction with other records such as driver's licences, compile and sell detailed information about individuals that would be prohibitively expensive to collect by other means. This threat to privacy has discouraged use of the Internet. According to the *Economist* (1998), 25 per cent of US consumers would use the Internet more if their privacy were better protected and 60 per cent considered that legislation was necessary to better protect personal information.

Defamation and disparagement

This covers publication of an untrue statement of fact that damages a person's reputation, a business or its products. Because web marketers are considered publishers, such online libel will be judged in the same way as any other mass media advertising medium. For example, McDonald's were defamed via a web site operated by a group of anarchists. Volunteers in 22 countries operated the web site carrying the defamatory messages. Identical mirror sites exist in four countries with liberal attitudes to freedom of speech (USA, the Netherlands, Australia and New Zealand). In the unlikely event of one being closed down, the others would continue to operate.

Example	*US law school professor learns lesson in UK law*

An adjunct professor of law from a Chicago law school ordered a CD via the Internet from a British web site, where it was advertised for £8.99 (US$ 14 approximately) and was sent an e-mail message confirming his order. Later he was contacted and advised that an error had been made and the price should have been £12.99. His reply was that he had accepted an offer to buy at £8.99 and insisted on getting the CD at that price. Under Illinois state law, the seller's action would have been deemed either an unfair trade practice or breach of contract. He filed a complaint in the UK under the Consumer Protection Act 1987, only to be told that the Act did not apply to him, since under English law the place of the offence is where the advertisement is read, not where it originates.

Source: Zugelder, Flaherty and Johnson (2000: 257)

Regional consumer protection laws such as those of the EU also apply to international e-business transactions. The issue of e-consumers dealing with overseas traders is the subject of both bilateral and multilateral discussions. One example is electronic commerce guidelines of the Organization for Economic Cooperation and Development (OECD). Its Guidelines for Consumer Protection in the Context of Electronic Commerce cover areas such as sellers disclosing information, payment policies, collection of personal information and secure payment systems. These guidelines provide a framework for regulating cross border electronic commerce. Table 7.1 summarizes some of the issues with consumer protection and the Internet.

Research by Poulson, Cavusgil and Kiyak (2000) involving 255 business to consumer retailing sites in the USA, Germany and South Korea found regional differences in disclosure of specific terms and conditions, procedures for handling complaints and resolving disputes, and in privacy policies and security arrangements. Effective complaint and dispute resolution mechanisms were difficult to find in e-business transactions. Very few sites specified an applicable

Table 7.1	Problem	Description
Unique problems with international electronic commerce	Global market	Incompatible national consumer protection laws impede cross-border sales.
	No prior relationship between contracting parties	Lack of knowledge about how the web site does business, takes orders, and handles fulfilment.
	Identification of the business	Identification of business is potentially much more difficult than in the office environment.
	Speed with which transactions are completed	Insufficient disclosure of the terms and conditions of online contracts prior to completion of contract.
	Information protection and privacy	Whether personal information will be transmitted securely and whether confidential information will be kept private.

Source: Poulson Cavusgil and Kiyak (2000: 6)

law for settlement of disputes and only a few subscribed to a professional code of practice. These findings were consistent with other studies such as that of the US Federal Trade Commission (1999), Consumers International (1999) and the Australian Competition and Consumer Commission (1999). This latter study of 700 international commerce sites found that many sites failed to meet basic consumer protection requirements.

Product liability in marketspace

One reason why Internet adoption in the B2C area has been slow is that there is concern by the e-consumer as to the legal protection available when making purchases on the Internet, especially from overseas. Unlike the marketplace, those buying in marketspace are often not given the opportunity to examine the goods in advance. Although the Internet facilitates the purchase of goods and services, the issue of responsibility for produce quality and product liability for purchases transacted in this manner is still to be resolved. Local laws may not count, especially as many Internet exchanges state in bold print that users absorb all product quality risks and related liability exposures. Furthermore, it is difficult if not impossible to find insurance that will cover the quality of goods or their merchantability when transacted through e-commerce. Because e-commerce enlarges the number of suppliers, many of which come from unfamiliar countries, the probability of product quality and product liability problems increases in marketspace. The answer in part may be to insist that buyers require letters of credit to draw upon if sellers fail to provide the product quality agreed upon and to insist they show evidence of insurance covering product liability.

Example	*Drawing a line in the sand*

An Australian company buying sand from Kalimantan for its cement operation may expect the quality to be consistent with Australian standards. However, if the sand has too much moisture content, causing the cement to fracture and result in injury, the cement manufacturer is liable. Seeking redress against the Kalimantan sand supplier would prove difficult, given that Indonesia does not fully recognize Australian legal judgements. Even if lawsuit could be filed in Indonesia and a judgement were awarded to the buyer, the sand company could be uninsured or financially unable to meet the terms of the award. Even if the company were solvent, the procedures for collecting an award in a lesser developed country are likely to be cumbersome at best and non-enforceable at worst.

Marketspace and national law

What is acceptable in one country may be unacceptable in another because of culture, social practices, religion, economic circumstances or politics. Due to its unbounded nature, the Internet can be used to enable citizens in a country where a practice is unacceptable to participate in the practice outside their national border of domicile. The most frequently cited example of this is pornography. Kobrin (2000) illustrates the issue with respect to Australia and the USA. In the USA, there is considerable opposition to online gambling because it enables citizens of states where it is forbidden to gamble. The US Senate passed an Internet Gaming Prohibition Act in late 1999. Online gambling is legal in Australia and 49 other countries. Australia's strict regulatory regime has the support of gaming operators as regulation is seen as a stamp of legitimacy and as a means for Australia to maintain its competitive advantage in this industry (Creed, 2000). This raises the question as to whether the US bill applies to Australian casinos accessible via the Internet in the USA. Even if it is deemed to do so, how practical is enforcement?

Cyberspace is a relational rather than a hierarchical network and the mode of transmission of data is over the net, and messages are broken into packets, sent separately and reassembled at their final destination. Because of this, it is impossible to know the route actually taken by a message from a given computer to a given server. The modern political system of territorial sovereignty and geographic jurisdiction does not provide an effective basis for governance of e-commerce. If countries insisted on the application of their local law, then at the extreme, every country, state or province in which a person had a virtual presence would have jurisdiction over that person's web site. As it stands at present, online businesses have no way of knowing whether their communications, advertisements, transactions or shipments of digital goods will actually comply with the regulations of the country where the digital goods end up.

Some advocate the solution as being self-regulation of Internet transactions. However, given that the impact of the Internet is pervasive in the real as well as the virtual world, and given the dubious uses to which the net has already been put by criminal and opportunistic elements of society, some degree of social control over economies and their actors is necessary (Kobrin, 2000). Although e-commerce is revolutionary, it is a market in which goods (in the form of bytes) are bought and sold. Markets require a social infrastructure to perform their function as a means of exchange.

Another answer might be to have different rules for marketplace to those for marketspace. However, given the intense interpenetration of physical space and cyberspace, this may not work either. The net is not a distinct space and cannot be totally divorced from society and politics because virtually all transactions in cyberspace effect the physical world. The following illustrates the point: If I solicit medical advice on the net from a practitioner in another country that is either incompetent or order medications that are ineffective or unsafe, then I am likely to end up in a hospital in the real world adding to the overcrowding and the cost of medical care (Kobrin, 2000).

Ethical issues and e-business in the international domain

The above gives rise to a number of ethical issues. In part, these arise because e-business creates a new set of power relationships between supplier and buyer in an environment where the traditional forms of protection of the innocent buyer against rapacious supplier do not apply because such protections were accorded via national legislations.

Another ethical issue arises because e-business empowers some consumers (usually the better off) whilst disadvantaging others (e.g. those who cannot afford a computer or Internet connection fees). As an example, US studies show that high income urban households are 20 times more likely to have Internet access than low income rural households (Whysall, 2001). At a national level, this 'digital divide' can discriminate between nations to the disadvantage of the most disadvantaged.

A further ethical issue relates to consumer privacy, especially as to what the information provided by the consumer is used for. Underlying concerns about consumer privacy are tensions between individual rights and marketing efficiency. Given the lack of legislation that applies to the Internet and its borderless nature, in the international environment individual rights generally take a back seat to marketing efficiency.

The Internet and taxation

Economic governance in the modern state system assumes geographic jurisdiction. Taxation is profoundly geographic and is usually determined by where the transaction occurs, where the income stream arises or where the person or entity that generates the income resides. National economies are defined and measured in terms of geographic borders and law and regulation applied within a geographic jurisdiction or to residents of that jurisdiction temporarily located elsewhere (Kobrin, 2000: 6).

In these circumstances, does every country, every state, every province or every locality in which I have a virtual presence via the Internet have jurisdiction over my site? Taxation is a driving force behind claims of jurisdiction, as authorities do not want to miss out, especially when Internet transactions replace marketplace transactions on which turnover or profit-based taxes are levied. The tax systems of most countries were not designed for an integrated world economy and were developed in an era when both international trade and large capital movements were limited. Globalization has already complicated the collection of taxes and taxing multinationals is difficult because of tax competition (related to attracting investment) and ability to take advantage of tax havens. Potentially, the Internet and e-business pose more serious problems for a system of taxation based on geographic jurisdiction. This is because the Internet has no physical location and users of the Internet have no control and little knowledge of the path travelled by the information they seek. This raises conceptual problems for a geographically based system of taxation (Kobrin, 2000).

Physical goods purchased on the net raise issues of sales tax and import duties. This is because with sales direct to customers in another country, the amount involved in single transactions is often not economical to collect. However, retailers in the marketplace have to pay taxes and duties and pass them on to their customers in the form of higher prices. A solution is to shift the burden of tax collection to sellers or third parties such as credit card insurers. Whilst this may work with domestic sales via the Internet, it would be difficult for the government of one country to make sellers in another act as their tax collection agency. The problem posed by digital transactions is even more difficult. In the absence of physical delivery of goods, the enforcement and collection of taxes may well be impossible, as there is no audit trail to alert the authorities that a transaction has occurred.

The above raises several issues. The first is why transactions via the Internet should be taxed. Some countries are deliberately avoiding the issue as they feel the greatest benefit is likely to be derived by encouraging citizens to become comfortable with the electronic environment and the avoidance of tax acts as bait. Olin (2001) argues that because the Internet has blurred the sense of place, traditional taxation criteria can be viewed in a flexible manner and that every e-business initiative should include an international tax plan to minimize the effective global tax rate. He argues that tax planning for an e-business is different from tax planning for a traditional company as historically the generation of income depended on the presence of physical assets and activities. This presence determined which jurisdiction had the primary right to tax the income generated. The new e-business models that have emerged allow taxpayers to both conduct business and generate income in a country with little or no physical presence in that country. To minimize the effective global tax rate, an e-business plan must address the following to avoid double taxation of income.

Permanent establishment

This determines which country may tax a transaction that crosses its borders. Tax authorities apply three tests to determine if a fixed place of business exists:

1. An asset test looks at what a company owns and where the assets are located.
2. An agency test looks at the activities of a dependent agent to determine if the agent performed work in that country.
3. An activity test covers activities in the foreign country to see if they meet certain thresholds.

Permanent establishment decisions made in the early stages of establishing the e-business give flexibility to select tax jurisdictions. Currently both the USA and its major trading partners do not consider that web servers or web pages alone constitute permanent establishment.

Character of income

This determines whether the income is considered local source or foreign source and it is also important for calculation of withholding taxes. When dealing with the sale of digital information, the taxpayer needs to determine whether the income is sales income, royalty income or service income. By setting contract terms classifying the income, the firm can influence how the authorities characterize the income for tax purposes.

Source of income

As foreign taxes are only credited in proportion to the taxpayer's foreign income, if the income is determined to have a local source, then the taxpayer will not get credit for any foreign taxes paid on that income. Sourcing rules differ according to type of income. Existing source of income rules rely on physical location to determine where the income has come from; and income from sale of personal property is determined by the location of the seller. The source of services income is determined by the location of the performance of the services and generally this is considered to be where value is added. A firm selling online services may determine the source of its income and create significant foreign income for the company by placing/maintaining e-business activities, intangibles and equipment in a favourable overseas tax country.

However, a basic principle of taxation is economic neutrality and it is difficult to justify why web-based competitors deserve a tax holiday compared with their bricks and mortar competitors. Possibly the answer is to create a specific tax system for e-business, but this will require all major trading nations to agree. Given the track record recently of transnational bodies such as the World Trade Organization, prospects for reaching a timely agreement are not good.

Summary

Table 7.2 provides a summary as to measures the international marketer should take when undertaking business on the Internet to guard against potential problems arising from the lack of international law governing cross-border transactions in marketspace.

Table 7.2	Objectives	Recommendations
Recommendations for international marketing managers	Avoid claims of unfair/ deceptive trade practices	Comply with domestic standards for marketing. Establish mirror web site in major overseas target markets, confirming to local standards for marketing. Direct inquiries from overseas to relevant mirror web site. Provide links to mirror web site in local language (e.g. German, Spanish, Japanese, etc.). Steer clear of misleading advertising, false claims, or endorsements. Avoid making statements about competitors or their products.
	Respect consumer's privacy	Include a statement of privacy policy on the site's home page. Allow consumer to opt out of receiving promotional offers, future e-mailings, etc. Participate in a 'seal of approval' programme (e.g. Better Business Bureau, TRUST) to reassure consumers.
	Gathering legitimate marketing data	Offer incentives (special offers, discounts, tailored information, etc.) in return for personal data.
	Respond to negative criticism on the Internet	Set up a counter web site to address legitimate complaints, link to this site from main home page. Contact owner(s) of rogue web site and attempt to resolve the grievance. Avoid a 'war of words'.

Objectives	Recommendations
Use material from another web site	Obtain permission to use copyrighted material from the site owner. If permission cannot be obtained, do not use the contents from that site. Before framing, obtain permission of the owner of the target site.
Link to outside pages from your site	Carefully select the web pages where your site will be linked. Avoid deep linking. Avoid linking to troublesome web site.
Protect contents of your web site	Place a copyright notice on the web site (in the local language in the case of mirror web sites). Register the web site with the resident copyright office. Register graphical and textual elements of the web site with the resident copyright office.
Acquire domain names	Thoroughly research availability of domain names. Register the domain name with the resident trademark office. Thoroughly research international trademark rights of potential domain names.
Limit exposure to suits brought in foreign courts	Limit the degree of web site interactivity. Limit the amount of non-Internet promotion and solicitation. Use contract provisions in the web site requiring choice of forum/ court. Decline business in undesirable jurisdictions.

Source: Zugelder, Flaherty and Johnson (2000: 266)

Questions

1. What are the underlying legal issues that influence the operation of the electronic environment for international marketing?
2. Under what circumstances does the application of law in marketspace conflict with the application of law in the international marketplace?
3. What do you believe is the long-term solution to protection of international property rights when Internet transactions are involved?
4. What are the arguments for and against creating a body of international law to govern e-business transactions?
5. What are the issues involved in taxing international Internet transactions?

References

Abel, C. C. (1997) 'Strategy and computers: Information systems as competitive weapons', *National Information Systems Education Conference Proceedings*, Jan–Feb.

Australian Competition and Consumer Commission (1999) 'E-commerce fails the test: International sweep day results show most sites don't provide basic consumer information', available at www.accc.gov.au.

Consumers International (1999) Consumers@shopping: An International Study of Electronic Commerce, available at www.consumersinternational.org.

Creed, A. (2000) 'Australian senate calls for distinctive gambling controls', *e-Commerce Times* 16 March, http://eccommercetimes.com/news/article/2000.

Economist (1998) 22 April, www.economist.com/archive.

Economist (2001) 9 June: 71.

Federal Trade Commission (1999) 'International web survey', available at www.ftc.gov.

Hansen, K. (2000) 'The world wide web and electronic commerce: Legal implications for marketers', *Proceedings of ANZMAC 2000, Visionary Marketing for the 21st Century: Facing the Challenge,* Griffith University.

Kobrin, S. (2000) 'There's no there. There: Gertrude Stein and the governance of cyberspace', *Proceedings of the eCommerce and Global Business Forum,* 17–19 May Santa Cruz, CA: Accentive Institute for Strategic Change.

Jarvenpaa, S. L., Tiller, E. H, and Beck, J. C. (2000) 'Regulation and strategy', *Proceedings of the eCommerce and Global Business Forum,* 17–19 May, Santa Cruz, CA: Accenture Institute for Strategic Change.

Johnson, S. (2000) 'Innovation in the networked firm: The need to develop new types of interface competence', in J. Birkinshaw, and P. Hagstrom *The Flexible Firm's Capability Management in Networked Organizations,* Oxford: Oxford University Press pp. 106–25.

Olin, J. (2001) 'Reducing international ecommerce taxes', *World Trade* March: 64–7.

Poulson, D, Cavusgil, S. T. and Kiyak, T. (2000) 'The regulation of global electronic commerce: strategies for building consumer confidence in online transactions', *Proceedings of the e-Commerce and Global Business Forum,* 17–19 May, Santa Cruz, CA: Accenture Institute for Strategic Change.

Whysall, P. (2001) 'Ethics and e-commerce: On nature and novelty', *Proceedings of the Academy of Marketing Conference,* 1–4 July, Cardiff: University of Cardiff.

Zugelder, M. T., Flaherty, T. B and Johnson, J. P. (2000) 'Legal issues associated with international internet marketing', *International Marketing Review* 17 (3): 253–71.

Case Study 7 *Microsoft Australia: The global issue of software piracy*
Stephen Teh and Richard Fletcher

Alex Mercer, Manager of Public Relations, South Asia Pacific Legal and Corporate Affairs, Microsoft® Corporation, is considering the issue of software piracy as pertains to her position within the organization. She is aware that the Chief Executive Officer of the monolithic Microsoft® Corporation, Mr William Gates III, is a pure advocate of intellectual property rights issues and will do almost anything to protect Microsoft's legal and commercial rights in this area.

Alex is also aware that the role that information technology is playing in the global economy has contributed to the problem in that it has assisted in the move towards a 'borderless economy' which is in turn dependent on packaged software. There is a necessity for businesses to have packaged software in order to remain competitive. It is this necessity that has created a rather large software piracy problem for all software manufacturers around the world.

Microsoft® Corporation in the USA has given Alex the task of creating a three-point plan to combat the pervasive issue of software piracy. Currently Microsoft® Australia is a licensed operation fulfilling the selling of Microsoft® products in Australia and New Zealand. However, the handling of software piracy issues for the Asia Pacific is spearheaded from Microsoft® Australia's offices in Sydney Australia. This provides Alex the challenge of finding a solution to curb software piracy in the Southeast Asian region (including Australia and New Zealand).

To begin her trek towards meeting this challenge, Alex assembles the following information from reports released by several

▶

organizations helping to combat the issue of software piracy on a global scale. It is from this information that Alex seeks to develop a clearer picture of what it is that Microsoft® is fighting against.

Global software piracy report (1998)[1]

In 1998, 38 per cent of the business software applications loaded onto PCs worldwide was pirated (Figure 7.1). This represents a contin-uous, albeit slow, reduction in worldwide piracy rates from the 1994 rate of 49 per cent. Annual piracy rates have fallen modestly each year since 1994. However, the decline in 1998 was less than that in previous years. There are several reasons for the decline in piracy rates:

1. Software companies have worked to keep up with the development of the worldwide PC marketplace and have an effective legal sales presence in all areas of the world.

2. Software companies have increased the availability of user support for their products outside of the USA.

3. The Business Software Alliance and Software and Information Industry Association have promoted the need to purchase legal versions of software and the importance of intellectual property rights. In an increasingly global marketplace, a company's risk of being found with illegal software extends beyond the legal implications, to the ethics of their business practices and their general credibility.

4. Governments worldwide are becoming increasingly supportive of protecting and enforcing intellectual property rights.

5. A strengthening of the world economy, combined with a continuing decline in world software prices, has made legal software more affordable.

Thirty-eight per cent piracy rates translates into US$11 billion lost as a result of software piracy in 1998, which is a slight improvement over the 1997 figure of US$11.4 billion. The year 1998 was economically difficult for many countries,

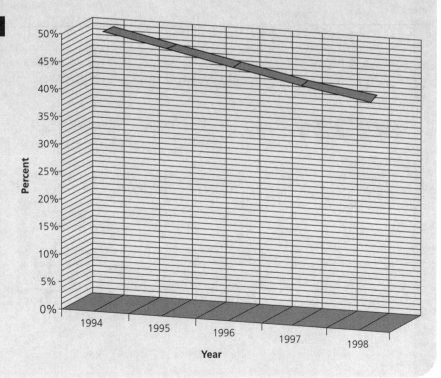

Figure 7.1

Worldwide percent piracy

particularly in Asia. PC and software sales, though strong in the USA and Western Europe, were weaker in Asia, Eastern Europe, and the Middle East (Figure 7.2). As a result, economic recession brought with it lower 1998 dollar losses in Asia, Eastern Europe and the Middle East than would have been expected without the recession. Importantly, this suggests the decline in piracy losses experienced in 1998 will not continue into the future without increased enforcement of software copyright laws. As Table 7.3 shows, the countries with the highest piracy rates in the world are in Asia, with Vietnam and China again topping the list in 1998.

The four common types of piracy[2]

The most frequent types of piracy are:

1. *End-user copying*. Simply put, it is unlicensed copying by individuals or business or, in the case of volume licensees, the under-reporting the number of computers on which software is installed. For example, when a company has 51 machines and only 50 software licences, instead of upgrading to a higher grade of licence it is much simpler to load one of the pre-existing programs and not pay for the extra licence cost = US$0.00.

2. *Hard disk loading*. Practised by the dishonest computer system builders who sell PCs with illicit software pre-installed. Dealers use one legally acquired copy for illegal installation on many machines. Disks and documentation are often missing or incomplete. Occasionally, the unlicensed software is counterfeit, which is then sold to end users who are unaware of the software's illegal status. Cost =initial cost of software template.

3. *Counterfeiting*. Software piracy on a grand scale, where software and its packaging are illegally duplicated, often by organized crime rings, then redistributed as the supposedly legal product. Cost = US$0.40 per CD, plus cost of CD replicator = US$20,000, plus cost of manuals = US$0.50 per manual.

4. *Mischannelling*. Software distributed under special discount licences, either to high-volume customers, computer manufacturers or academic institutions, that is then redistributed to others who do not hold or qualify for these licences. Cost = discount for volume purchase.

A June 1999 survey[3] of PC software distributors, retailers and developers in the Australian market revealed the following:

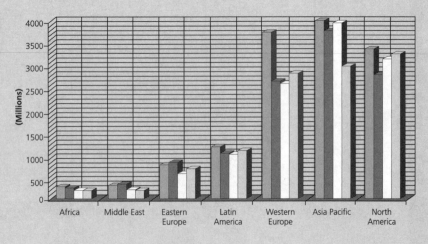

Figure 7.2

Dollar losses due to piracy by region

(Millions)

Africa · Middle East · Eastern Europe · Latin America · Western Europe · Asia Pacific · North America

■ 1995 ■ 1996 □ 1997 □ 1998

- Of respondents 91 per cent said they have seen evidence of software piracy in the Australian market.

- Of respondents 87 per cent said that they believed software piracy is a problem in their sector in Australia.

- Of respondents 53 per cent said they were losing sales and turnover because of software piracy.

- Of the sample 34 per cent believed they would increase their investment in their business if software piracy was substantially reduced.

- Private individuals copying from colleagues is the main area of concern in regard to types of piracy, followed by counterfeit imports from overseas and corporate piracy (copying in business)

Further to this report it is generally known within the industry that piracy in Asian countries is exacerbated by the following key factors:

- There exists a general culture of software piracy.

- Software piracy is easy to engineer.

Table 7.3	Country	Piracy rate %
Highest piracy rates in 1998	Vietnam	97
	China	95
	Oman	93
	Lebanon	93
	CIS – less Russia	93
	Russia	92
	Indonesia	92
	Bulgaria	90
	Bahrain	89
	Kuwait	88
	Turkey	87
	Qatar	87
	Bolivia	87
	El Salvador	87
	Romania	86
	Pakistan	86
	Guatemala	85
	Egypt	85
	Paraguay	85
	Thailand	82
	Nicaragua	81
	Jordan	80
	Mauritius	78
	Philippines	77
	Honduras	77
	Greece	74

- Intellectual property rights are not strictly policed.
- There are no major deterrents to software piracy such as enforcement or education schemes.

Contribution of the packaged software industry to the Southeast Asian economy[4]

In 1996, the packaged software market in the region accounted for US$15.6 billion in retail sales. The rapidly developing market for the same software segment in these countries brings numerous economic benefits. In the same year, a total of 169,513 job opportunities were created by the packaged software industry. In that period the software industry generated over US$2.7 billion in tax revenues.

Despite recent economic constraints in most of these economies, few industry sectors can expect to exceed the performance of the software industry. Every country in the region acknowledges that they must build and enhance their own information infrastructure in order to compete globally. The region's average annual growth rate is projected at 13.6 per cent per year which means that by 2001 sales should exceed some US$29.7 billion. This in turn will stimulate US$11.2 billion in total economic activity (based on data from China, Hong Kong, Indonesia, Korea, Malaysia, Phillippines, Singapore, Taiwan, Thailand and Vietnam).

Not surprisingly similar results were replicated by the Business Software Association of Australia[5] for the Australian market. In this instance the package software industry created more than 25,000 jobs in 1996 and generated more than US$2 billion in sales revenue. Based on Price Waterhouse Coopers market projection of 15.1 per cent, the report predicted the packaged software market in Australia will be worth over US$4 billion by 2001, with total employment of 36,000.

According to Jim Macnamara the Chairperson of the Business Software Association of Australia, 'This report pinpoints software piracy as the major obstacle for the software industry in Australia with an average software piracy rate of 32 per cent (BSA 1997 statistics). This represents not only serious revenue losses for the industry, but a significant number of lost jobs and diminished tax revenues'.

The stark reality of the above is reflected in the following dialogue[6] relating to Vietnam:

As a developing country it has been publicised that Vietnam cannot afford software. Let's take a step back and look at the 100,000 PCs bought every year, the $2,500 scooters and the high number of cellular phones and you quickly realise there are plenty of people who can afford PCs and software, more importantly technology that provides access to a global marketplace.

Coming from the perspective of a country with high piracy (over 97 per cent), it is more difficult to assess a true benchmark for software prices. As a consumer you compare counterfeit pricing with that of a genuine product without assessing its true value and acknowledging the extensive R&D and time it takes to bring a product to market.

Hardware costs approximate the same across the world, in fact in most developing countries including Vietnam there are import duties that actually make it more expensive than in developed markets. Why can software not be developed the same? The answer: software is easier to copy, counterfeit software is easy to access, and intellectual property rights are not enforced which results in an attitude that software appears to have less value in the eyes of the consumer.

Piracy harms local business. Microsoft employs a handful of people in Vietnam, their resellers, support providers and trainers employ a large multiple of this number of people, and their ability to grow and build business is much more dependent on the legal use of software. Microsoft® can survive piracy in Vietnam, however, many of the local companies that depend on being paid for software cannot survive, or do not even get started in the first place.

Microsoft® requires partners for success. They don't build hardware, they don't build vertical applications, they don't provide many services such as training, systems integration, custom development and support. They need local companies to be successful to provide these services, and they will need the Government's help to create a real market for these companies.

As software increasingly becomes the critical ingredient to productivity and economic success, it is essential that the Government takes the lead in showing how:

a) *It can be a model user and gain the benefit of software for its own use.*

b) *It can help enforce intellectual property rights issues*

c) *It can help create a market for local Vietnamese software companies.*

Attracting investment in a Vietnamese software industry will only occur if there is a local market. With 70 per cent of PCs in use within the government, it has a critical role to play to create a market for software from local companies.

Indeed this should be a philosophy accepted by all governments of developing economies. Ultimately black and grey markets in these developing economies, whilst self sustaining for those organizations within those countries, and indirectly beneficial to the economy in the short term, will not assist in the growth of a country's economy in the long run. Major corporations such as Microsoft® have a big part to play in the development of a global economy, and as such will better serve the masses by doing what they do best – that is create software technology for a continuously evolving 'borderless' world and for the next generation of a global economy.

Questions

1. What do you see as the main global issues pertaining to this case study?

2. How does Information technology contribute to a global economy?

3. What do you see as the challenges Alex Mercer will face when attempting to combat software piracy in the Southeast Asian region?

4. How can software piracy be combated from a technological perspective?

5. What three-point plan should Alex Mercer effect to combat these software piracy issues in the Southeast Asia region?

Notes

1 A study conducted by International Planning Research Corporation for the Business Software Alliance and Software & Information Industry Association (1998).
2 www.microsoft.com
3 *PC Software Distributors, Retailers and Developers Survey on Piracy* (1999) conducted by CARMA International for the Business Software Association of Australia.
4 *The Contribution of the Packaged Software Industry to the Southeast Asian Economy* – research conducted by Price Waterhouse Coopers for the Business Software Alliance, May 1998.
5 *The Contribution of the Packaged Software Industry to the Australian Economy* – research conducted by Price Waterhouse Coopers for the Business Software Association of Australia, December 1998.
6 This was part of a dialogue between Alex Mercer and a Vietnamese reporter via e-mail. As such the reporter wishes to remain anonymous.

8 The political minefield of marketspace

Learning objectives

After studying this chapter, you should be able to:

- Appreciate the political impact government can have on marketspace transactions.

- Recognize the national benefits that can flow from government encouragement of the adoption of e-business.

- Assess the likely involvement of Internet-related issues in future bilateral, regional and multilateral trade relations.

- Identify ways in which the Internet has the potential to both positively and negatively impact national sovereignty.

Introduction

De la Torre and Moxon (2001) identify a number of interesting issues about the impact of the information and communications technology (ICT) revolution on the political aspects of conducting international business. They point out that whereas distance is a central concept in economic geography, national sovereignty is a defining concept of the nation state, and both are threatened by the ICT revolution. The questions De la Torre and Moxon raise include whether ICT will bring states together both physically and culturally; whether such transformation will allow peripheral nations to compete in the global economy or increase the 'north–south' divide; will existing national clusters become less relevant as outsiders tap into them via ICT; will ICT weaken sovereignty and make firms 'stateless'; and will global governance become the inevitable response to the emergence of the Internet as a truly global marketplace?

In this chapter, the positive and negative impact of the Internet on government is discussed, as well as how different governments are responding to the e-business revolution. Then we explore the influence of the Internet on international trade diplomacy at the bilateral, regional and multilateral levels.

Finally, the impact of the Internet on national sovereignty is discussed in detail. Impact on sovereignty will influence whether future policies of national governments will encourage or impede the spread of e-business.

General issues

E-markets are vulnerable to certain imperfections in that they shift power away from buyers in favour of sellers. While the Internet empowers customers, it enables sellers to have unprecedented access to data related to customer preferences and buying profiles (Sarkar, 2000). The Internet can diminish the rights of citizens of a country and the ability of governments to both control its citizens and what happens economically within its borders.

Crawford and Bray-Crawford (1995) view the Internet as a vehicle for achieving self-determination. Evolving information and communication technologies play an expanding role in the self-determination of peoples and emergent nations. Internally, access to information and facilitation of communication provides new and enhanced opportunities for people to participate in the process of self-determination and enjoy political, economic, social, educational and cultural advancement beyond the scope of traditional institutions and forms of governance. Externally, regional and global information networks expand the voice of emergent nations and provide an electronic forum to seek support for issues of self-determination. Thus, the Internet can threaten national sovereignty and political stability by providing a force for minority groups within a national boundary to seek self-determination. No longer do national governments have a monopoly either over the media or over the content of the messages. The Internet facilitates access to information, usually uncensored.

An analogy can be drawn between the criteria for sovereignty in the marketplace (having territory) and the criteria for sovereignty in cyberspace (having a virtual territory via a presence on the WWW). In cyberspace, the home page is the capital and all related documents are the territory. However, to gain virtual territory the basics must be in place, and in many developing countries they are not. Some of these basics are infrastructure to access the Internet, basic literacy, and absence of control by the government of the Internet gateway (e.g. in Singapore the government controls the only gateway).

Another issue is the control of free speech. Some nations, intent upon preserving their national interests, seek to regulate certain forms of speech – the content of which is classified as being reprehensible or offensive to national well-being. However, control over Internet content is not possible because censoring the Internet has not proved possible to date. The attitude of government towards e-business varies markedly from a total ban to very unregulated. Firms need to check on the attitude of a nation's government towards the Internet before attempting to do business with firms in that country via the Internet.

Impact on government of marketspace transactions

E-business has the potential to influence the ability of government to control the money supply, to protect individual privacy and to safeguard data (especially that involving national security). Until now, government has regulated national commerce in the interests of the physical safety and economic security of its citizens. E-business makes this more difficult. For example, how will government license service providers such as doctors and lawyers who practise globally via the Internet?

Gawthorne (2000) defines e-government as the application of tools and techniques of e-business to the business of government for the benefit of both government and the citizens it serves. Forces driving governments to address the changes caused by e-business are:

- convergence between communication, content and computing are making international boundaries less relevant
- blurring lines between public and private sector
- demands from business and citizens for choice, convenience and control
- economic competitiveness.

The market pressures on government to respond quickly are not the same as for the private sector and the entrenched nature of bureaucracy slows the adoption of new technologies. Governments cannot choose their customers and much of what they do involves dealing with the poor and disadvantaged – sections of society least likely to have access to the Internet. Transactions with government are rarely a matter of choice and agencies collecting taxes or administering entitlement programmes do not see e-business as a challenge to their existence. Reality is that with moves by government to outsourcing, e-business is a challenge if it enables the private sector bidder to deliver the service more competitively than the government department. This aspect requires research in overseas markets if business is sought from or involves government agencies.

Security and trust are bigger concerns for government than for the private sector. Nothing in the private sector matches the range and detail of information that governments collect about their citizens. Unless the integrity of that information can be guaranteed, the ability of a government to make constructive use of the information is constrained. Another issue with implications for national security is the potential lack of privacy of personal information. Kobrin (1995, 2000) suggests several issues related to personal privacy that also have implications for national interests if such details were available to external interests in an aggregated form:

- Is privacy a commodity that can be bought and sold: (e.g., can I agree to give up my rights to some personal information in exchange for discount coupons, or is privacy an inalienable right that cannot be traded?)
- What is the proper balance between personal privacy (limits to the transmission and sharing of personal information) and market efficiency? Is the citizen's right to privacy more important than the efficient functioning of society?
- How do we value the rights of individuals vs. the rights of business firms and other organizations? Is name-linked data the property of the individual or of the organization or business that collected it?

- Will protection of personal data hinder the rapid development of information technology or should society be willing to slow down the pace of development in their countries so as to protect privacy?

Countries take different positions on these questions. Whereas in general, Americans see privacy as a commodity and the issue as one of control over property rights, Europeans tend to view privacy as an inalienable human right that should not be traded in the marketplace. For example, the European Parliament has considered banning cookies, the small computer files used to store information about a user's Internet browsing patterns. From a practical point of view, if cookies are banned, people who regularly shop and bank online may be put off using the Internet by having to re-register or re-enter their preferences every time an online shop is visited.

Benefits to government of e-business

If a government adopts e-business, a range of benefits can accrue including:

- *benefits to government* – such as reduced costs of service delivery and enhanced image by providing better quality services
- *benefits to citizens/businesses* – such as better quality service, more choice, convenience and control, and increased ease and reduced costs of compliance
- *mutual benefits* – such as reduced reliance on human interaction for most transactions and greater resources diversion to those in the most need.

Table 8.1 shows a categorization of countries in terms of government leadership in e-business adoption. The profile of a leading country is mature technical infrastructures, a high per capita adoption of the Internet, a clearly articulated programme for online service delivery, a continual search for ways of maximizing level of online service quickly, a willingness to tackle complex services with e-business components and effective leadership from elected officials.

More needs to be done on the part of government in adopting e-business. Even the most advanced national governments have only realized 20 per cent of their potential for online service delivery. To date, much government effort has been devoted to maximizing the volume of published material online. In fact, many government agencies are only now beginning to understand the online environment. In part, this is because privacy concerns have inhibited development.

E-business regulations can either advantage or disadvantage one country over another. ISP fees and discriminatory Internet taxes can hinder national competitiveness. According to Jarvenpaa, Tiller and Beck (2000), governments can either stimulate or stifle e-business depending on how the regulations imposed affect knowledge, investment flows, cost and price structures of industries compared with their counterparts in other nations. In the electronic age, the issue of national competitiveness is different. In the international marketplace issues are addressed by public choice with a focus on how firms in host countries might raise protectionist barriers against foreign firms. However, a different situation operates in international marketspace. Local firms seek

Table 8.1

Government
leadership in
Internet adoption

Early leaders	Cautious implementers
• Australia	• Italy
• Canada	• Japan
• Singapore	• USA
• Netherlands	• South Africa
Visionary followers	**Slow starters**
• France	• Belgium
• Germany	• Brazil
• Hong Kong	• Ireland
• New Zealand	• Malaysia
• Norway	
• Mexico	
• Spain	
• United Kingdom	

Source: Accenture Institute for Strategic Change (2000)

regulations that will give them local advantages over other countries in attracting Internet companies. In short, the emphasis shifts from protecting what a country has to attracting what a country needs.

Examples of government involvement in the e-business environment

Australia – an example of adoption by government in a developed country

The Australian government has addressed the need for rules to regulate e-business on both a national and an international basis. It sees the need for a balance between unfettered markets on one hand and non-restrictive ground rules on the other to cater for the needs of big suppliers of information technology and users of all sizes. In its publication *Creating a Clearway on the New Silk Road* (Dept of Foreign Affairs, 1999), the Australian government indicates that this will be achieved by:

- working with other governments, both bilaterally and in the WTO, APEC and OECD, to create a non-restrictive international trading environment for online traders. This would involve restricting attempts to introduce unduly prescriptive or overly intrusive regulations.
- Monitoring overseas policy developments and developing better data on the level and direction of Australia's online trade.
- Building understanding in the three tiers of government (federal, state and local) and in business, that e-business has major trade and trade policy implications.

- Creating awareness among the general community that Australia's approach to e-business across borders needs to be based on Australia's national interests being best served by an open international trading environment and a business community confident in its capacity to provide competitive goods and services.

<table>
<tr><td>**Example**</td><td>*Australian government procurement goes online*</td></tr>
</table>

Electronic procurement is one of the fastest growing areas of e-business because it can save time and money. The same web-based technologies that are saving firms such as GE and Ford hundreds of millions of dollars could have an even more dramatic effect on the public sector. The state government of Australia's Victoria has worked with Oracle to improve the purchasing efficiency of its Department of Natural Resources by 70 per cent. The Department has deployed a paperless system with access for 5000 users that provides complete transparency between vendor and user. Payments are electronic and fraud is kept down by random sampling. As well as saving money, the department is providing better value thanks to the enforcement of business rules and the accountability inherent within the system. This model is likely to be adopted in government throughout Australia.

Source: *The Economist* (24 June, 2000)

Singapore – an example of an Asian tiger economy whose government has deliberately positioned it for e-business

This small island nation has been 'wired' so all of its citizens who wish to can easily and affordably access the Internet. Not only does the government offer copious information via the Internet, but it has cut red tape by offering online transactions at its web site (www.citizen.gov.sg). Underpinned by the concept of 'Your One-stop Citizen Service Portal', Singapore sets out its services as a 'journey through life' from registering births to retirement from the workforce.

Citizens can use the web to attend to their business with the government, including paying taxes, applying for exit permits to leave the country, paying parking fines, notifying change of address, applying for patents and for import/ export licences. The level of filing tax returns online (about 30 per cent) is the same as in the USA. Conducting government business online saves Singaporeans time, and saves the government about US$1.50 in transaction costs per filing.

Of the Singapore government's 121 e-services available on its main portal, 21 offer transaction capabilities such as filling in online forms. Not only is the web used as a primary tool for government procurement but offering services online is viewed as a crucial vehicle for attracting business and investment to the island state (*Far Eastern Economic Review*, 2001: 52).

Africa – an example of the situation faced by most of the least developed of the developing countries

The problems in the least developed of the developing countries as far as government adoption of the Internet include:

Table 8.2	*Major domain*	*Major domain*	*Major domain*	*Major domain*
The four major domains	General management factors	Information systems management factors	Cultural factors	Environmental factors
	Subdomain	*Subdomain*	*Subdomain*	*Subdomain*
	Collaboration and communication competence factors	Africans as end users	African cultural diversity	Virtual environment and information management effectiveness
	African economic volatility factors	Connectivity factors	Regional expectations	Tangible and intangible resources
	Bureaucratic standards	Systems securities		Information technology and electronic commerce

- multilingual cross-cultural communication
- different legal systems
- varying government regulations
- political and geo-economic challenges
- various bureaucratic processes.

Specific examples of the above include policies prohibiting or regulating the transfer of data across borders, policies restricting imports and exports of software and hardware, and policies requiring overseas firms to spend part of the revenue earned in the host country. Table 8.2 shows the factors at stake in implementing business information systems in Africa.

Unless the developing countries receive assistance, the Internet will accelerate the gap in economic development between rich and poor countries and the so-called 'north–south' divide will expand further.

International trade diplomacy

This section explores the role that the Internet is likely to play in relationships between countries. The solution to the disparity in e-business between the developed and the developing countries and to harmonization within and between groups of countries lies in international trade diplomacy and using existing instruments to address e-business issues and create specific bodies to address global issues in marketspace.

E-business is an issue that affects the ability of countries to compete with each other, which has the potential to confer monopoly power on some countries at the expense of others. It also affects the sovereignty of nations due to its interactive, borderless and timely nature. E-business increasingly appears on the agenda of countries' multilateral, regional and bilateral trade relationships. Historically nation states have had only limited success at creating global treaties that succeed in practice. Moreover, such treaties take a long time to negotiate and, given the pace of Internet technology, it is possible that such treaties will forever follow economic reality.

Multilateral bodies

World Intellectual Property Organization

This body has established benchmarks for treating various forms of intellectual property in cyberspace. They have set up an arbitration and mediation centre which may result in setting aside of territorial issues and national jurisdiction. The impact of e-business on protection of intellectual property will require countries to work together to modify existing approaches to consider the Internet in ways that do not disadvantage individual parties. Some developed countries have updated their copyright regimes to both take account of new technologies and the principles of the two relevant WIPO treaties of 1996.

Organization for Economic Cooperation and Development (OECD)

The OECD is principally a forum for discussion. However, this body hosted an international conference on e-business in 1998, and hosts a number of working parties on e-business issues of interest. This body is involved in preparing draft declarations on privacy, authentication, consumer protection and taxation.

World Trade Organization (WTO)

This body now devotes more attention to services following the Uruguay Round of GATT. Its focus in the e-business area addresses issues such as privacy, customs duties, mode of delivery, international procurement, intellectual property, standards and access to and use of telecommunications networks. The General Agreement on Trade in Services (GATS) applies to e-business, especially as far as its transparency requirements are concerned. Also relevant is the Agreement on Basic Telecommunications 1997 by which countries agree to provide other countries with fair access to their telecommunications markets. The WTO's current focus is on addressing the implications of electronic commerce for existing agreements. In particular, it is concerned that governments may use national legislation on the regulation of electronic transactions to create a barrier to trade. The Information Technology Agreement 1996 aims to eliminate duties and charges on IT products and enhances access opportunities. However, while it may be possible to apply GATT disciplines to trade via the Internet where there is a parallel in the marketplace, situations unique to the Internet mean that GATS will be the only vehicle for regulating such commerce.

GATS is the closest mechanism in the armoury of the WTO that can be applied to governing and regulating international trade conducted via the Internet. However, much trade can only be conducted via the Internet (e.g. digital transmission of music) and the issue here is whether such trade should be subject to the regulations of GATS. On the other hand, there are many cases where trade conducted via the Internet is a substitute for trade conducted in the marketplace and here there is potential for the Internet to be used as a vehicle for evading existing regulations. The issue is whether GATS should apply to all trade conducted via the Internet or to only that portion where physical counterparts also exist. In essence, the issue boils down to differences between access to Internet services and access to services that can be traded electronically. The former deals with access to Internet infrastructure whereas the latter relates to specific commitments in electronically tradable services (Panagariya, 2000: 10).

Given that one of the concerns of the WTO is to improve the situation of developing countries by freeing up international trade, the role of the Internet in relation to the developing countries should be considered. It is argued that the developing countries stand to gain much because of the Internet, not only because size is no longer as important, but also it overcomes the disadvantages such countries previously encountered because of the barriers of information technology infrastructure. The potential in such countries, however, will be constrained by both the level of demand for goods and services that can be traded via the Internet and the existence and affordability of the necessary infrastructure. Panagariya (2000: 19) argues that for the Internet to benefit developing countries, three conditions must be met:

- The hardware and software necessary to develop electronically saleable services should be available at reasonable prices.
- The basic infrastructure necessary for the smooth functioning of the Internet should be in situ (including facilities to conduct financial transactions on the net).
- Developing countries must negotiate access to developed country markets in sectors to which they can export services electronically.

Other UN bodies

United Nations Commission for International Trade Law (UNICITRAL)

The UNICITRAL has finalized a Model Law on Electronic Commerce and is now engaged in drafting uniform rules on digital and other electronic signatures, certification authorities and other related matters. The Model Law sets out what constitutes the equivalent of a written document signature and original in the electronic environment. It also outlines the admissibility and weight of evidence that electronic messages are considered to contain.

World Customs Organization (WCO)

This body supports customs authorities in using electronic means for processing international trade. It is reviewing the International Convention on the Simplification and Harmonization of Customs Procedures (the Kyoto Convention) to account for electronic trading.

Asia Pacific Economic Cooperation Group (APEC)

Although a regional group which develops voluntary non-treaty arrangements, APEC has an interest in facilitating e-business among member countries. The

APEC Interconnection Framework, which aims to foster competitive network development and arrive at equitable solutions to the question of Internet charging, and the APEC Authentication Task Group that aims to foster user confidence in e-commerce through effective systems of electronic authentication, institutionalize this. APEC is also building a virtual APEC electronic commerce/multimedia resource network and working towards a paperless trading situation for developed countries by 2005 and for developing countries by 2010.

Bilateral agreements

As e-business grows in international trade, it is likely to become part of the bilateral negotiations and agreements between countries. The topic may be included in general trade agreements between countries or be the subject of specific agreements such as the Australia–United States Joint Statement. This statement on Electronic Commerce (December 1998), provided that both countries would work together to provide certainty and build confidence for government, business and consumers in key areas of e-commerce. Specific issues addressed include domain names, consumer protection, content, privacy and tax.

Any attempts at global, regional or bilateral governance of marketspace will need to involve government, business and interested elements of civil society. As events such as the Seattle Round of WTO talks have shown, the Internet empowers a wide range of civil society groups and it is better to include them rather than exclude them from issues likely to have a major impact on society.

Multilateral bodies are also beginning to factor the Internet into their programmes, especially for assisting the developing countries. As an example, the International Telecommunications Union has created an Electronic Commerce for Developing Countries Project (EC-DC) whose objectives are to:

- enable developing and least developed countries to use existing infrastructures and services to participate in electronic commerce
- facilitate the transfer of electronic commerce technology and increase public awareness
- stimulate the planning and deployment of the telecommunication infrastructure.

The hope is that this initiative will broaden markets for developing countries by providing low-cost access to international markets. The low-cost access model provided enables more rapid connection to the electronic world than would be possible if these countries were to wait until a complete infrastructure for electronic commerce was in place.

The Internet and national sovereignty

Of major concern to government is the threat of the Internet to national sovereignty, especially, but not confined to, the ability to collect taxes and duties and control capital flows into and out of their geographical jurisdiction.

The Internet enhances access to information as it enables the customer to obtain details of what is on offer on a global basis rather than just within their own country. Because of potentially increased interactivity between supplier and customer, the Internet also enables greater customization of products. In many instances, customers can participate in the specification and design of the item they want. While notionally of benefit to a nation's consumers, government is no longer able to exercise control over what products its citizens buy, particularly in cases where the product can be downloaded electronically as is the case with pornography. Governments wish to control what their citizens buy for:

- economic reasons (protect local industry and create jobs)
- cultural reasons (maintain a moral standard and adhere to religious mores)
- social reasons (prevent entry of products that damage health or the environment)
- security reasons (prevent entry of items in either physical or text form which could threaten national security or destabilize the regime in power).

The Internet makes price information more transparent and customers more aware of how prices in their own country compare with prices in other countries. Over time, this may cause price differentials between countries to contract, especially as consumers pressure governments to reduce those differentials that are due to government taxation. In addition, suppliers of goods via the Internet may be able to undercut marketplace competition due to economies of scale in Internet purchasing. Governments, however, have traditionally used price controls as a vehicle for implementing economic, social and political policies. Using the Internet can enable the evasion of government controls on dumping, price fixing and price discrimination. The Internet also enables evasion of import duties and sales taxes on imported items. This is because many Internet purchases from offshore by individuals may fall below the threshold where customs authorities levy duty. Firms may also be encouraged to move offshore to a low tax country to avoid local taxes and conduct business via the Internet. This places national firms at a competitive disadvantage with online firms and causes the government to lose tax revenue.

The Internet provides a new promotional medium, although the appeal of online advertising is more to the visual than to the aural, tactile or taste/smell senses. Because of its interactivity, the Internet enables targeted promotion on a one-to-one basis and is particularly useful where a special event or a special offer with a limited time horizon is involved. Thus, governments have difficulty controlling the messages its citizens receive. This can be particularly sensitive in transitioning and developing economies where 'opulent' advertising could lead to dissatisfaction and in Islamic countries where 'Western' advertisements might offend religious mores. In order to address such problems, most governments impose regulations on the content of promotional messages and their delivery. As Internet advertising is not subject to restrictions of this kind, national sovereignty is impaired.

The Internet enables real-time processing of orders. The ability to order online from the supplier is likely to result in disintermediation and consequent cost savings. However, governments will have difficulty tracking the distribution of goods sold via the Internet for purposes of levying imposts. In addition, disintermediation could have an adverse impact on national retailing, wholesaling and distribution, especially as far as employment is concerned. These trends are particularly evident in service industries such as stockbroking and travel agencies. Although to some extent there will be a replacement requirement for electronic intermediary functions, these can be performed offshore as with call centres.

The transformation wrought by the Internet impacts national sovereignty, both directly and through the factors discussed above. Cultural uniqueness is threatened because the Internet is a stimulus to globalization, which leads in turn to a more global culture for the conduct of business. One possible consequence of this may be moves towards a more universal set of ethical behaviours and approach towards civil and political rights. The Internet is developing its own culture, especially as far as the development of virtual communities is concerned. On the other hand, there are national cultural values that in turn affect industry cultural values and these in turn impact on the cultural values of firms. Of concern is whether these national, industry and firm cultural values are likely to be replaced or undermined by the cultural values being propagated by the Internet?

At the level of economic management, the Internet may facilitate a nation competing more effectively in the international marketplace. However, the Internet can have an adverse effect on traditional economic management by influencing the management of both current and capital accounts and by placing government in a position where it is subject to interference from and confronted by evasion of national obligations by transnational companies and their subsidiaries.

At the political level, the Internet can make the regime and the nation more appealing as a member of the world economic order, especially by communication of information. However, there is a downside in terms of national sovereignty. The Internet can be a vehicle for the communication of messages from external sources that may be destabilizing to the current regime in a country. It can also act as a medium for external forces to influence a nation's domestic policies. In addition, the Internet has the capacity to increase the influence in a nation of non-elected bodies. In the process, there is the potential to undermine national identity and the nationality of a nation's business enterprises. On the other hand, the Internet is a communication medium that the government in power can use to reinforce its political influence.

In the domain of legal enforcement, governments have a role to support domestic products and impose barriers against foreign sourced offerings. However, globalization via the Internet calls the reality of this role into question. Governments aim to enforce the laws of the country on individuals and corporations within its domicile, but the Internet with its borderless marketplace makes this difficult because sovereignty is traditionally defined by geographical boundaries. In marketspace many transactions are beyond the reach of national jurisdictions.

Finally, the Internet has the potential to enhance a nation's national sovereignty by upgrading the country's technological capability. This is because it relies on an infrastructure of technology that enables firms to serve markets previously beyond their scope. Wired countries like Singapore have a competitive advantage. On the downside, the Internet threatens the protection of a nation's intellectual property (Figure 8.1).

Research carried out in Australia shows that as far as political influence was concerned respondents saw the Internet as having a positive influence on national sovereignty (73 per cent) and considered that governments should use it to their advantage as a medium for both polling and swaying audiences (Bahargi, 2000). Respondents thought that information flows were enhanced by the Internet, and that the Internet would influence the creation and implementation of policies. Some respondents acknowledged that the Internet could adversely affect national sovereignty through promoting political instability. Some specific findings are:

- Sixty-one per cent of respondents considered that the Internet could negatively affect national security, as it was easy for people to copy and paste sensitive information.
- Seventy-four per cent considered that the infrastructure associated with the Internet was in itself a threat to national sovereignty. (This was because whereas formerly government had control of communications infrastructure, now such control can be easily bypassed.)
- Seventy-nine per cent considered that the Internet negatively affected the ability of government to implement regulations on the messages its citizens send or receive. Particularly the Internet undermined government's ability to prevent the spread of misleading and deceptive practices (58 per cent) and complicated enforcement of consumer protection legislation (84 per cent).
- Thirty-one per cent felt that the availability on the Internet of global prices reflecting supply and demand would reduce the ability of government to determine prices within its national borders.

Figure 8.1	

Model of the impact of the Internet on national sovereignty

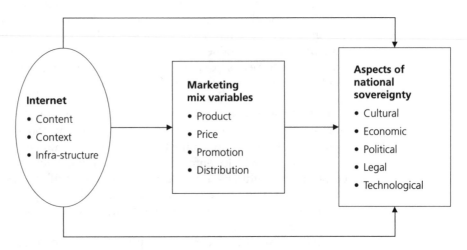

Source: Fletcher and Bahargi (2001)

- Most respondents (95 per cent) believed that the Internet negatively affected the government's ability to collect taxes due to inability to track Internet transactions and tax evasion by Internet users.
- Eighty-four per cent of respondents believed the Internet is a likely a vehicle for evading national laws governing intellectual property.

Almost all respondents considered that the Internet would cause changes in the government's management of the economy, as the Internet would require a shift from resource-based to information-based activities. A downside would be loss of jobs as people purchased products and services from overseas that they previously sourced in Australia. Some respondents predicted that in future, economic issues would be more tied to corporations than to governments. Unless government fostered adoption of the Internet, 90 per cent of respondents believed that Australia would face a lessened comparative advantage with its major trading partners. Adoption would in fact improve comparative advantage as it reduces the tyranny of distance from which Australia suffers. Ninety-five percent of respondents believed that the Internet would change distribution patterns both within Australia and internationally. Most saw the future as involving disintermediation rather than re-intermediation. Some respondents also viewed the Internet as reducing government control over which goods were imported and exported.

Overall, this research reveals that, in order of importance, the national sovereignty elements impacted by the Internet were thought to be economic management, legal influence, political influence and equally cultural uniqueness and technological capability. These results, although specific to Australia, indicate that there is a need for governments to address a wide range of issues related to the affect of the Internet on national sovereignty. They also identify a paradox: on the one hand governments need to encourage widespread adoption of the Internet and facilitate the creation of the necessary infrastructure in the interests of improving national competitiveness, while on the other increased Internet use can diminish the influence and control of government.

Questions

1. How have recent events illustrated the use of the Internet by minority, disenfranchised or radical groups to communicate their views on issues of national or global economic management?
2. What is the problem national governments face in controlling marketspace transactions undertaken by their citizens?
3. How does the Internet assist transnational companies to evade national regulations that influence the profitability of their activities in individual countries?
4. Do you consider your national government has achieved the right balance between encouraging Internet adoption on the one hand and minimizing an adverse impact on national sovereignty on the other?
5. In its future international trade relations activities, what should a government lobby for to give advantage to its national firms in the Internet age?

References

Accenture Institute for Strategic Change (2000) *Proceedings of the eCommerce and Global Business Forum*, 17–19 May, Santa Cruz, CA: Accenture Institute for Strategic Change.

Barhagi, J. (2000) 'Modeling the impact of the internet on national sovereignty', Honors thesis, University of Technology, Sydney.

Crawford, S. C. and Bray-Crawford, K. (1995) 'Self-determination in the information age', *Proceedings of Internet Society 1995 International Networking Conference*, 29 June, Honolulu.

De La Torre, J. and Moxon, R. W. (2001) 'Introduction to the Symposium E-Commerce and Global Business: The impact of the information and communication technology revolution on the conduct of international business', *Journal of International Business Studies*, 32 (4): 617–39.

Department of Foreign Affairs and Trade, East-Asia Analytical Unit (1999), *Creating Clearway on the New Silk Road: International Business and Policy Trends in Internet Commerce*, Canberra: Australian Government Printer.

Economist (2000) 'Government and the internet survey', 24 June: 9.

Far East Economic Review (2001) p. 52.

Fletcher, R. and Barhagi, J. (2001) 'Evaluating the impact of the internet on national sovereignty', *Proceedings of the Academy of Marketing Annual Conference*, 1–3 July, Cardiff.

Fletcher, R. and Barhagi, J. (2003) 'International marketing and the impact of the internet on national sovereignty', in G. Ogunmokun and R. Gabbay (eds) *International Business and Cross Cultural Marketing: Contemporary Research in Selected Countries*, Nedland, Western Australia: Academic Press International.

Gawthorne, T. (2000) 'Implementing eGovernment – rhetoric and reality', *Proceedings of the eCommerce and Global Business Forum*, 17–19 May, Santa Cruz, CA: Accenture Institute for Strategic Change.

Jarvenpaa, S. L., Tiller, E. H. and Beck, J. C. (2000) 'Regulation and strategy in the global network economy: National competitiveness and new entrant power', *Proceedings of the eCommerce and Global Business Forum*, May 17–19, Santa Cruz, CA, Accenture Institute for Strategic Change.

Kobrin, S. J. (1995) 'Beyond symmetry: State sovereignty in a networked global economy', working paper, *Carnegie Bosch Institute for Applied Studies in International Management*, 95 (8).

Kobrin, S. J. (2000) 'There's no there there: Gertrude Stein and the governance of cyberspace', *Proceedings of the eCommerce and Global Business Forum*, 17–19 May, Santa Cruz, CA, Accenture Institute for Strategic Change.

Panagariya, A. (2000) *E-Commerce, WTO and Developing Countries*, New York and Geneva: United Nations.

Sarkar, M. (2000) 'Show me the money: Cybermediation in global eMarkets', *Proceedings of the eCommerce and Global Business Forum*, 17–19 May, Santa Cruz, CA: Accenture Institute for Strategic Change.

Case Study 8 *HavenCo: Business opportunity or a political threat?*
Bill Todorovic and Francine Schlosser

The development and widespread utilization of information technology have changed our world forever. Allowing instantaneous communication across the world, and access to the Internet, information technology is seen as an opportunity by some and a threat by others. The sudden onset of information technology left governments trying to regulate it on the one hand, while individuals and organizations are trying to maximize it. Exploiting the situation, HavenCo found a business opportunity – to provide a 'data haven'. In the midst of the waves of controversy, a group of 'American cypherpunks' transferred a windswept island of Sealand into the world's first satellite-linked internet data management and storage facility

▶

(McCullagh, 2003a). HavenCo, incorporated in May 2000, has become a home to individuals and businesses looking for a place to store and manage sensitive and controversial data.

The HavenCo business proposition

HavenCo targets customers who require servers that are safe from lawsuits, seizures or other legal/government interference. Further, HavenCo claims to offer the world's most securely managed servers in the world including:

- security from subpoenas, search and seizures of equipment and data
- redundancy and reliability
- tamper resistance – machines are encrypted using a FIPS 140–1 level 4 coprocessors, and offsite unlock codes (HavenCo, 2003).

The founders of HavenCo see themselves not as rebels against the authority, but rather as strong believers in unfettered individual freedom. Although offering to host sites that are illegal in some parts of the world (e.g. gambling, explicit material, etc.), their sites will not permit spamming, obscenity or child pornography (Appendix I).

Although no customer sent hardware is accepted for security reasons, new customers are offered the following hardware and support services (HavenCo, 2003):

- ultra-high bandwidth IP communications directly into the Internet backbone, STM-1 to STM-16 and higher, and gigabit speed internal networks, with superior routing and management
- fully redundant power, cooling, network and management systems, using 2N redundancy when possible
- tamper-resistant computing hardware, designed to protect customer transactions from all possible attackers, including HavenCo and its staff
- advanced cryptographic protocols to support access control, financial

transactions, and secure transaction back-up
- open-source software modifications to allow customers to use existing, reliable, well-understood software while exploiting the features of tamper-resistant and cryptographically secured servers (HavenCo, 2003).

One would expect these services to be extremely expensive. However, HavenCo claims that they are very competitively priced. For example, their Linux servers costs only US1500 per month. It takes about 3–5 days for the new accounts to be set up and running (HavenCo, 2003). The company is publicly audited, with a substantial investor pool supporting its venture (minimum investor involvement is US100,000).

Geography – a part of the advantage?

Perhaps the most unique element of this business activity is the geographical location, positioned on the only 'man-made sovereign island', the Principality of Sealand (McCullagh, 200b). The Principality of Sealand is a small island, with a windswept tower, positioned six miles off England's coast. Originally erected during the Second World War (WWII), it was used by the British Navy to shoot down incoming Nazi aircraft. The island is about 10 by 25 yards in size and was founded as an independent Principality by Roy Bates in 1967 (Sealand, 2003a). Roy Bates declared himself a prince (and his wife a princess) of the newly established sovereign country of Sealand just outside the territorial waters of England. Its official language is English and the Sealand dollar is comparable to the US dollar. The principality of Sealand also has its own passport and security (Sealand, 2003a). In 1986, a British court effectively recognized Sealand as an independent state (McCullagh, 2000a). This rather uncertain legal independence has been further supported by several subsequent legal challenges.

Sealand is closed to visitors or tourists, a reasonable position considering the security requirements of HavenCo. Before deciding on the site, HavenCo was also attracted to this unique location by the lack of data traffic reporting and regulatory requirements of the Principality of Sealand. HavenCo has been given assurance that there will be no such requirements implemented in the future.

Positioned in the 'First World', the Principality of Sealand offers some impressive benefits (HavenCo, 2001c). These are presented in Table 8.3.

The political angle of data havens

The rest of the world appears to be greeting the developments at HavenCo with a mixed response. While some are praising HavenCo as the champions of freedom, others are recognizing the need to ensure this does not become a haven for illegal activity. In their recent meeting, the Group of Eight (G8) nations recognized the need to hammer out an agreement on the international law relating to Internet and data traffic regulation. This is in part an attempt to minimize the existence of digital or Internet havens (McCullagh, 2000a). This could impact HavenCo, since the London office could restrict the microwave links that connect HavenCo. Further, the apparent sense of freedom could be curtailed if satellite connection companies were to come under pressure from their own governments to disconnect HavenCo. HavenCo could even see its bank accounts imperiled (McCullagh, 2000a). HavenCo may not be as 'independent and free' from the rest of the world as they would like to be. This is crucial to HavenCo, because it is this independence and freedom that makes HavenCo so unique.

Questions

1. How much freedom does HavenCo have? How much freedom should they have?

2. Does HavenCo present a threat to governments' ability to collect taxes, duties or control capital flow? How does this impact national sovereignty?

3. How might HavenCo influence international trade diplomacy?

References

HavenCo *Frequently Asked Questions*, www.havenco.com/about_havenco/faq.html, 23 September.

HavenCo *Products and Services*, www.havenco.com/products_and_services/index.html, 23 September.

HavenCo *Why HavenCo?*, www.havenco.com/products_and_services/why.html; 23 September.

HavenCo *Acceptable Use Policy*, www.havenco.com/legal/aup.html; 23 September, 2003.

HavenCo *HavenCo Services Rate Sheet*, www.havenco.com/products_and_services/rates.html, 23 September.

HavenCo *HavenCo Home Page*, www.havenco.com/, 23 September.

McCullagh, D. (2003a) *A Data Sanctuary is Born*, www.wired.com/news/business/0,1367,36749,00.html 23 September 2003.

McCullagh, D. (2003b) *HavenCo: Come to Data*, www.wired.com/news/politics/0,1283,36756,00.html 23 September 2003.

Sealand, P. O. (2003a) *About Sealand*, www.sealandgov.com/, 23 September.

Sealand, P. O. (2003b) *History of Sealand*, www.sealandgov.com/history.html, 23 September 2003

Table 8.3		*First World*	*Third World*
The differences between the First and Third World	Infrastructure	High quality/low cost	Low quality/high cost
	Regulations	Random/high enforcement	Negotiable/low enforcement
	Taxation	High/high enforcement	Negotiable/low enforcement

Source: HavenCo (2001c)

Accommodating culture in international business strategy

Introduction

There are a number of comparisons published showing differences in Internet adoption between countries. Figure 9.1 is an example. Although availability of technical infrastructure and ability to afford the infrastructure (e.g. PCs) are major reasons for differences in rates of adoption between countries and although research has shown a positive correlation between gross national product (GNP) and Internet adoption (Park, 2000), a major factor is that of cultural differences. Culture impacts on the way information is used, the credibility attached to information and the degree of trust exhibited in the Internet as a medium for information. The Internet is geared to the American cultural norms of anti-government, individualism, populism and egalitarianism. This means that some in other countries will consider that American culture is embedded in the Internet and this will lead to resistance to Internet adoption in cultures that are different to the USA.

Figure 9.1   Internet adoption by country

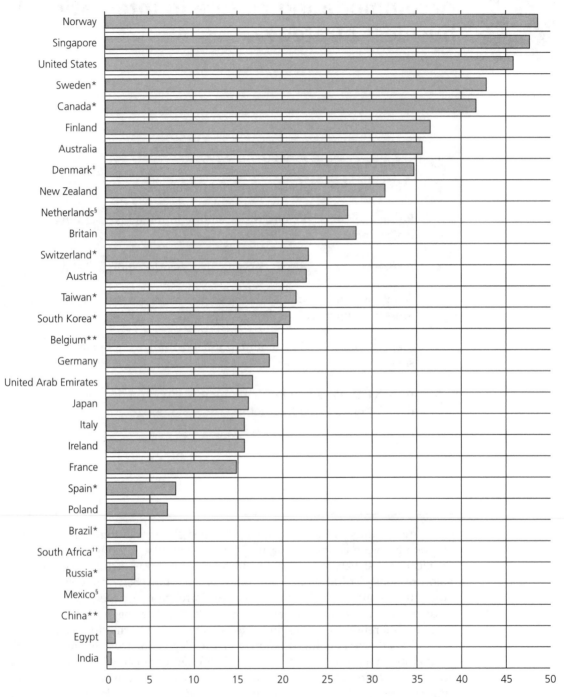

*December 1999   †November 1999   ‡October 1999   §February 2000   **January 2000   ††August 1999

Source: Economist Intelligence Unit (EIU), cited by Bauer (2000: 74)

Dimensions of culture and the Internet

One of the characteristics of the Internet is its global reach. This means that e-marketers must address the diversity of the consumer's global culture if Internet marketing is to be effective. This is because nations and subcultures within nations differ from each other on various cultural dimensions. Those that appear to apply to Internet adoption and usage include the following:

Time

The Internet is regarded as a medium that saves time because of its interactivity, its ability to consummate a sale and the speed of its information exchanges. This means that it will be valued in cultures where 'time is money' and punctuality is prized. In cultures that adopt a more relaxed approach to time and where time is subordinated to creating or maintaining relationships, the timeliness of the Internet is not likely to be valued as much. In societies where the focus is on the past (e.g. Iran), innovations like the Internet are not likely to be as prized as is the case in societies where the focus is on the present or the future (e.g. the USA).

Materialism

Because of its association with Americanness, the Internet is regarded in many countries as being associated with materialism and the dollar, rather than quality of life or improvement in the welfare of the average citizen. This perception is reinforced by the association of the Internet with transnational companies endeavouring to become global firms, and the Internet is regarded as being a vehicle for achieving these aspirations. Adoption of the Internet in societies that are critical of materialism may be delayed because of this association.

Technical orientation

Technical orientation is a dimension along which countries differ. The Internet is strongly associated with new technology. Countries that are not strong in new technology creation may be those that are not innovators or early adopters as far as diffusion of innovation is concerned. They are also less likely to invest funds in embracing the Internet or creating the necessary infrastructure, because of its association with new technology.

Language

Language in its structure, content and form manifests the culture of those who speak it. This is reflected in word order, grammatical structure, number of words used to indicate shades of meaning (e.g. for snow for an Eskimo and heat for someone living near the equator), in discourse analysis (where the emphasis in the sentence comes), and specificity vs. vagueness of meaning. As the Internet is specific rather than contextual and associated with American direct style of communication rather than with oblique style of communication, in many Asian countries its adoption may be delayed because its directness could lead to giving offence.

Another related issue is the use of English on web sites. Although the demographic and social characteristics of international web users are such that they are likely to speak English as a second or other language, they are likely to be more proficient in their native language. Navigating sites in English represents an additional burden and non-native English speakers still prefer local language sites. Research by Luna and Peracchio (2000) supports the notion that processing of stimuli in the second language is likely to be more difficult than processing of stimuli in one's native language. They advocate that if a second language site is used, it should be designed so that non-verbal cues can help visitors process the verbal content.

Business customs and practices

Cultures vary in terms of acceptable business customs and practices. In some cultures, these should be specific and transparent while in others they are opaque, providing room to manoeuvre, to repay favours and to make a commercial return in circumstances where regulations eliminate the incentive. Because of the transparency of the Internet and the traceability of Internet transactions, people in cultures where business customs and practices are opaque and negotiable may be more reluctant to adopt the new technology than people in cultures where business activities are more transparent. This is particularly the case where bribery is common or a significant percentage of international trade flows through unofficial channels.

Cultural concepts and the Internet

There are a number of underlying cultural concepts that influence the impact of culture on international marketing The relevance of these to marketing via the Internet is reviewed below.

High vs. low context

Hall (1976) pointed out that cultures differ in terms of being high context or low context. A high context culture is one where what is said conveys only a limited portion of the meaning and the balance of the meaning must be interpreted in terms of how it is being said, where it is being said and the body language of the speaker. In high context cultures, much of the message will be implied in the context of the communication and is influenced by the background and basic values of the communicator. In low context cultures, messages are mostly explicit and the words convey most of the meaning in the communication. In low context cultures, the impact of non-verbal cues is far less significant and the status of the speaker is less important in attaching meaning to what is said. Figure 9.2 shows where various countries lay on a continuum between high and low context cultures.

It is interesting to compare context with rates of Internet adoption in Figure 9.1. It would seem that low context countries are more likely to adopt the

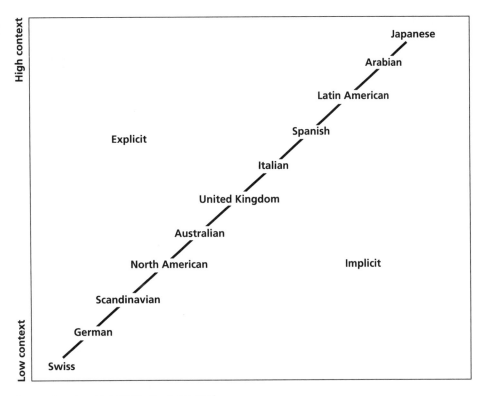

Figure 9.2

Cultural contexts of various countries

Source: Based on Hall (1976: Ch. 7, 91–101)

Internet than high context countries. This may be because the Internet is not contextual and Internet messages convey all the intended meaning. This has led Fock (2000) to propose that communication behaviour of Internet visitors from high context cultures will be different to those from low context cultures and that perceptions of web messages by web visitors from high context cultures will also be different to the perceptions of messages by visitors from low context cultures.

Psychic distance

This is based on a range of perceptual variables that differentiate an overseas market from one's own country. Although these variables include language differences, literacy and education, the nature of the political system, stage of economic development and extent of infrastructure, the most important variable is culture as all the other variables are influenced to some degree by culture. Psychic distance is a measure of how far away a country is perceived to be from one's own country in terms of an aggregation of the above factors. It is also a measure of the extent to which a country is perceived to be different. As an example, Table 9.1 provides psychic distance measures from Australia for a range of countries.

To extend the example further, a comparison of these distances with rates of Internet adoption in Figure 9.1 provides some indication that psychic similarity with Australia is linked to a higher rate of Internet adoption. There is some logic

Table 9.1		Index of psychic distance ratings of countries from Australia			

Country	Index	Country	Index	Country	Index
United States	0.1	Sweden	8.8	Mexico	17.6
Great Britain	0.6	Argentina	9.2	Greece	18.0
Canada	0.6	Iran	9.3	Indonesia	18.3
New Zealand	0.7	India	9.7	Singapore	19.3
Switzerland	1.5	Kenya	12.2	Korea	20.3
Germany	1.7	Zimbabwe	12.2	Taiwan	20.4
Ireland	1.7	Tanzania	12.2	Hong Kong	20.5
South Africa	2.0	Rwanda	12.2	Chile	20.7
Italy	2.2	Brazil	12.3	Portugal	21.9
Finland	4.7	Turkey	13.6	Yugoslavia	21.9
Netherlands	5.5	Japan	15.2	Peru	23.3
Belgium	6.1	Philippines	15.7	Colombia	23.5
France	6.1	Russia	16.0	Malaysia	23.6
Austria	6.3	Nigeria	16.3	Costa Rica	25.0
Israel	7.1	Ghana	16.3	Venezuela	26.2
Denmark	7.3	Uruguay	16.4	Ecuador	27.4
Norway	7.4	Thailand	16.5	China	29.2
Spain	8.6	Pakistan	17.3	Panama	31.4

Note: A high index number for a country indicates that the country is further away from Australia in terms of psychic distance. It also indicates that the higher the index number of a country with which a firm does business, the less the extent to which psychic distance is perceived by that firm as a barrier to undertaking international business.

Source: Fletcher and Bohn (1998)

to this as Australia is close to the USA in psychic distance terms and Internet uptake in Australia has been extremely high in world terms. There are some exceptions to this conclusion which lead to it being tentative; for example, Singapore, although psychically distant from Australia, has a very high rate of Internet adoption. Research into the psychic distance of various countries from the USA supports the above. Park (2000) concludes that the greater the psychic distance between the American culture and the host culture, the less the host culture is encouraged to use the Internet.

Ethnocentrism

Perlmutter (1995) developed a typology whereby firms could be classified according to the orientation of their management:

- *ethnocentric* (the home country is superior and its standards should be applied to all countries with which the firm does business)

- *polycentric* (every country is different and approaches and products need to be tailored to the differences in each country)
- *regiocentric* (things should be viewed from the point of view of the region in which the host country is based and approaches should take into account both similarities and differences between the host country and other countries in the region)
- *geocentric* (which is a world marketing strategy, viewing the whole world as a market but one that recognizes that countries have both similarities and differences).

Some researchers have found a relationship between ethnocentrism and reluctance to adopt the Internet. They believe that ethnocentrism is related to reluctance to adopt new technology. Cunningham (1995) found Europeans are not comfortable with new electronic communication methods and prefer traditional methods. Kirkpatrick (1997) attributes this to an antipathy to things with an American association and cites the French as the most prominent example. Wheeler (1998) found that Islamic societies in the developing world reject technology associated with the Western world as imperialistic, morally corrupt and harmful to local identity. She found that Kuwaiti companies do not use the Internet for business deals but rather to reinforce local identity or spread Islamic conservatism. Hedley (1992) claims that the relative lack of Japanese participation in the Internet is due to the structure of the Internet itself. He found that because the Internet is loosely configured, continuously evolving and mainly accessed by individuals, it is not compatible with the structure of Japanese society that is clearly delineated, highly formalized and paternalistic with people bound together by face-to-face relationships. When an American culture situated and embedded in the Internet is exported to other countries, it can clash with local culture and create resistance to Internet adoption in cultural environments where anti-statism, individualism, populism and egalitarianism are not the norm.

Hofstede, Trompenaars and Internet adoption

Hofstede's dimensions

Hofstede (1991) provides the first and most influential study of underlying cross-cultural dimensions. He arrived at five measures, which were originally developed for the measurement of management values of executives. Park (2000) researched their applicability in relation to Internet adoption. The dimensions were uncertainty avoidance; power distance; individualism vs. collectivism; masculine vs. feminine; and long-term vs. short-term orientation.

Uncertainty avoidance

Those with high uncertainty avoidance are not tolerant of ambiguity and strive for certainty in their lives. Technology, particularly information technology, provides a means to reduce uncertainty. From this, it would be reasonable to assume that a weak uncertainty avoidance culture does not lend itself to adoption and use of Internet technology. However, when the Hofstede's classification of countries on this dimension is considered (Figure 9.3), the results are mixed as far as Internet adoption is concerned. Park (2000) found that it was low uncertainty avoidance rather than high uncertainty avoidance cultures that were most likely to adopt the Internet. This was the reverse of what had been hypothesized.

Power distance

This is defined as the extent to which members of a society accept unequal distribution of power as the norm. In low power distance cultures, it is believed that all human beings are equal. Hofstede found that in high power distance cultures, there is an unwillingness to accept change in the distribution of power and to accept new technology The Internet provides egalitarian access to communication networks and makes it possible for non-traditional power holders to access information which has previously been denied them. Cairncross (1997) claims that new technology enables minorities to communicate with one another more easily than before, thus accelerating the democratization process. This suggests that the Internet may be more compatible with low rather than with high power distance cultures. Hofstede's classification of countries on this dimension, as shown in Figure 9.3, tends to support this view. In his research, Park (2000) found that there was no support for the proposition that low power distance cultures were more likely to use Internet services than high power distance cultures.

Individualism vs. collectivism

The individualism dimension refers to the relationship between the individual and the collectivity that prevails in a given society. Many agree that the culture embedded in the Internet is basically an individualistic culture, which is not surprising if the Internet is a manifestation of American culture. Park (2000) argues that there are two major elements of individualism that can affect the use of Internet services. These are autonomy (independence and freedom) and variety (diversity). In individualistic societies, citizens are provided with considerable autonomy. The Internet provides a vehicle for exchanging views that diverge from the mainstream and an ability to check on divergent views without embarrassment. By contrast, collectivist cultures put considerable pressure on members to conform and this pressure for conformity and uniformity in collective cultures is not conducive to adoption of the Internet where diversity and different viewpoints are encouraged. The foregoing would suggest that individualistic cultures are more likely to use the Internet than collectivist cultures. Hofstede's classification of countries on this dimension, as shown in Figure 9.3, tends to support the above suggestion. In addition, Park (2000) found that individualistic cultures are more prone to adopt the Internet than collectivist cultures. This he attributes to the autonomy, freedom and optimal flexibility that the Internet provides.

Masculine vs. feminine

People in feminine cultures believe there should be equality between the sexes. Another aspect of this dimension is that in feminine cultures, people care more for each other. The Internet provides a forum for communication on an equal basis regardless of gender. The Internet provides a good mechanism for people to maintain relationships with each other. The function of the Internet is more compatible with feminine cultures where they value interdependence, interrelationships with other people and caring for other people. This suggests that feminine cultures are more likely to adopt the Internet than masculine cultures. Hofstede's classification of countries on this dimension, as shown in

Figure 9.3

Hofstede's dimensions and country differences

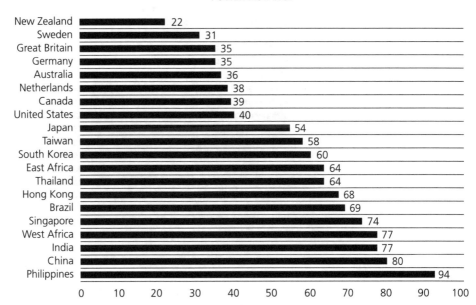

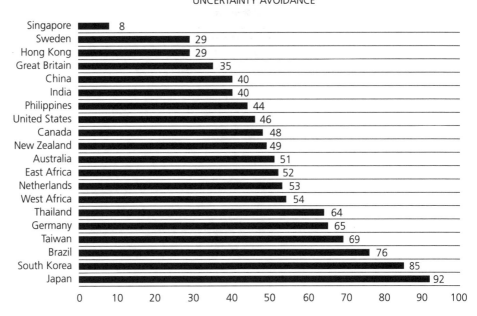

Figure 9.3

(*continued*)

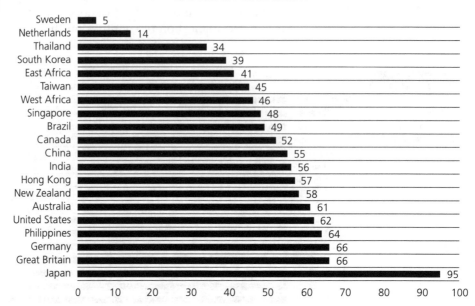

MASCULINITY VS. FEMININITY

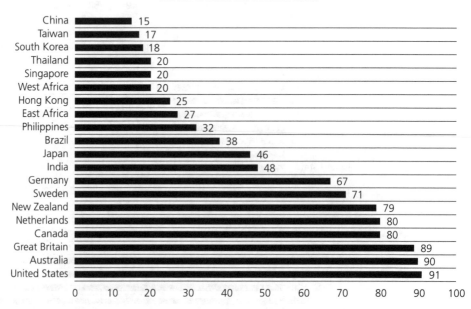

INDIVIDUALISM VS. COLLECTIVISM

Figure 9.3

(continued)

LONG-TERM VS. SHORT-TERM ORIENTATION
(OR CONFUCIAN DYNAMISM)

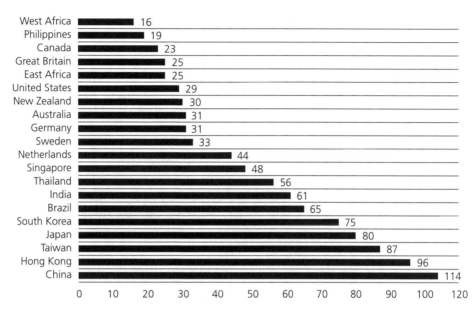

Source: Fletcher and Brown (2002: 83–86)

Figure 9.3, provides some support for this proposition although there are some exceptions such as Sweden, the Philippines and Japan. Park (2000) found strong support for the argument that feminine cultures were more likely to use the Internet than were masculine cultures. This he attributes to the fact that people in feminine cultures enjoy the anonymity that the Internet provides to avoid gender or ethnic identity.

Long-term vs. short-term orientation

This later dimension was developed in response to criticism that the previous four dimensions were 'Western' based and did not take account of uniquely Asian cultural dimensions. Long-term vs. short-term orientation is the extent to which cultures exhibit a pragmatic, future-oriented perspective as opposed to an historic short-term point of view. Cultures having a long-term orientation reflect the values of thrift, perseverance, concern for proper ways of doing things, building market share rather than chasing immediate returns to shareholders, respect for tradition, fulfilling social obligations and a focus on causing others to gain rather than lose face in business dealings. In Figure 9.3, cultures with a short-term orientation tend towards zero and those with a long-term orientation tend towards one hundred or more. This figure shows that countries in West Africa are most likely to have a short-term orientation, whereas the country with the greatest tendency to have a long-term approach is China. It is not possible to draw any conclusions as to whether Internet adoption is more likely with countries having a short-term orientation based on the country ranking in Figure 9.3. Park (2000) did not include this dimension in his research.

Trompenaar's dimensions

A more recent attempt to measure cultural differences on a global basis was by Trompenaars and Hampden Turner (1997). They arrived at five dimensions as follows:

Universalism vs. particularism

For the universalist, what is good and right can be applied everywhere, whereas for the particularist the obligations imposed by relationships are more important than general rules.

Individualism vs. communitarianism

This is similar to the Hofstede dimension of individualism vs. collectivism and is a matter of whether people consider themselves as individuals first or whether group obligations outweigh individual desires.

Neutral vs. affective

In affective cultures, expression of emotion is viewed as natural, whereas in neutral cultures expression of emotion is repressed to give the impression of objectivity and 'being in control'.

Specific vs. diffuse

People in specific cultures get straight to the point, whereas people in diffuse cultures discuss business only after relationships have been established. Should involvement in the contract or activity be confined to that contract or activity or should the 'whole' person be involved? In part, this dimension approximates that of high context vs. low context.

Achievement vs. ascription

In the achievement culture, status derives from one's own achievements, whereas in ascribing cultures status comes from age, gender, kinship, education, connections, etc.

A comparison of rankings of countries in the study by Trompenaar and Hampden-Turner (1997) with extent of Internet adoption by country (Figure 9.1) indicates that Internet adoption tends to be associated with universalism, individualism and achievement orientation. Although it might seem that Internet adoption could also be associated with being neutral rather than affective and with being specific rather than diffuse, this is not supported by the above comparison.

Cultural aspects of consumer behaviour and the Internet

Luna and Peracchio (2000) researched the relationship between the individual's behaviour towards the adoption and use of the Internet and the individual's cultural value system. These value systems are developed over time as individuals are socialized within a particular group. The individual's value system is also influenced by societal culture, regional subcultures and family values. An individual's consumption behaviour may be imitated or rejected by others and become the group's norm of behaviour and part of the culture of a given population. Figure 9.4 shows how culture affects consumer behaviour. Culture influences behaviour through its manifestations such as values, symbols, heroes and rituals.

- *Values.* These lie at the heart of most definitions of culture. The values preferred by one group of people separate them from other groups, so that cultures can be compared with each other using values as a standard.

- *Symbols.* These are a broad category of processes and/or objects that carry meaning unique to a particular group of people. As a consequence, a society's symbols may not exist in another culture, or if they do their meaning is different. Language is a symbol expressing the values embedded in culturally influenced cognitive schemas. For example, the language used when navigating a web site may activate culturally specific concepts and values that another language may not.

- *Heroes.* These are persons (alive or dead, real or imaginary) who possess characteristics that are highly prized in a culture. In marketing, these can be extended to include reference groups or opinion leaders. Heroes may influence consumer behaviour through their association with specific products or brands.

Figure 9.4

A model of the interaction of culture and consumer behaviour

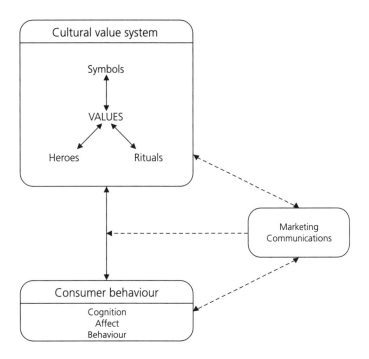

Source: Luna and Peracchio (2001)

- *Rituals.* These go beyond religion and include a wide variety of social actions. They are pervasive in society and often involve the consumption of goods and services.

Luna and Peracchio (2000) argue that these manifestations of culture impact on the navigational experience of visitors to the web site. They attribute this to the degree of congruity between the site and the consumer's cultural manifestations. They also claim that other site characteristics such as pictorial cues and the language used can influence the site's effectiveness in reaching global visitors. They argue that web sites can achieve cultural congruity by:

- *content congruity*: inclusion in the site of verbal and non-verbal material that is congruent with the culture of the targeted group. For example, the site could include pictures of the targetted country and text describing product usage situations that are culturally appropriate.
- *structural congruity*: structuring the site and its appearance to conform to expectations of the culture of the targeted group. For example, the site could have a hierarchical or a search-based structure depending on whether the target visitors belong to a high context or a low context culture.

Therefore, a web site should include content and have a structure that is consistent with the values, symbols, rituals and heroes of likely visitors. Such an approach allows for the creation of a standard set of materials by head office, but also provides for the possibility of including culture-specific content allowing for localization of marketing communications. Culturally sensitive site localization can also be achieved by site links to pages that address different values as well as symbols, heroes and rituals. For example, a firm's home page could contain links to pages that address culturally specific values. From there the visitor could click through to pages that describe symbols, heroes and rituals that are consistent with the values previously chosen. Alternatively, where language is indicative of a culture, clicking onto a specific language version of the site would mean opening a version of the site consistent with the values symbolized by that language. For example, the English version of the site could emphasize the technical attributes of the product while the Korean version could focus on relationship building (Luna and Peracchio, 2000).

Ethnicity and e-business

One way of exhibiting cultural sensitivity on the Internet is to use global ethnic portals. Dou, Yoo and Donthu (2000) advocate that firms, especially MNCs, should use ethnic portals as a vehicle for communicating with audiences in culturally different environments. They point out that ethnic portals are a vehicle for reaching both Internet active and Internet inactive customers in overseas countries.

Recently there has been a rise in the number of sites targeting specific ethnic groups because Internet user profiles are becoming increasingly multicultural and the expanding mobile global workforce wish to stay connected to their ethnic culture regardless of their physical location. Global ethnic portals can be classified in terms of the following:

- *International brand portal extensions*: e.g. Yahoo! Japan. These are extensions of well-known brands that enjoy instant recognition.
- *Ethnic portals with strong international flavour*: designed to target Internet users of a specific ethnic group worldwide without emphasis on a particular country (e.g. Spanish speakers).
- *Locally brewed ethnic portals*: sites built by local entrepreneurs for local Internet users, which usually reflect a deep understanding of the needs of these domestic Internet users.
- *Joint-brand portals*: sites established jointly by a local media firm and a global portal brand, e.g. www.ninemsn.com.au, which was formed by MSN and a local media firm in Australia, Publishing and Broadcasting Ltd (PBL).

Example	*Asian cultures and internet adoption*

Chinese societies throughout the world have maintained their distinct cultural identity through adherence to such traditional value concepts as guanxi or special relationships, 'face' and renqin or human obligation. These powerful social norms have traditionally acted as a strong deterrent against the widespread Western practice of buying and selling secondhand household goods. Guanxi binds people through the exchange of favours and such exchanges tend to benefit disproportionately the weaker members of society. Therefore, unwanted items are traditionally reserved for needy family members rather than sold for money. By giving away these items, the donor gains renqing. It is good for one's social status and the recipient now owes the giver a renqing that has to be returned when asked. In addition, to be seen to be buying or selling secondhand possessions means a loss of face under the traditional value system. However, the user anonymity characteristic of the Internet is bringing about an e-cultural revolution among the Chinese community in Singapore. Unwanted items can be disposed of and ready cash raised via the Internet without anyone knowing the identity of those involved.

Source: Tay *et al.* (2000: 1252–56)

Traditionally, communication via advertising usually stops at the brand awareness stage and there is little opportunity for the advertiser to move potential consumers along the buying process using closer integration of communication and sales activities. The Internet enables this closer integration of communication and selling to occur. This is because it may be cheaper to reach global consumers using the Internet and communication in an online setting, due to it enabling MNCs to engage consumers in interactive communications that facilitate their buying decision-making. Figure 9.5 provides a comparison of traditional and Internet driven communications. The CIA aspect of the Internet model reflects the fact that the information flow from the sender may be amplified through intermediaries such as opinion leaders and then reach a broader audience of followers who may be Internet inactive.

The Internet makes feasible the targeting of consumers who are not residing in their home country, which given the increasingly mobile nature of the global

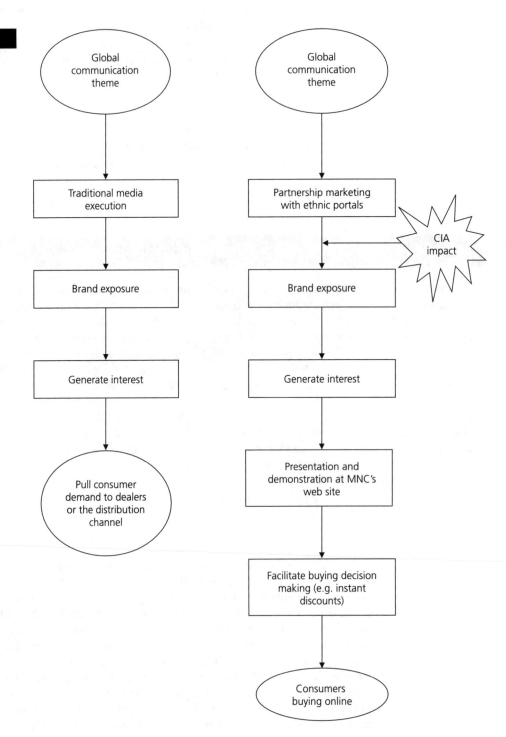

Figure 9.5

Comparison of traditional and Internet-oriented global communications strategy

Source: Dou, Yoo and Donthur (2000: 27)

workforce, especially professionals, could be an advantage. For example, United Airlines could promote round trips to Kuala Lumpur for Malaysians worldwide using a Malaysian portal (Dou, Yoo and Donthur, 2000: 2). There are problems, however, in reaching a worthwhile percentage of an ethnic group worldwide via ethnic portals as the Internet reach in many countries is limited. Only 259 million of the global population of 50 billion are connected to the Internet.

In designing ethnic portals for markets that are worthwhile in numbers or purchasing power, it is necessary to take host country culturally influenced preferences into account. Procter & Gamble has designed country-specific localized web sites of a different style and content, targetted at the ethnic audience for each of its major markets, e.g. Brazil (www.pantene.com.br), China (www.pg.com.cn) and Germany (www.procterundgamble.de).

The above suggests that MNCs need to energize their web site exposure as a complementary communication channel to their existing communications activity. One way of achieving this is to collaborate with an existing web portal that is a popular gateway for Internet users, as 46 per cent of Internet users find web sites via search engines. These portals can be an Internet service provider such as AOL or a search engine such as Yahoo!. For many MNCs, it may be more effective when entering a new market such as China to partner with a strong local ethnic portal (china.com), than building a local web site from scratch.

This attention to cultural differences is reflected in the fact that almost every major search engine portal site has ethnic-oriented portals for different country markets. Yahoo! has 19 localized ethnic portals including one specifically for Australia. In addition, there are specific ethnic portals, set up within countries such as the USA to provide non-US users with a gateway to the Internet in a familiar interface mode as far as language and content are concerned. The MNC may be able to capture a portion of the ethnic Internet market that does not normally access ethnic portals by the ethnic portal promoting its existence on specialized ethnic web sites.

The rise of global ethnic portals can provide an important medium for reaching Internet active consumers outside the USA and a vehicle to promote to non-Internet active consumers through rippling exposure effects in the traditional media (Dou, Yoo and Donthu, 2000: 4).

Negotiation and the Internet

The Internet can be a useful medium for international negotiations if used carefully in conjunction with, but not instead of, face-to-face contacts. Because many countries have high context cultures, the initial contact phase does require a 'touch and feel' content which involves meetings at which verbal signals can be compared with body language to establish consistency between what people say and what they think or intend – i.e. test sincerity and establish trust.

Trust and confidence are difficult to establish by the Internet alone. This is particularly the case when one party is mainly interested in price and exchanges and counter-exchanges on price via the Internet are unlikely to resolve the issue. Therefore face-to-face meetings may be required to create a climate where price is not the only consideration and price differentials can be offset by long-term relationships, quality issues and supply factors.

Following these initial encounters, the Internet can be useful for follow-up dealings and save both time and cost. According to Cellich (2001), the Internet enables you to negotiate from your office. When you do so, you save time and money on travel, you have access to your files and expertise as needed is close at hand. Selecting the place at which the negotiations are to be conducted is no longer an issue and the Internet provides instant access to information as to competitor's activities, buyer specifications and related market intelligence.

The instant response facility of the Internet can be a trap and it is wise not to reply to messages instantly but rather take sufficient time to create a reply that will not commit you to more than you are prepared for nor obligate you legally. Sending an interim reply acknowledging the message you have received is a good ploy to gain time. Initially negotiation on the Internet should be confined to exchange of information, clarification of key issues or finalizing specific clauses in the agreement. Once the relationship has become established and trust formed, then an increasing proportion of the negotiation can take place via the Internet. The Internet at the initial stage is also useful for establishing details for forthcoming face-to-face negotiations such as travel bookings, fixing the agenda, selecting a location, establishing the reciprocal composition of negotiating teams, etc. Table 9.2 provides a summary of the advantages and disadvantages of using the Internet for international negotiation. Table 9.3 provides guidelines for the effective conduct of international negations via the web.

Table 9.2	Benefits	Disadvantages
Pros and cons of e-negotiations	• Overcome time zones, location and distances • Minimize social barriers, e.g. age, gender, position • Obtain instant feedback to your offers and counter-proposals • Use inexpensive and reliable communications • Reduce the need to deal through intermediaries and agents • Negotiate simultaneously with several parties • Negotiate from home base	• Can be difficult to build trust, if used in isolation • Can lead to single negotiation issues centred on pricing • Insufficient information may be exchanged and shared • Greater risks due to dealing at a distance with unknown parties and markets • Intensifies competition • Reinforces buyers' negotiating power

Source: Cellich (2001: 11)

Table 9.3	How to use e-negotiations	
E-negotiations are best to	**Provided you**	**But be careful when**
• Negotiate repeat business	• Send well-crated e-messages	• Dealing with clients directly when you have agents with exclusive territorial rights
• Take and confirm orders	• Consider long-term implications	
• Initiate trade leads	• Consult others before replying	• Charging different prices in the same target market
• Test the market	• Carefully review your messages before sending them	
• Clarify specific points		• Collecting payments
• Furnish additional information	• Be selective in replying to incoming inquiries	
• Provide after-sales service	• Refrain from using negative or irritating expressions	
• Give details on shipping and deliveries		
• Communicate with existing clients	• Adopt cooperative strategies	
	• Avoid discussing pricing issues from the outset	
• Check up on competition	• Prepare thoroughly as for conventional negotiations	
• Prepare for face-to-face negotiations	• Avoid developing 'screen myopia'	

Source: Cellich (2001: 11)

Summary

In this chapter the aspects of culture that influence international marketing via the Internet were reviewed, especially as far as consumer adoption of the Internet was concerned. How culture influences web site navigation is explored, as is the role of the Internet in the conduct of international negotiations.

Questions

1. To what extent does the fact that the Internet is a manifestation of US cultural norms reduce its usefulness in international marketing?

2. Discuss Hofstede's and Trompenaar's cultural dimensions in relation to Internet adoption.

3. How does the Internet erode cultural influences and culturally determined business practices as far as international marketing is concerned?

4. Do ethnic business portals provide a new means of market segmentation in global business?

5. Under what circumstances should the Internet be used as a vehicle for international negotiation?

References

Bauer, M. J. (2000) 'The E-ffect of the Internet on supply chain logistics', *World Trade* September: 72–80.

Cairncross, F. (1997) *The Death of Distance: How the Communications Revolution will Change our Lives*, Boston: *Harvard Business School Press*.

Cellich, C. (2001) 'Frequently asked questions about business negotiations on the internet', *International Trade Forum* 1: 10–11.

Cunningham, C. A. (1995) 'Europe not ready for Multimedia' *Computer World* 29 (6): 76.

Dou, W., Yoo, B. and Donthu, N. (2000) 'Building global e-commerce presence through global ethnic portals', *Proceedings of the eCommerce and Global Business Forum*, 17–19 May, Santa Cruz, CA: Accenture Institute for Strategic Change.

Fletcher, R. and Bohn, J. (1998) 'The impact of psychic distance on the internationalisation of the Australian firm', *Journal of Global Marketing*, 12(2) pp. 47–68.

Fletcher, R, and Brown, L. (2002) *International Marketing: An Asia-Pacific Perspective*, Sydney: Prentice-Hall.

Fock, H. (2000) 'Cultural Influences on marketing communication on the world wide web', *Proceedings of the Multicultural Marketing Conference*, 17–20 September, Hong Kong: Academy of Marketing Science.

Hall, E. T. (1976) *Beyond Culture*, Anchor Press/Doubleday, New York, pp. 91–101.

Hedley, R. A. (1992) *Making a Living: Technology and Change*, New York: Harper Collins.

Hofstede, G. (1991) *Cultures and Organizations*, London: Harper Collins.

Kirkpatrick, D. (1997) 'Europe's technology gap is getting scary', *Fortune*, 135(5): 26–8.

Luna, D. and Peracchio, L. A. (2000) 'The effect of culture and language on web site navigation: A cognitive framework', *Proceedings of the eCommerce and Global Business Forum*, 17–19 May, Santa Cruz, CA: Accenture Institute for Strategic Change.

Park, H. (2000) 'A cross-cultural analysis of internet connectivity', *Journal of Current Research in Global Business* fall: 97–107.

Perlmutter, H. V. (1969) 'The tortuous evolution of the multinational corporation', *Columbia Journal of World Business* Jan–Feb: 9–18.

Tay, L., de Bussey, N., Pitt, L. F. and Ewing, M. T. (2000) 'The e-cultural revolution: Internet auctions and their impact on buyer behaviour in Singapore's Chinese community', *Proceedings of ANZMAC 2000 Visionary Marketing for the 21st Century: Facing the Challenge*, 28 November–1 December, Griffith University, Gold Coast.

Trompenaars, F. and Hampden-Turner, C. (1997) *Riding the Waves of Culture: Understanding Cultural Diversity*, London: Nicholas Brealey.

Wheeler, D. L. (1998) 'Global culture or culture clash: New information technologies in the Islamic world – a view from Kuwait', *Communication Research* 25(4): 359–77.

Case Study 9 *Language as a source of communications difficulty*
Takayuki Tsutal and Richard Fletcher

Introduction

This case is based on one of the author's actual working experience during February 1998 to May 1999 in Japan Telecom America, Inc., when located in New York as one of the marketing directors.

Japan Telecom America, Inc. (JTA) is a wholly owned foreign subsidiary of Japan Telecom, Co. Ltd (JT). In 1997, JT headquarters in Tokyo decided to expand its international operations in the USA in order to meet the demand from multinational companies that need to have end-to-end global network services. JTA obtained a facilities-based telecommunications licence in the USA in January 1998. Then Japan Telecom (JT) increased the capital of JTA to $15 million to establish

▶

their own telecommunications switch in Los Angeles. JTA originally planned to operate their business in the following areas:

1. Data transmission service between the USA and Japan for corporate customers.
2. Voice circuit wholesalers to US secondary telecommunication carriers.
3. Technical and marketing support for multinational corporate customers.

JTA has three sites in the USA (1) New York: headquarters, and location of marketing, planning, general affairs responsibilities; (2) San Jose: location of R&D, engineering, technical support; (3) Los Angeles: location of facilities maintenance.

As of June 1998, there were approximately 30 full-time employees in three sites in the USA. These were mainly managers and above, including CEO and executive vice president, and were recently transferred from JT headquarters as expatriates. They were in their late twenties to fifties. The local employees were assistant managers or lower and were aged in their twenties, with the exception of a senior

marketing director, Tony, and a strategy consultant, Chen.

Figure 9.6 shows a partial organizational chart of JTA. As can be seen from the chart, the formal authority is clearly allocated in a hierarchal structure. The CEO assigned responsibilities to the expatriates based on the formal rank in JT and many of them were given director or higher positions in JTA. Although the size of JTA was relatively small, the authority to make strategy and decisions was highly concentrated among the top executives. This was because major business decisions had to be approved by JT headquarters, especially at the initial stage of a new project. JT had great influence and control over JTA's strategy and direction. Inevitably, this resulted in an increase in the need to have discussions or negotiate issues with JT headquarters.

Issues and networks

Japanese expatriates were able to use English, but it was their second language. On the other hand, many of the local workers could not use Japanese language, including Tony and Chen.

Figure 9.6 Organization chart (Partial/Japan Telecom America)

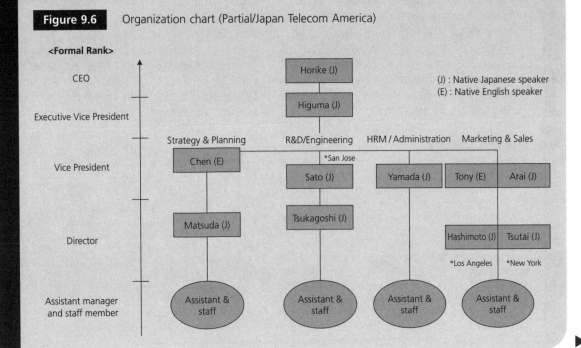

In JTA, English had been used as a formal language ever since its original establishment as a representative office. Therefore, Japanese expatriates also used English in formal meetings even though the majority of workers were Japanese at that time (see Figure 9.7).

Although every Japanese expatriate could speak sufficient English in JTA, there was still a gap between Japanese and non-Japanese. Because much information was provided by JT headquarters in both verbal and written Japanese, non-Japanese workers had difficulty in accessing the important information and knowledge. In fact, non-Japanese workers became gradually excluded from important decision-making processes.

To overcome the information gap, the CEO commenced conducting staff briefing meetings every morning. It was expected this would present a good opportunity to share information among all levels of workers. Unfortunately, this did not work because many decisions were made in informal casual discussions or at formal meetings only attended by senior executives. It is often said that Japanese workers take part in Japanese-style group consultation sessions for important decisions. Japanese are to a large extent controlled by their peer group rather than by their manager due to a high degree of collectivism.

Figure 9.8 shows a 'political' map of JTA, including the information channels to JT headquarters. Because the CEO of JTA was inclined to adopt the views of headquarters, the views of local individuals and groups became weaker under this management. The information gap has more serious consequences when executives are isolated from the rest of the organization or from other decision makers. For example, a local marketing VP, Tony, and a strategy consultant, Chen, gradually lost their power and influence in JTA because they could not get important up-to-date information from JT due to it being conveyed in the Japanese language.

If the formal organization is the skeleton of a company, the information is the central nervous system driving the collective thought processes, actions and reactions of its business units. The informal organization has an important influence, on the morale, motivation, job satisfaction and performance of staff. Furthermore, much of the real work of an organization is achieved through this informal organization with its complex networks of relationships that cross functions and divisions.

Figure 9.8 shows the informal network in JTA including links to associated departments in JT's headquarters. Clearly, the informal network in JTA was based on the language and cultural background simply because it was easy for the Japanese to communicate with each other in their mother tongue. It can be seen from the map that, even in the informal network, the groups or individuals who have a connection with JT can exercise power in JTA. Non-Japanese workers were at a great disadvantage in establishing communication channels with JT

Figure 9.7

Language in JT and JTA

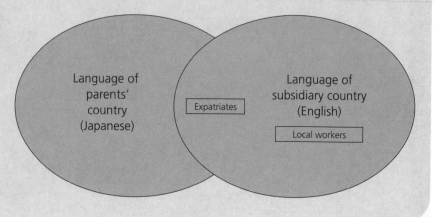

because of their lack of Japanese language skills. Individual success in an organization is frequently a matter of working with and through other people, and organizational success is often a function of how successfully individuals can coordinate their activities.

The impact

The language differences discussed above were not a serious matter for the lower ranked workers in JTA because the higher ranked Japanese expatriates could translate and deliver the necessary information to those at the lower levels. However, for the two vice presidents, Tony and Chen, the communication gap mainly caused by different languages lowered their motivation and satisfaction. They were placed in an ambiguous and unclear situation when many of the important decisions were made by informal Japanese-style group consultation. This resulted in inefficient and lower productivity for the organization. It also meant that some of the

executives failed to utilize their experience and knowledge of doing business in the USA because they developed a mistrust of each other.

Questions

1. In which way would language differences affect international communication in marketspace compared with communication in the marketplace?

2. To what extent would the communication problems have been reduced by use of the Internet?

3. How are cultural differences likely to impact on the management of relations between a headquarters and a subsidiary of another country when e-business is involved?

4. How would cultural differences influence interpretation of instructions and company policy when conveyed via the Internet, especially between managers in HQ and the US subsidiary?

| **Figure 9.8** | Power and informal network map (partial) |

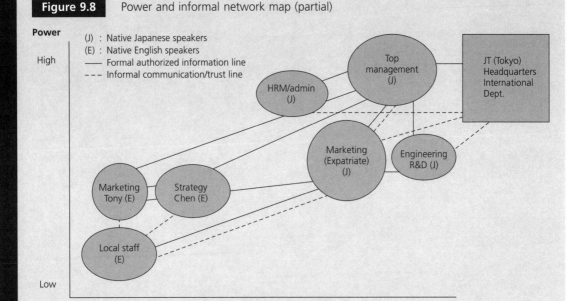

Marketing tactics and e-business

Products, services and pricing in marketspace

Products and services in marketspace

Rayport and Sviokla (1994: 141) provide an excellent example of how information and communications technologies – even those that preceded the Internet – can profoundly affect the selling and price of both products and services. Until the mid-1980s, used cars in Japan were transported each week to one of several locations where they were sold to retailers at a live auction. This method was inefficient because at any auction on average only 45 per cent of inventory was sold. In 1985, Masataka Fujisaki transformed the market by creating a proprietary computer and satellite communications system called AUCNET. Each week sellers called AUCNET with a list of the cars they are offering. Then the AUCNET inspector travelled to the sellers' lots, verified the information, inspected the cars and collected photos of them. The information was digitized, put on laser disks and sent to the dealers who subscribe to the system. Every weekend, an AUCNET employee moderated an auction that took place on computer screens all over the country. The purchased cars are then delivered to the appropriate lots. The AUCNET system made the physical location of inventory and the actual site of buying and selling irrelevant. The traditional marketplace interaction between buyer and seller had been eliminated.

Everything about these electronic transactions is different from what happens in the marketplace. In this marketspace transaction:

- the content of the transaction is different in that information about the cars replaces the cars themselves
- the context in which the transaction takes place is different in that an electronic, onscreen auction replaces the face-to-face auction
- the infrastructure that enables the transaction to occur is different as computers and communication lines replace car lots.

Thus:

- The traditional marketplace of a bundle of physical locations, inventory and tangible products has radically changed.
- Customers learn about products differently, buy them differently and have them delivered differently.
- Buyer loyalty will be different as the traditional means by which sellers and buyers differentiate their offerings no longer are appropriate. This is because content may no longer mean product, distribution may no longer mean physical location and brand equity can become ephemeral.

Rayport and Sviolka (1994) cite as an example of how e-business has changed the nature of the offering, the case of voice message services. Here, a physical product (the answering machine) is rapidly being replaced by an information-based service (that provided by one's telecommunications company). In the process, this new offering in marketspace has provided consumers with new features and functions for which consumers are often willing to pay more with the result that profitability to the provider is enhanced.

Value creation

A key to the trends commented upon above is the issue of value creation. In the marketplace, brand equity is created and managed by manipulating content, context and infrastructure through the traditional marketing mix. Both customers and sellers see brand as a representation of customer perceived value that is provided by the product or service being offered. In order for customers to perceive the value, the content, context and infrastructure must be aggregated into a single value proposition. In marketspace, however, content, context and infrastructure can be disaggregated to create new ways of creating value, reduce costs and developing relationships with new partners. This is because in marketspace information technology adds or alters content, changes the context of the interaction and enables delivery to take place over a variety of different infrastructures.

Rayport and Sviokla (1994) illustrate this by comparing traditional newspapers with Internet news services such as America Online (AOL). With the former, content such as news, sports and weather information must be aggregated with context such as format, logo and editorial style and with infrastructure such as printing plant, trucking services and door-to-door delivery, into a single value proposition. By contrast, with AOL content, context and infrastructure are disaggregated. The content belongs to a dozen newspapers that supply the editorial product. The context is the willingness of AOL to provide a 'front end' for consumers that allows them to customize the information they wish to read and the infrastructure is a series of assets, none of which are owned by AOL, such as telephone lines, electronic networks and the PCs owned by the customers.

The Internet and different types of products and services

To some extent, the disaggregation mentioned above relates to the service elements of the offering. International marketing of service elements via the web is easier than with product elements because the provision of the service does not involve physical shipment of an item, thus facilitating provision of the service elements by electronic means. According to Berthon *et al.* (1999), many of the problems encountered in international marketing are reduced in marketspace because of the following characteristics of the medium.

Quantization

This is the process in which services are reduced to their smallest constituent elements. This facilitates mass customization of the service as it enables the various elements of the service to be reconfigured according to the needs of individual customers.

Search

This enables questions from buyers to be matched with answers from suppliers (and vice-versa), needs and wants with satisfaction and customers with suppliers. The web is a hyperefficient vehicle for the exchange of information and can match supply and demand at a level that was previously unattainable.

Automation

In marketspace, many activities previously undertaken by humans are now undertaken by machine. This allows service bottlenecks to be bypassed, offerings to be more uniform in quality, returns power and choice to the consumer and overcomes the traditional limitations of time and space.

Interactivity

The process of two-way communication available via the Internet allows customers to become producers and customize the service they are provided with and it facilitates both communication and coordination.

Product

Big-ticket items and consumer durables may be difficult to sell through the Internet as customers may want to touch and feel them. Usually this is related to the 'ticket' price, as the tendency to touch and feel is likely to be greater the more the item costs and hence the risks of purchase. This is why at the retail level cars are not usually sold via the Internet. However, in such cases, the Internet still has a role in providing information, which the buyer can use to narrow down the range of final choices based on price, quality, style or features. The technical specifications and other information can be viewed via the Internet before the customer arrives at the location where the purchase is to take place.

Likewise, large mechanized and technical machinery is not usually sold via the Internet. However, the augmentation of these products is often provided via the Internet such as servicing details and maintenance manuals. The ability to communicate and troubleshoot via the Internet improves the attractiveness of the marketplace offering in this category as it allows the products to be better utilized with the assistance of support information on the web site. It has recently been shown that the Internet is being more widely adopted for B2B rather than B2C transactions. This reflects the fact that much B2B purchasing is repetitive and of consumables that are price sensitive. Such consumables as opposed to capital plant and machinery are ideally suited to be traded on the Internet as the specifications are well known and the innovation or customization required are limited. It also reflects the fact that in B2B, firms are using the Internet to link international supply chains and reduce time and cost of moving goods between countries (supply driven) rather than as a vehicle for communicating with their customers (demand driven).

Rayport and Sviokla (1994) cite the case of Pacific Pride (PP) to illustrate that e-business can be successfully applied to a commodity type product. In this case, the firm created a unique distribution system for delivering diesel to truckers in the US Pacific Northwest. They set up unattended PP stations in strategic locations and installed automatic teller type facilities so truckers could get diesel at any time of the day or night. The content for the truckers was the diesel, but for the fleet owners it was the accounting reports that detail fuel purchases with time, date and volume recorded, resulting in higher quality information for control purposes. The context for the trucker was the ATM-like network with 24-hour accessibility, shorter lines and self-accessibility. The infrastructure was a series of gas stations conveniently located for the commercial user and specially outfitted for trucks. Again in this case, it is the service elements of the offering that are being delivered electronically.

Product innovation

The Internet can play a major role in product innovation. This is because it facilitates each element in the organization communicating with the R&D function in the firm. Hollensen (2001) sees the major linkages impacting on innovation as:

- *Design*: data is gathered directly from the existing product and is then integrated directly into designing, modifying or developing the new product. New product features can be built directly into the product from the Internet.

- *Service and support*: the service department can perform troubleshooting and correction directly through the Internet (e.g. software repairs on line to the computer in a car).

- *Customer relations*: the Internet facilitates customer feedback, which can be directly taken into account in future product innovation. In addition the statistics gathered via the Internet can enable the firm to target its most likely profitable customers and strengthen existing customer relationships.

- *Logistics*: the Internet can facilitate locating the best delivery modes to serve customers as well as the most suitable channels of distribution.

- *Link to other products*: this is facilitated by the Internet and can lead to the firm offering a better solution to the buyer's needs or problem.

The above are illustrated in Figure 10.1.

Projects

Project marketing overseas is an offering combining services and product with the competitive ingredient usually being the ability to coordinate a series of

Figure 10.1

Product innovation through the Internet

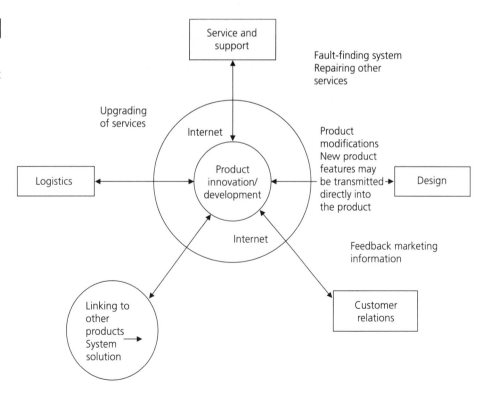

Source: Hollensen (2001: 428)

different inputs to deliver the solution to a problem. Costs are driving construction firms to consider the use of online exchanges. Two large exchanges are being developed to service the Australian market. One being developed in the USA, AECventure, involves Bovis Lend Lease, AMEC, Hotchief, Turner Corporation and Skanska and is aimed at the global market including Australia. The other, a local grouping, the Construction Industry Trading Exchange, involves Leighton Holdings and its subsidiaries, Barclay Mowlem, Baulderstone Hornibrook, Clough, Henry Walker Eltin, Transfield, Walter Construction and Multiplex. The construction industry has been attracted to online exchanges because of the potential for accessing a wide range of products and facilitating collaboration among the many parties involved in a single project. The exchanges will aim to offer one-stop shops for cataloguing and purchasing goods and services, managing jobs, bidding for tenders and other industry services. In addition, they will facilitate electronic tendering, obtaining updates on new products, support for transactions, streamlined document flows and speedy access to industry news and information – all most important when involved in a project in a developing country.

Services

Whereas consumers can touch, hold and see goods, they cannot do so with services as these are intangible. This intangibility creates marketing problems as intangibles cannot be stored or displayed. Because of this and the fact that many services are produced and consumed simultaneously, identical services cannot be produced in advance of being sold. This means that the quality of the services offered cannot be controlled and that services exhibit the characteristic of heterogeneity. Additionally, consumer goods can be produced and stored until needed, but services cannot because they are produced and consumed simultaneously. This provides another service characteristic of perishability.

In the international domain, these problems are compounded as the greater physical distance between the parties causes problems with simultaneity (coordination difficulties between service providers and overseas customers), and perishability (difficulty in balancing the supply of services and foreign demand). Heterogeneity is compounded by problems of sociocultural distance and the political–legal distance can have a negative impact on all characteristics of services, as can technological and economic distance.

Most online trade across borders is in digitally delivered services such as software, telecommunications, financial services, gaming and entertainment (DFAT, 1999). It is argued that in respect of the Internet, while trade in services will vary from country to country:

- Competition is likely to reach unprecedented levels as services increasingly become part of the traded economy.
- The extent of online digital import penetration is likely to be directly related to the competitiveness of countries' service sectors and the richness of their online environments.

- Some governments will find it difficult to balance free-flowing digital services across borders with domestic social and economic objectives. In such cases, they may seek to erect barriers to international transactions using the Internet.

In international marketing, the unique characteristics of services as opposed to products, such as intangibility, perishability, heterogeneity and simultaneity, are exacerbated. This is because of additional elements unique to the international environment such as the technical, economic, physical, socio-cultural and political–legal distance between domestic and overseas markets.

- Physical distance compounds the problems of simultaneity (production and consumption at the same time) and perishability (balancing the supply of services with overseas demand).
- Sociocultural distance compounds the problem of heterogeneity (differences in expectations between overseas buyers and local sellers).
- Political–legal distance can have a negative impact on service attributes because many aspects on which the service depends are removed from the supplier's control.

Figure 10.2

Services in the international electronic environment

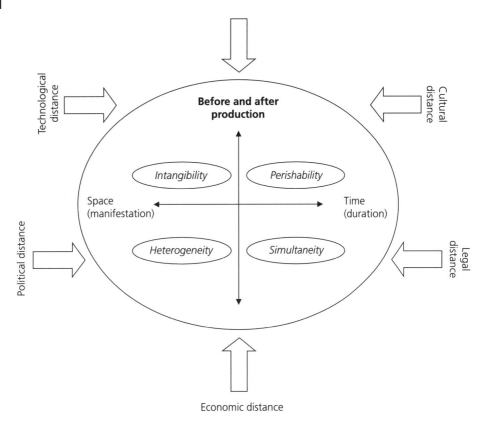

Source: Berthon *et al.* (1999: 88)

The characteristics of services in the international environment are shown in Figure 10.2.

Berthon *et al.* (1999) take the unique features of services in international marketing and examine them in relation to the electronic environment. They have conceptualized the web as a developing market channel that transcends national boundaries and encompasses elements of informing, investigating, interacting, distributing, transacting, eliciting feedback and supporting transactions. These elements are illustrated in Figure 10.3. Berthon *et al.* examine the role of the web at each stage of the purchasing process.

Figure 10.3   Service delivery via the web in international marketing

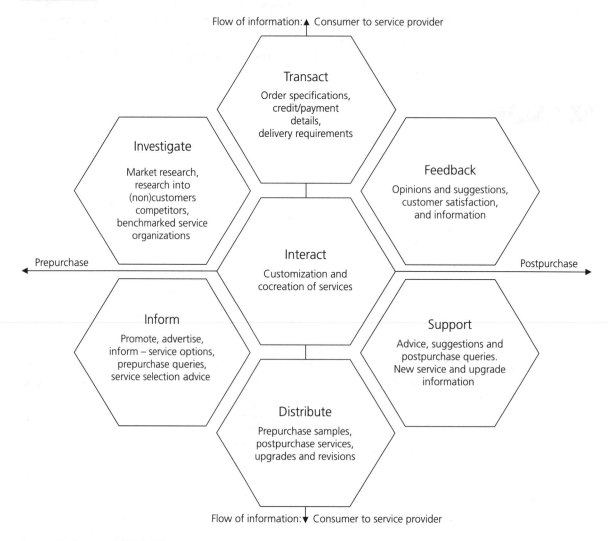

Source: Berthon *et al.* (1999: 91)

1. *At the pre-purchase stage*. The web can be used to investigate, for example conduct market research into attitudes, needs, competitor activity, etc., and inform by promoting and positioning the service and its options.
2. *At the purchase stage*. The web can be used to facilitate transactions in which the consumer provides information as to specifications, payment details and delivery to stimulate interaction for the joint creation of a desirable service and distribution to get the service to the customer.
3. *At the post-purchase stage*. The web can be used to elicit feedback and provide support following the sale.

Because the web is able to encompass the above elements, it is most useful in the distribution of symbolic, informational and knowledge services. However, its weaknesses lie in the distribution of matter-dependent or physically embodied services. As an example, although technical engineering information and designs can be conveyed between countries over the web, the related physical parts to which the advice or drawings refer cannot.

As pointed out earlier, difficulties in the international marketing of services are sometimes created by the fact that they are characterized by intangibility, simultaneity, heterogeneity and perishability. These difficulties can often be reduced by using the web as a vehicle for international services marketing as follows.

Intangibility

The web can be used to provide tangible cues when marketing the intangible (i.e. something to compensate for the fact that the customers cannot see the service they are receiving). This happens when airlines sell an electronic ticket and confirmation is received via electronic means. The web can also address the issue of intangibility by providing the customer with a sample in cyberspace as happens with the MP3 music site. Having a 'visitor's book' on your site also addresses this issue as it provides a record of who visited the site and when.

Simultaneity

Because of the simultaneous nature of production and consumption of the service, demands for a customized offering are frequent. The web is ideally suited for customization because its capacity is based on information technology, data storage and data processing instead of reliance on employees at a physical location. The web facilitates the customer both innovating and offering suggestions to improve the service outcome. It also facilitates interactivity between customer and provider, both with the medium as exemplified in a customer being able to customize the content of a web page and through the medium when it allows people to interact with each other.

Heterogeneity

The web facilitates standardization of customer treatment as when you receive the same form of greeting when logging onto a web site. It removes some of the variable treatment in the service encountered due to different personalities encountered in the marketplace. This is evident, for example, when booking travel via the web as opposed to booking travel through a travel agent. Data gathering is facilitated by a web usage. The conduct of focus groups via the Internet enables them to be conducted with more customers, more attentively and in real time. It also means that everyone in the firm can listen to what the customer has to say about the service, not just the interviewer.

Perishability

To overcome this problem, international service marketers are using web sites to manage both supply and demand. On the supply side, the web gives the international marketer the ability to provide 24-hour service to customers anywhere in the world. On the demand side, firms can use the web for promotion, pricing and service bundling to stimulate demand (e.g. to dispose of last minute remaining seats on a flight).

The foregoing leads to strategic implications for using the Internet in marketing services internationally. Lovelock, Patterson and Walker (2001) identify the strategic implications:

- *Customer service.* The web enables SMEs to provide almost the same level of service when marketing services internationally as would be the case if they had used a sales person. Given the cost differences, the web enables SME service providers to internationalize more easily.
- *Pirating the value chain.* Participants in the value chain have the opportunity with the web to take over the role of other members in the chain and provide customers with better value as a consequence. This happens when the producer of the service uses the web to replace physical delivery and the use of intermediaries overseas. An example would be when a publisher delivers content of publications to libraries in other countries.
- *Digital value chain creation.* Innovation can be achieved and new services provided from afar. SMEs located anywhere can engage in online collaboration in R&D, service design and promotion with overseas alliance partners.
- *Creating a customer magnet.* Firms that create strong brand equity on the Internet will create customer confidence to return to the site.

Service quality is considered to be very important in the marketplace. Yang (2001) argues that it is even more important in marketspace. For online customers service quality is the means for customers, to realize the potential benefits of Internet commerce. For online suppliers on the other hand, it is also extremely important as non-price competitive advantages are much more critical on the Internet as customers are more easily able to make instant price comparisons. What brings customers back, he argues, is loyalty that comes from an online company offering better service than anyone else. He identifies six underlying dimensions of service quality in marketspace as being: reliability/responsiveness, attentiveness, access, and ease of use, security and credibility.

| Example | *CUCME for cooperation in distance education* |

An example of the 'see-you-see-me' (CUCME) technology that uses a small video camera mounted on a personal computer in addition to the Internet is a project between the University of Otago in New Zealand, Nanyang Technological University in Singapore and RMIT University in Australia. This involves collaboration on an electronic marketing paper, whereby the outcomes of student learning are shared between sites and students communicate via e-mail or web boards and use CUCME to interact visually in real time. CUCME is also used to conduct interactive discussions and presentations by both faculty and students. Participants can view presenters and web-based course materials or other visuals simultaneously in a manner which is as close to reality as a virtual medium allows.

Source: Bell, Deans and Sinkovics (2001)

Business and professional services and the Internet

As the Internet enhances the opportunities for small firms to become internationalized, it has had a profound impact on firms in the business and professional services sector. This applies to all the subsectors in this category – accounting and legal, technical, computing and marketing/business management services. In many of these subsectors, a majority of client contact is already conducted electronically (e.g. 70–80 per cent for accounting) or soon will be (40 per cent of legal services within 10 years). In the case of technical services, exporting has been closely aligned with advances in information technology and communications. These advances have allowed both transmission of blueprints and designs electronically across borders and the performance of an increasing proportion of consulting work online (Allen Consulting, 2000: 44). The constraints on Internet-led exports in this sector, as with many other sectors, is the extent to which countries have secure servers and Internet hosts. Table 10.1 shows how countries differ in this connection.

Global online populations

The population statistics and the number of Internet Service Providers (ISPs) in each of the countries listed are taken from the CIA's *World Factbook*. The number of active users is available for Internet users in more than 20 nations tracked by the Nielsen//NetRatings service, which account for more than 90 per cent of the world's Internet users. The number of active users is an estimate of the number of people that actually go online in a given month, rather than the number of people with access.

Table 10.1 Number of Internet hosts and secure servers in OECD countries

Worldwide Internet population as at 21 March 2002 445.9 million (eMarketer) 533 million (Computer Industry Almanac)			Projection for 2004 709.1 million (eMarketer) 945 million (Computer Industry Almanac)	
Nation	Population	Internet users (source)	Active users (Nielsen/Net Ratings)	ISPs
Argentina	37.4 million	2.0 million (D'Alessio IROL)	1.9 million	33
Australia	19.4 million	5 million (eMarketer)	5.6 million	718
Austria	8.2 million	2.7 million (Austrian Internet Monitor)	1.3 million	37
Bahrain	645,361	<40,000 (DIT.net)	NA	1
Belarus	10.4 million	100,000 (Belarus Embassy)	NA	4
Belgium	10.3 million	2.7 million (InSites)	1.6 million	61
Brazil	174.5 million	6.1 million (eMarketer)	6.0 million	50
Bulgaria	7.7 million	585,000 (GFK-Bulgaria) 386,000 (BBSSGallup)	NA	26
Canada	31.6 million	14.2 million (Media Metrix Canada)	8.8 million	760
Chile	15.3 million	1.8 million (Int'l Telecom. Union)	NA	7
China	1.3 billion	33.7 million (CNNIC)	NA	3
Colombia	40.3 million	700,000 (IDC)	NA	18
Croatia	4.3 million	300,000 (IDC)	NA	9
Cuba	11.2 million	40,000 (Cuban Government) 60,000 (Int'l Telecom. Union)	NA	4
Czech Republic	10.2 million	2.2 million (GfK)	NA	>300
Denmark	5.4 million	1.6 million (NetValue)	1.6 million	13
Djibouti	460,700	<1,000 (Djibouti Dept. of Statistics)	NA	1

			Projection for 2004 709.1 million (eMarketer) 945 million (Computer Industry Almanac)	
Worldwide Internet population as at 21 March 2002 _445.9 million (eMarketer)_ _533 million (Computer Industry Almanac)_				
Nation	_Population_	_Internet users (source)_	_Active users (Nielsen/Net Ratings)_	_ISPs_
Egypt	70 million	455,000 DIT.net	NA	50
Estonia	1.4 million	462,000 (TNS Interactive)	NA	28
Finland	5.2 million	2.0 million (eMarketer) 2.15 million (Taloustutkimus)	1.0 million	23
France	60 million	11 million (Nielsen//NetRatings)	5.5 million	62
Germany	83 million	26 million (Forsa)	15.1 million	123
Greece	10.6 million	1.3 million (VPRC)	NA	27
Hong Kong	7.2 million	3.9 million (Nielsen//NetRatings)	NA	17
Hungary	10.1 million	730,000 (NetSurvey)	NA	16
Iceland	278,000	167,000 (Int'l Telecom. Union)	NA	7
India	1 billion	5.0 million (NASSCOM)	NA	43
Ireland	4.0 million	1.0 million (Amarach)	560,000	22
Israel	6.0 million	1.2 million (eMarketer)	976,000	21
Italy	57.7 million	11.0 million (Nielsen//NetRatings)	8.3 million	93
Japan	126.8 million	22 million (eMarketer)	20 million	73
Jordan	5.2 million	25,000 to 30,000 (Human Rights Watch)	NA	5
Kuwait	2 million	63,000 (eMarketer)	NA	3
Lebanon	3.6 million	approx. 420,000 (Arab Advisors)	NA	22
Libya	5.2 million	7,500 (Internet Arab World)	NA	1

			Projection for 2004 709.1 million (eMarketer) 945 million (Computer Industry Almanac)	
Worldwide Internet population as at 21 March 2002 445.9 million (eMarketer) 533 million (Computer Industry Almanac)			*Active users (Nielsen/Net Ratings)*	*ISPs*
Nation	*Population*	*Internet users (source)*		
Lithuania	3.6 million	320,000 (SIC Gallup Media)	NA	14
Malaysia	22.2 million	2 million (IDC Malaysia)	NA	7
Mexico	101.8 million	2.3 million (eMarketer)	1.7 million	51
Morocco	30.6 million	50,000 (Internet Arab World)	NA	8
New Zealand	3.8 million	1.3 million (Nielsen//NetRatings)	1 million	36
Norway	4.5 million	2.2 million (Norsk Gallup)	1.4 million	13
The Netherlands	16 million	6.8 million (Nielsen//NetRatings)	4.5 million	52
Oman	2.6 million	50,000 (DIT.net)	NA	1
Philippines	82.8 million	2.0 million (DigitalFilipino.com)	NA	19
Poland	39.0 million	4.9 million (Zycie)	NA	33
Portugal	10.1 million	3.055 million (ICP/Anacom)	NA	16
Qatar	769,000	47,000 (Internet Arab World)	NA	1
Romania	22.4 million	630,000 (European Survey of the Info. Society)	NA	38
Russia	145 million	7.5 million (Computer Industry Almanac)	NA	35
Saudia Arabia	22.8 million	300,000 (Internet Arab World)	NA	42
Singapore	4.3 million	1.3 million (Singapore IDA)	956,000	9
Slovakia	5.4 million	approx. 700,000 (TNS Factum)	NA	6
Slovenia	1.9 million	approx. 400,000 (RINE Project)	NA	11
South Africa	43.6 million	1.5 million (Nielsen//NetRatings)	611,000	44

Worldwide Internet population as at 21 March 2002 445.9 million (eMarketer) 533 million (Computer Industry Almanac)			Projection for 2004 709.1 million (eMarketer) 945 million (Computer Industry Almanac)	
Nation	*Population*	*Internet users (source)*	*Active users (Nielsen/Net Ratings)*	*ISPs*
South Korea	47.9 million	16.7 million (Gartner Dataquest)	13.1 million	11
Spain	40.0 million	7 million (Telefonica)	4 million	56
Sri Lanka	19.4 million	<50,000 (NUA)	NA	5
Sudan	36.0 million	10,000 (Internet Arab World)	NA	1
Sweden	8.9 million	4.5 million (Nielsen//NetRatings)	3.0 million	29
Switzerland	7.3 million	3.4 million (Nielsen//NetRatings)	1.8 million	44
Syria	16.7 million	20,000 (Internet Arab World)	NA	1
Taiwan	22.3 million	6.4 million (iamasia)	5.0 million	8
Thailand	61.8 million	4.6 million (Bangkok Poll Center)	NA	15
Tunisia	9.7 million	<120,000 (Internet Arab World)	NA	1
Turkey	66.5 million	3.7 million (IBS)	NA	22
UAE	2.4 million	920,000 (EIM)	NA	1
Ukraine	48.8 million	750,000 (Committee on Comm. and Info.)	NA	32
United Kingdom	59.6 million	33.0 million (Jupiter MMXI)	13.0 million	245
United States	278.0 million	149 million (Computer Industry Almanac)	102.0 million	7,800
Vietnam	80.0 million	22,000 (CommerceNet)	NA	5
Venezuela	24 million	1.2 million (Cavecom-e)	NA	16
Yemen	18.0 million	12,600 (Internet Arab World)	NA	1

Source: M. Pastore (2002) 'The world's online population', accessed on 14 September 2002 online at: http://cuberatlas.Internet.com/big.picture/geographics/article/0..5911_151151,00.html

Adapting the offering to global e-business

One of the driving forces to switch from marketplace to marketspace is to retain customers. If your largest or most affluent customers commence using the web, you are likely to lose their business unless you are where they do their shopping. The switch to the web appears to progress through a series of stages, according to Rosen (2000). She characterizes these stages in terms of generations:

- *Generation 1.* Initially companies create simple 'brochures online' web sites as a first step in creating a web presence.
- *Generation 2.* Companies become more aware of the potential of the web and begin using it to reflect corporate issues such as company mission statements, investor relations issues and messages from the CEO. This stage may involve some interaction.
- *Generation 3.* As companies begin to appreciate the potential of the Internet for fostering both B2B and B2C transactions, web sites become simpler, faster and more focused on the needs of the person visiting the site.
- *Generation 4.* These sites are now dynamically created and tightly integrated into the operations of the company. In this phase, the web has connections to each aspect of the company, not just customer marketing.

One of the adaptations that needs to be made is that of mass customization, which is a result of the interactivity of the new medium between supplier and customer. This is forcing firms to tailor products and services to local online markets. Shoppers are demanding that they have local online experiences. For example, Amazon.com will not be able to sell Harry Potter books in Germany if the texts are not translated and sold through German distributors in conjunction with online German book reviews. After price, possibly the greatest influences on online shopping experiences are good descriptions and photos of products or services, local language options and brands that can be trusted. Findings of the American Express Financial Services study are that consumers are more comfortable doing business over the Internet with a retailer or supplier they have grown to trust in the offline environment. This points to the need to link the online to the offline offering and tailor the latter with an eye to going online.

Customer choice issues

The web facilitates bundling of services and goods because of its interactive nature and speed of accessing information. Being able to offer the consumer a range of connected products and services provides benefit, which is greater than that which would accrue if each item were purchased individually. In addition, because the customer is often willing to pay a premium for this facilitation, profit margins increase. This is particularly evident in the online travel industry. The US travel agent www.expedia.com operates in marketspace. They assist customers through their web site to bundle a range of services and tailormake a tour of Africa. Their service includes booking flights, car rental, bus travel, tour guides and other facilitation as required.

A second customer choice issue relates to the facility offered by the web to the customer to contribute to the make-up of the product or service they purchase. Not only does this customization result in a more appealing offering, but it also enables the provider to maintain smaller inventories when operating a 'build to order' business. It also reduces information-processing costs as internal systems are linked to those of the trading partners. The level of service provided is increased through more timely and accurate delivery of goods (Commonwealth of Australia, 1999).

A third aspect of customer choice concerns the issue of buyer loyalty when electronic transactions are involved. This is much different in marketspace than in the marketplace and certainly this applies in the international domain. Rayport and Sviokla (1994) illustrate this with the example of Time Warner in the USA:

> In the marketplace, a video casette of *Terminator 2* is branded by the title of the film, its price is set for sale or rental, it is advertised by Time Warner via its media and its channels such as video rental stores or media retailers bring the product to the customers. Here the customer interface is managed, not by the producer of the film but by Time Warner's channel intermediaries. When Warner Cable markets the same film, the transaction occurs in marketspace as the customer is placing an order by phone on a pay-per-view basis via cable. While the content purchased is *Terminator 2*, both the purchase and consumption of the film take place in a context – the cable channel. The customer must have some loyalty to the context through which the film is vended (eg HBO). For Time Warner Cable, the content is the film, rather than the video cassette and the infrastructure is Time Warner's cable system. In marketspace, Time Warner has the opportunity to directly manage the interface with the customer at the levels of content, context and infrastructure. It can define and control the contexts through which its content is distributed and achieve brand differentiation and customer loyalty as far as both content and context is concerned. In those areas where it is the dominant cable operator, it can even cement brand loyalty at the infrastructure level also. It no longer needs to rely on channel members to maintain relations with customers because the company can manage relations with its customers on a direct basis. It is particularly important that customer loyalty be developed at the context level (ie to the cable offering via HBO), as this provides a window to a wide variety of new offerings from the company, Time Warner, which transcend national boundaries.
>
> (Source: Rayport and Sviokla, 1994: 4–5)

Standardization vs. localization and the Internet

While superficially it might seem that e-business has the potential to foster standardization because of its global reach, this is not necessarily the case as it does empower the individual via information. As a result, the individual is better placed to comparison shop across national boundaries and to demand suppliers cater to specific wants and needs via a customized offering. As consumers are better able via the Internet to buy products on their terms, with the Internet there is a shift of bargaining power from supplier to buyer. Given the borderless nature of the Internet; this improvement in bargaining power and move towards customization is likely to apply in the international arena.

Pricing in marketspace

Introduction

There are a number of general features of the Internet that can impact indirectly on pricing. In some cases, these force suppliers to lower prices and in others to raise prices, in others to set prices in a more flexible manner. The Internet lowers the cost of customers acquiring information and, especially in a B2B context, this may affect affordability. Therefore, the Internet may widen the market for a product. The Internet also reduces transaction costs and achieves this by improving economic efficiency, which enables the supplier to charge a lower price. Examples of this are disintermediation and improved physical distribution.

The Internet gives power to the buyers and this reduces switching costs. Price search engines (such as Bookbrain.co.uk and Shopsmart.com) enable consumers to compare online prices with little effort. In addition, the Internet, because of its global nature, allows vendors to buy products in the cheapest markets and sell them in other markets bypassing authorized distributors, with the consequence that prices become less (Rettie, 2001). As a result, the Internet can be bad for profits. On the other hand, the Internet enables customization, which can be good for profits as the buyer may be prepared to pay a higher price for the customized item. With the Internet geography becomes largely irrelevant, which means that prices are likely to be affected by international competition to a greater extent than in the marketplace. Finally, the Internet threatens government measures to influence prices charged within their domain or regulate price-related promotional techniques. For example, some governments ban the use of price-off coupons. Government can do little in the case of price discount coupons on the Internet. Therefore, the environment of pricing in marketspace differs markedly from that in the marketplace.

Impact of the Internet on price setting

Although price setting on the Internet is influenced by demand and supply, the Internet facilitates the management of this relationship because of its timeliness, direct contact with the final customer and its interactivity. Qantas can use the Internet to tailor the availability of flights to anticipated demand. Should the demand lag behind the supply of seats, it can use the Internet to manage demand by employing discount procedures to fill the balance of capacity on a given flight. In this case, the airline is able to sell cheap tickets without having to pay commission to travel agents and fill for some revenue seats that would otherwise have been empty.

The paperless world of the Internet has the capacity to reduce shipping costs by as much as 30 per cent (Coia, 2000). In addition, the online networks are being devised so as to facilitate the fulfilment and settlement of international trade transactions. TradeCard has formed an alliance with Thomas Cook Group to provide secure B2B global payment and foreign exchange functions. Once buyers and sellers decide to transact, TradeCard provides a payment guarantee charging customers one-tenth of the average cost of a letter of credit.

The above is part of a trend towards a single source for international trade transactions enabled by the Internet. Associated with this is the concept of trade portals which maximize trade efficiency for shippers by providing a single source for services such as banking, insurance, transportation and customs clearance. For example, MeetChina.com has its headquarters in San Francisco and offers a system that enables buyers and sellers of Chinese merchandise to connect and locate the components for international trade such as banking, finance and freight forwarding under one roof (Coia, 2000: 53). This enables suppliers to lower prices or improve profits as their competitive position will be advantageous compared with those who operate solely in the international marketplace. In addition, these portals enable smaller firms to compete with larger firms for better rates as happens with shipping. It facilitates small firms combining their requirements.

As an example, if a shipper wanted to insure US$10 million worth of goods, the rate might be 30 cents per US$100. If the shipper were to join forces with other shippers under the aegis of a trade portal, the total insured could amount to US$500 million and the rate reduced to 10 cents per US$100. In this case the shippers would have individual insurance policies but these would all be under one master policy.

Another situation relates to tracking shipments online. Software with inventory management capabilities is linked to warehouse management systems. As an example, a firm might have a manufacturing operation in Thailand, ship by sea freight to Genoa, from where it is shipped to Egypt. The firm does not have an office in Genoa. They use a freight forwarder and need to know the whereabouts of the consignment at any time from point of shipment to arrival at the warehouse of the buyer in Egypt. The Internet enables the tracking of the consignment during its complex transit. These examples reflect the ability of e-business to improve efficiencies and reduce costs, which in turn can influence the pricing approach adopted by firms. Due to the electronic communication, brokerage and electronic integration effects, e-markets are likely to benefit consumers as producers are forced to reduce profit margins.

Although there are many instances where the Internet shifts power away from sellers to buyers, there are some aspects of the Internet where the reverse is the case. This happens when the Internet gives suppliers unprecedented access to data related to the preferences and buying profiles of customers. While this enables customization of offerings, it allows firms to price discriminate between segments. In the global environment, institutional imperfections and cultural dissimilarities will enable dot.coms to further fragment markets and facilitate heightened price discrimination. (Sarkar, 2000).

In the B2C domain, the Internet allows for lower costs as goods do not have to be moved around. In the case of auctions in marketspace, because a larger number of potential buyers are 'present', sellers may be able to command a premium over the price they would get at a physical auction and buyers may be prepared to pay more because of greater convenience. Without an auction to search for the price at which buyer and seller are willing to trade, buyers may be forced to be price takers. This is especially so with low-value retail goods. The widest application of electronic auctions outside of the securities market is in moderately valued consumer goods.

Duties, taxes and quotas

Taxation is a debatable issue as far as Internet commerce is concerned. Those in favour of taxes point to the fact that bricks and mortar firms have to pay taxes and will be unfairly disadvantaged if marketspace firms do not pay taxes. Those against taxing Internet transactions claim that anyone can do business via the Internet and it is up to bricks and mortar firms to take advantage of the tax situation on the Internet (as many of them do). They also argue that it is against public interest to place barriers in the way of the spread of electronic commerce and for this reason the Internet should not be taxed. Also, if one country taxes Internet transactions and another does not, then the taxing country is likely to be disadvantaged as far as international business via the Internet is concerned.

Duties and quotas can be evaded when doing B2C business over the Internet as this business often involves small size shipments from supplier direct to customer the value of which is below the threshold at which it is worthwhile to collect duty or check whether the import quota for the product category has been used up (e.g. importing a book from amazon.com). When this occurs, the Internet becomes a vehicle for evading protection.

The issue of taxing Internet transactions has become a subject of debate in multinational trade fora such as the World Trade Organization (WTO) and regional fora such as the European Union. The WTO has imposed a moratorium on taxing Internet transactions whereas the EU is about to impose a VAT on e-business. In the latter case, virtual merchandise will be taxed within Europe. Virtual merchandise is regarded as items downloaded from the Internet where no physical delivery is required such as music, software and video. In the USA, there is a federal moratorium on Internet taxes. Online merchants are exempt from collecting sales taxes while offline merchants are still required to collect and remit sales taxes to the states in which they conduct business.

There is also the issue of jurisdiction with cyberspace transactions. Tracking a taxable sales transaction in marketspace is difficult even within the one country, let alone between different countries. At issue is which government has the jurisdiction to levy taxes when a person in one country logs onto the site of a firm in another, ships the product from a third country and charges the sale to a bank in a fourth country. In this case, in which country or state did the purchase actually occur, where did it originate and where should it ultimately be taxed? E-commerce does not recognize national borders or tax laws outside the home country of an e-business. Online business can operate internationally in any jurisdiction without leaving a 'footprint' that will expose them to taxation.

Pricing and payment issues

An issue for consideration is the impact on pricing of the uncertainties regarding the security of Internet transactions. Use of the Internet involves making credit card numbers available over the web. Although there are encryption techniques to protect the security of this information, consumers are still wary of using credit cards on the net. According to Bryan (2000), research by Citibank shows that 60 per cent of consumers will not entrust their credit card details, while 50 per cent said they would not enter private information online for fear of credit card fraud, hacking or other security-related problems. These aspects have cost implications that are likely reflected in the pricing of goods sold via the Internet.

Summary

In this chapter, the unique features of the Internet as they impact on the marketing mix variables of product and pricing were discussed. As far as product is concerned the Internet impact is primarily on the service element of the offering. For this reason, the chapter also covers the impact of the Internet on services and projects.

Questions

1. Why are some product categories more suitable for marketing internationally via the Internet than others?
2. Are the unique characteristics of services better catered for when marketed internationally by marketplace or marketspace approaches?
3. Discuss issues involved in customer choice when using the web to market internationally.
4. In what ways does the Internet (a) facilitate and (b) constrain the setting of prices?
5. How does the potential of the Internet for the evasion of duties, taxes, quotas and other government imposts impact on international competitiveness?

References

Allen Consulting Group (2000) *Creating Value by Transforming Knowledge: Australia's Business and Professional Services Sector*. Report prepared for the Service Industries Section of the Department of Industry, Science and Resources and Austrade, December.

Bell, J., Deans, K. and Sinkovics, R. (2001) 'Towards the "Internetalisation" of international marketing education', *Marketing Education Review* (forthcoming).

Berthon, P., Pitt, L., Katsikeas, C. S. and Berthon, J. P. (1999) 'Virtual services go international: International services in the marketspace', *Journal of International Marketing* 7(3): 84–105.

Bryan, M. (2000) 'Consumers still wary of using credit cards on net', *Australian Financial Review* 12: 14.

Coia, A. (2000) 'Paperless transactions in your (near) future', *World Trade* October: 52–4.

Commonwealth of Australia (DFAT)(1999) *Creating a Clearway on the New Silk Road: International Business and Policy Trends in Internet Commerce*. Australian Government Publishing Service.

Firoz, N. M. and Banta, C. (2000) 'Business in the age of the internet – strategy for success on the e-playing field', Paper presented at the 5th International Conference on Global, Business & Economic Development, Managing Global Business in the Internet Age, 21–4 June, Beijing.

Hollensen, S. (2001) *Global Marketing: A Market-Responsive Approach*, 2nd edn, Harlow: Prentice Hall.

Levaux, J. P. (2001) 'Adapting products and services for global e-eommerce', *World Trade* January: 52–4.

Rayport, J. F. and Sviokla, J. J. (1994) 'Managing in the marketspace', *Harvard Business Review* 11 January: 141–8.

Rettie, R. (2001) 'How will the internet change marketing?', *Proceedings of the Academy of Marketing Conference*, 1–4 July, Cardiff, University of Cardiff.

Sarkar, M. (2000) 'Show me the money: Cybermediation in global eMarkets', paper submitted to Conference and Symposium on Electronic Commerce and Global Business, *Journal of International Business Studies*.

Yang, Z. (2001) 'Consumer perceptions of service quality in internet-based electronic commerce', *Proceedings of the Conference of the European Marketing Academy Conference*, 8–11 May, Bergen: Norges Handelshoyskole.

Case Study 10 *Tom Hilton's Donuts: On location?*
Francine Schlosser and Bill Todorovic

Tom Hilton's Donuts is a fast food franchise serving the North American market. The operation has grown steadily, by providing a 'healthier' fast food option to customers; expanding its menu from original donuts and coffee to sandwiches and other lunch fare.

One franchisee, Monica Peters, is currently considering new location-based e-marketing advertising alternatives based upon wireless mobile technologies. Although advertising and promotion is usually controlled at the franchise level, she felt it was important for her to be involved in this decision. As the owner of three stores, she felt threatened by the continuing expansion strategy endorsed by the franchiser.

In the past three years (since the opening of her newest location), an additional six Tom Hilton's stores were built within its one-mile radius. The market seemed to be over-saturated, and her profits had dropped by 15 per cent in the past two years, in spite of adding the new location. The franchise had a seven-year renovation policy, requiring costly improvements to multiple locations. Additionally, the franchiser required changes in the way that the donuts were made had forced her to remodel all three kitchens, and invest in new ovens. Finally, to top it off, various streets accessing her locations were intermittently under construction, making it difficult for customers to choose her store over other more accessible Tom Hilton locations.

Monica knew that drastic actions were necessary before her market share further deteriorated. She had to find a way to draw customers to her particular franchise location. Current advertising and promotions designed by Tom Hilton's corporate office were targeted toward non-franchise competitors. It was important that she find a way to market her location, without attracting attention and resistance from corporate head office and other franchisees. Perhaps newer location-based advertising strategies, utilizing mobile handheld devices, might provide a way to do this.

Key success factors

At a franchise level, its key success factor was consistency, especially with respect to: (1) high quality product; (2) clean stores; (3) dependable service; (4) value pricing. Monica's stores competed against other franchise locations, based on easy accessibility, parking, good (and attractive) staff, and attention to detail.

The chain, famous for its coffee, drew customers of all ages, but senior citizens liked to spend time in the coffee shop. Interestingly, a newspaper article recently described Tom Hilton locations as mobile offices, where mobile professionals, such as teleworking employees or real estate agents increasingly conducted business.

Monica often received faxed corporate orders because her stores were located close to the corporate head offices of many high-tech firms, including a manufacturer of handheld devices. These demographics increased the potential for location-based e-marketing.

Current advertising and promotions

Tom Hilton's donuts advertised using a combination of radio and television advertising and in-store promotions. The advertising promoted the key success factors for the chain. For example, they recently tested a new bacon, lettuce and tomato bagel (BLT), by advertising in only certain locations, with plans to go national in six weeks. However, whenever they promoted a new product they found that it cannibalized their other products.

Currently, they were undertaking a customer appreciation initiative, handing out 37 coupons daily between 8:00 am and 9:00 am in return

▶

for completion of an in-store survey. The coupons were put into a draw for free coffee for a year. Monica wondered what type of promotion (if any) would be suitable for location-based e-marketing.

Location-based e-marketing

Location-based e-marketing describes the ability of a retailer to reach individual customers via a mobile wireless handheld device, such as a cellphone, pager or handheld computer. Equipped with a tracking device, the retailer would be able to send location-based messages to customers. For example, at lunch, customers walking by McDonald's, may receive a message from McDonald's inviting them to come in and take advantage of a special 'two for one' offer on hamburgers.

This locational tracking ability would soon be present on all wireless devices as manufacturers rushed to meet the requirements of new US legislation. The US Federal Communications Commission (FCC) tabled Enhanced 911 (E911) legislation, which required location tracking of handheld wireless devices to within a few metres. Specifically, handsets must be tracked within 50 metres for 67 per cent of calls, and 150 metres for 95 per cent of calls (Evans, 2002). Such tracking features would enable emergency service providers to cover 911 calls from mobile devices. Additionally, knowledge of a customer's physical location would facilitate a targetted type of e-marketing based on location.

Handheld devices included vfeature phones, smart phones (voice/data with colour display), handheld organizers and pagers, industrial handhelds, and pocket PCs. Recent announcements by Research in Motion (RIM) and Palm demonstrated the tendency toward technology convergence, as pagers acquired sound capability, and cell phones acquire greater data transmission and processing capability. These technological advances made it more likely that customers would be carrying a cell phone with the ability to surf the Internet and send short messaging.

In setting location-based e-marketing strategy, Kalakota and Robinson (2002) suggested that the retailer must consider elements of value creation. The value proposition must be measurable, tangible and brandable. The network provider within a location-based e-marketing value chain directed advertising messages to customers meeting a certain demographic profile through the location tracking facility on the handheld. This link played an increasingly valuable role in connecting product providers and new customers located in the relevant geographic area.

The introduction of the Internet created new, more efficient and less expensive direct advertising opportunities for small businesses to keep up with large international retailing operations. This mobile channel targetted customers through informational services such as brochures. Channel extension strategies could also be used that would allow customers to access current services through their handhelds. New services were made possible through mobile channels, such as m-ticketing, m-shopping, m-banking and m-trading (Kalakota and Robinson, 2002). The market for location-based services was projected to climb to US$6.5 billion in the USA and US$9 billion in Europe (Evans, 2002).

The consumer buying decision

Monica researched the buying decision facing mobile consumers from the perspective of the consumer's decision involvement, responsiveness to advertising and decision economics.

Decision involvement Consumer researchers (Kover and Abruzzo, 1993; Rossiter and Percy, 1997) suggested that there is a higher likelihood of brand loyalty for a low involvement decision, or one in which the consumer needs little convincing (either it is of small relative importance or the consumer has established purchasing norms). In contrast, high involvement decisions demand more search and conviction prior to purchase. Her research indicated that the most appropriate advertisements for location advertising are those that target repeat customers, or a less important buying decision.

Decision-maker responsiveness to advertising Monica found out that decision makers responded to location-based e-marketing of large volume brands with average brand loyalty of 50 to 70 per cent, and with new or more demand elastic products (East, 1997). This implied that successful advertisers using a location-based strategy should push strong brands, or new products associated with proven brands.

Decision economics Revenue models included access-based fees, subscription-based fees, advertising and sponsorship, transaction fees (i.e. commission based), and pay-per-use micro-transactions. The varying economics of these revenue models would also influence customer acceptance of less desirable location information features. Monica wanted to make sure that the location-based e-marketing strategy she chose was affordable to her customers.

Technology attitudes In addition to these marketing issues regarding the decision and the advertising distribution, Monica realized that it was important to understand how consumers viewed the technological medium used to convey the marketing message.

A prerequisite to any buying decision, consumers must be open to using the technology before they would pay attention to its content. For example, advertisers using traditional telephone solicitation and bulk mail already discovered that messages would not be received if they were conveyed in a time-wasting or inconvenient way. Similarly, if a buyer found the location-based information service annoying, the buyer could choose another network provider's service. Location-based e-marketing created opportunities for Monica to reach buyers when need and impulse opportunity were the greatest. This

opportunity would be lost if buyers did not elect to use the medium to receive product information.

Privacy attitudes Consumer concern for protection of privacy has been fuelled by media coverage. The advent of 'big brother' type technologies such as smart cards and video surveillance raised concerns publicly expressed by the Canadian Federal Privacy Commissioner. In marketing, controversy erupted over the marketing 'cookies' laced on consumer computers during Internet usage. These cookies used consumer Internet surfing to provide an invasive picture of an individual's interests and buying patterns. Open Profiling Standard (OPS) enabled consumers to erect boundaries to protect their personal privacy, resisting pervasive types of technologies, such as those that allowed a service network provider to track their movements and act upon this information by sending unsolicited spam (junkmail).

Although the location-based service potentially provided useful and efficient information to customers via handheld wireless devices, it also created the potential for privacy invasion, as network providers tracked consumer movements and sent targetted emails. As Monica considered the possibilities of location-based e-marketing, she realized that she would need to respect consumers' desire for privacy. Monica realized that she must understand how receptive her customers would be to location-based advertising. She would need to do some pilot research in order to design a winning location-based advertising strategy.

Monica's pilot research

Monica decided to test market three different location-based e-marketing alternatives by surveying 15 customers who owned a wireless device. The participants were exposed to three different types of mobile advertising. They were not allowed to collaborate and were asked to rate these scenarios comparatively, that is to determine which mode of advertising they preferred. Each scenario included attributes reflecting varying levels of discretion, privacy, ease of use and usefulness. Upon rating the three tools, participants were given a survey questionnaire.

Scenario #1: personal navigation tool The participants were given a demonstration of a personal navigation tool, used by a customer to locate needed services in a certain geographic location. Customers input their location coordinates, and selected desired services. Then the software provided a list of potential restaurants and provided contact and location information for the chosen service. Vindigo (2002), the tool used in the demonstration, was a low-cost directory service for Palm PDAs, used to find restaurants, retailers and movies in specific cities. As consumers scrolled through their choices, related advertising appeared in pop-up or banner style boxes.

Scenario #2: discount coupons via text marketing A customer elected to receive certain types of coupons. These coupons were selected through the network provider, based upon past usage and specified consumer preferences. Alternatively, the customer signed up at individual retail locations by sending a message to a common short code address. The short code address substituted for a normal ten-digit phone number.

Scenario #3: discounted service with unsolicited advertisement In this scenario, participants could agree to accept location-prompted coupons and advertisements in exchange for reduced network service rates. The advertisements were targeted at the discretion of the network provider and retailer, based on desired demographics. The customer was not able to restrict these offers.

Pilot study results

Table 10.2 indicates how participants rated each advertising alternative. Table 10.3 indicates the reasons for these preferences, noted by each participant. As Monica read the results of the market survey, she considered her options. Should she move ahead with this new type of advertising? If she did, what type of location-based e-marketing tool should she select? How might she address consumer privacy and control concerns?

Questions

1. What criteria would you recommend that Monica use to assess the readiness of her product for location-based e-marketing?

Table 10.2	Scenario	Rank	Frequency
Frequencies of technology rankings	1 Personal navigation tool	1	13
	1	2	1
	1	3	1
	2 Discount coupons	1	2
	2	2	9
	2	3	4
	3 Free service for unsolicited ads	1	0
	3	2	5
	3	3	10

2. Is the product line of Tom Hilton's Donuts suited to this product channel?

3. Discuss the location alternatives from the perspective of the target customer. Consider how criteria such as ease of use, usefulness, privacy and discretion might shape attitudes and intention to buy.

4. What are the implications of the new value chain structure – i.e. what role does the network provider play? (in terms of power , knowledge of the customer).

References

East, R. (1997) *Consumer Behavior: Advances and Applications in Marketing*, Harlow: Prentice Hall.

Evans, N. D. (2002) *Business Agility: Strategies for Gaining Competitive Advantage through Mobile Business Solutions* Upper Saddle River, NJ: Prentice-Hall.

Kalakota, R. & Robinson, M. (2002) *M-Business: The Race to Mobility*, New York: McGraw-Hill.

Kover, A. J. & Abruzzo, J. (1993) 'The Rossiter-Percy grid and emotional response to advertising an initial evaluation', *Journal of Advertising Research* 33(6): 21–7.

Rossiter, J. R. & Percy, L. (1997) *Advertising Communications and Promotion Management*, New York: McGraw-Hill.

Table 10.3	Participant	Comment
Test group reasons for technology rankings	1	The personal navigator tool is the highest because it is actually under my control. I do not use coupons, so that is the lowest rank.
	2	Discount coupons are good since I can control the nature of content, but I don't travel enough to use the navigator.
	3	For the discount coupons and service within unsolicited ads, I can easily get them from services every day. I would rank the navigation tool first, but it might be expensive.
	4	I can easily ignore the navigator – it's the least invasive so I ranked it first.
	5	I ranked the navigator first because I can get information whenever I want. I can black out the undesired information.
	6	Junk info would be annoying. Being able to find a map for what I want when I want would be very helpful. I have issues with junk e-mail, so junk information would waste a lot of time.
	7	I want to choose when to get information (chose navigation tool first). Although I also like coupons (I'm a poor student) so scenario #2 is a close second (discount coupons) and scenario #3 a very distant third (discounted service with unsolicited ads).
	8	Scenario #1 is useful for people to find places. However, scenario #3's unsolicited ads are disruptive and annoying.
	9	Scenario #1 makes me feel more comfortable.
	10	Service #1 because it would help you when travelling.
	11	I can't keep track of coupons. Don't like the ads 'white noise'.
	12	I would prefer to get information when I need it or for services that interest me.

11 International e-business distribution and logistics

Learning objectives

After studying this chapter, you should be able to:

- Recognize the relevance of disintermediation and reintermediation when the Internet is used for international transactions.

- Appreciate under what circumstances Internet auctions improve efficiencies in international marketing.

- Appreciate how the value chain needs to be configured for effective distribution of goods across national borders.

- Identify how B2C distribution techniques in international marketing compare with B2B techniques.

- Understand how the Internet transforms international logistics.

International e-business distribution

Firms engaged in international commerce spend considerable effort to establish effective distribution channels in overseas markets. Such channels involve intermediaries, all of whom operate in a regulated environment involving issues such as territorial exclusivity, price differences between countries and an established sequence in the distribution channel such as manufacturer, agent, distributor, subdistributor, wholesaler, retailer. The adoption of the Internet threatens this pattern of distribution, which has often been established at considerable expense and consists of parties who know and trust each other.

On the other hand, the nature of recent changes in international marketing facilitate the use of the Internet. A major change has seen firms move from being manufacturers to designers and branders who outsource the actual manufacture to operations in a variety of countries.

The most promising products for trading via the Internet are those where existing intermediaries do not perform traditional wholesaler functions due to the high cost of servicing small, diverse and geographically dispersed players. This is particularly the case in international marketing and is one reason why the Internet may enable formerly excluded small and medium sized enterprises (SMEs) to engage in international trade. Manheim, the largest wholesale automobile auction house has developed an online site to overcome the limitations of both size and geography in the buying and selling of used cars by dealers.

Quelch and Klein (1997) claim that the following market characteristics favour electronic marketmakers:

- *Inefficiencies in traditional distribution channels*: buyers cannot find all possible sellers and consequently prices paid are not optimal.
- *Market fragmentation*: markets with many geographically dispersed buyers and sellers are operating suboptimally in terms of transaction costs.
- *Minimum scale barriers*: in traditional markets where smaller firms may be excluded from traditional channels by larger ones who benefit from economies of scale and have been able to negotiate exclusive distribution agreements.
- *Commodity type products*: products with well-known technical specifications or brands that enable easy price comparison and products that do not require substantial after sales service.
- *Short life cycle products*: this generates large quantities of obsolete or discontinued items. In such markets, there are also difficulties for users in locating spares or compatible accessories.
- *Trade association involvement*: in those industries where associations play an active role in organizing members, the endorsement of marketmakers by such associations creates credibility (e.g. the partnership between TRADEex and the Australian Chamber of Manufacturers).

In addition to the above, the potential for the Internet to transform international marketing is likely to be enhanced because customers in most foreign markets do not enjoy the breadth of product or vendor choice found in the USA. This results in there being less competition in many of these markets because of which prices may be higher. As the US and other developed markets lead in product innovation, sophisticated customers in other markets may want to secure these products before they are available through local distributors. On the other hand, less sophisticated customers in these other countries often need what vendors in developed countries consider earlier generation products. The prices for these products are likely to be less via the Internet than from local distributors. The Internet addresses the problems of both groups.

Market leader dot.coms have the ability and funds to enter foreign markets with advanced business models, to leverage their brands globally and the financial liquidity to enter such markets via acquisition. For example, Amazon has entered the UK and Germany through acquisition of large booksellers. However, while introducing a supplier through a B2B hub to a new buyer in an overseas market is terrific, not knowing the creditworthiness of this new buyer or how much it will cost to move the transacted goods there erodes the effectiveness of the Internet in the international domain.

As a result, a number of new Internet start-ups are emerging to cover servicing logistics, credit needs and other requirements of electronic commerce in international marketing. Examples in the credit area are Bolero and eCredit.com. Their aim is to enable companies to make credit analyses and financing happen at web speeds.

Disintermediation/reintermediation

The travel business is loaded with intermediaries who all want to be paid. They keep the industry-wide profit margins at less than double figures. With a system that doesn't require call-backs, fax-backs or consultants dealing with 'what-if' customers on the phone, the costs of making a sale plummet.

(*Bulletin*, 19 December–2 January 2001–02: 62–3)

If the Internet can perform a useful set of functions undertaken in marketplace distribution channels, then potentially it can absorb or render unnecessary the jobs of existing providers of those services. It is for this reason that it is argued that the Internet can reduce transaction costs because it cuts out the need for intermediaries. Disintermedition is the term used to describe the withering away of intermediaries as firms use new technology to contact their customers directly.

However, while you can eliminate the intermediary, you cannot eliminate the function performed. Either you do it yourself or your customers do it. However, the consumer–supplier relationship is a complex one and is information intensive. It is not one that consumers or producers always wish to manage directly. Therefore, despite the Internet, channel functions are unlikely to disappear entirely. In fact, there is evidence that marketplace channels will be replaced with marketspace channels (sometimes called cybermediaries), rather than evaporate. For example, the Internet has given rise to a new group of booksellers, airline reservation and ticketing agencies and music distributors. In short, the functions that a channel performs (e.g. providing information and distributing goods and services) are largely fixed, but the institutions that perform these functions are not. For this reason, the Internet should be regarded as a component of a firm's marketing plans rather than as a new phenomenon that replaces conventional methods of doing business. Electronic business eliminates intermediary institutions by substitution or consolidation using computer and communications technology, but does not generally eliminate intermediary functions. Rather it automates or shifts intermediary functions forward or backward along the supply chain.

Disintermediation is less likely to be the case in international marketing than in domestic marketing as one of the reasons for intermediaries in international marketing is to replace the absent principal in the overseas country. This function will still need to be performed in many cases, especially when the product is being introduced to a market or to a new customer in an overseas market. In fact the disintermediation, the eradication of channel intermediaries and the forging of closer producer to consumer relationships, has not occurred to the extent anticipated (Strutton, Srivastava and Pelton, 2000)

Reintermediation occurs when intermediaries whose continuing roles are threatened find new niches for themselves in the electronic marketplace by gathering customers and information, extending online credit and providing services to complete transactions (Klein and Quelch, 1997). Sarkar (2000) argues that three types of cybermediary have evolved:

1. *Physical cybermediaries*. These handle inventory and physical distribution, e.g. e-tailers.
2. *Virtual cybermediaries*. These are virtual resellers that do not have inventory or physical distribution capabilities, e.g. online stores.
3. *Facilitating cybermediaries*. These direct traffic to or perform niche servicing and merchandising for online stores, e.g. aggregators such as large portals.

The above is illustrated in Figure 11.1.

Despite the hype, these cybermediaries will still have to cope with the trust gap between buyer and seller. While it can be argued that new forms of intermediary will arise to perform necessary functions when conducting international trade via the Internet, these new distributors will have to coexist

Figure 11.1

Rebuilding the value chain

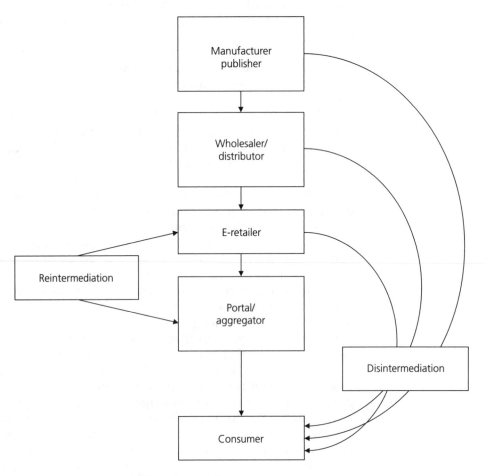

Source: Craig, Douglas and Flaherty (2000: 33)

alongside traditional intermediaries and could involve established intermediaries sharing a declining margin with newcomers. This will only work provided that the newcomers can deliver a higher value to the final customer. The travel industry provides evidence that situations could develop where you have bricks and mortar intermediaries for functions requiring high touch/high feel and Internet intermediaries for the actual purchase (travel agents and e-tickets).

New forms of intermediary are springing up to operate as electronic marketplaces to buy goods for firms via the Internet. This is particularly useful with indirect goods (e.g. light bulbs) rather than direct goods (e.g. components). RightWorks sells e-procurement services that link buyers to sellers of both indirect and direct goods. PointSpeed offers a full-scale electronic purchasing system, which it hosts on its own server, relieving small businesses of the need to buy costly software. Such firms operate in effect as outsourced purchasing departments for their customers. This form of purchasing is more up to date as it replaces a roomful of catalogues that are out of date.

The effects of disintermediation on distribution channels and the reintermediation caused by the Internet are shown in Figure 11.2.

Internet usage in international distribution channels

Manufacturers and wholesale export enterprises are the most likely users of the Internet as a business process tool. A business process embedded in the Internet (i.e. an extranet) should be viewed as a strategic tool that differentiates the firm from its competitors when performing export related operations. The wholesale exporter may develop customized Internet-based technology for tracking orders

Figure 11.2 Disintermediation and reintermediation

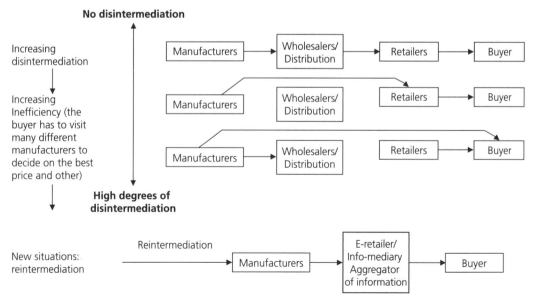

Source: Hollensen (2001: 355)

and transactions, negotiating contracts with customers, evaluating and entering new markets, etc. In general, using the Internet and its own software, the exporter can exchange inventory information with suppliers, reorder and request bids.

There are two different types of retailers that use the Internet to obtain orders. The first are the major catalogue firms who take title to the goods they sell and maintain an inventory of the products they handle. In some cases, they develop customized catalogues for export markets. They have also developed specialized web sites for these markets. Land's End is an example of this type of Internet retail operation. The second type of retailer is the firm that maintains little or no inventory. They buy merchandise under agreements with manufacturers or suppliers that is either shipped direct from supplier to the customer or reshipped by the retailer to the customer. Amazon is an example of this type of retail operation (Samiee, 1998).

International Internet exchanges and auctions

These are of particular appeal to SMEs. They were preceded by electronic data interchange (EDI), which automated standard data exchanges between existing trading partners. This was followed by companies in the mid-1990s establishing extranet connections with their suppliers and customers so as to facilitate real-time communication up and down the supply chain. These extranets drove down purchasing costs, shortened order cycles, reduced errors, provided instant order status information and notification of shortages. This then led to the development of e-hubs. These bring together buyers and sellers in real-time trading communities at relatively low cost. The differences between auctions, exchanges, extranets, etc. are shown in Figure 11.3. The difference depends on the number of markets on the one hand and the number of buyers on the other.

A number of major transnational Companies (TNCs) have moved into e-hubs. Examples are General Motors, Ford and DaimlerChrysler who have

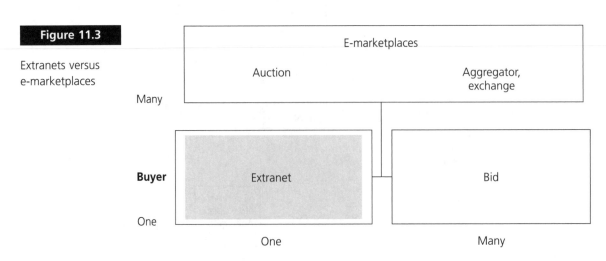

Figure 11.3

Extranets versus e-marketplaces

Source: Forrester (1999)

announced that they would abandon plans for individual enterprise portals in favour of collaboration. Table 11.1 shows the differences between web sites and e-hubs.

A further distinction can be made between vertical e-hubs that have sprung up to serve the needs of particular industries and horizontal e-hubs that run across several or many industries characterized by common buyer needs.

Electronic auctions

In international marketing, situations arise where either the buyer or seller does not know precisely how much their offering is worth. In other circumstances, there may be a constraint on capacity to supply. In both instances, posting a price is unlikely to elicit the price that the other party is willing to pay. When this happens, it is better to buy or sell at auction than to post a price.

Electronic auctions are online marketplaces where the negotiation of price between independent buyers and sellers is implemented via a system-wide standard auction open to all participants. Auctions remove the right of the seller to set the price (except to post a reserve). Leading auction sites (such as www.eBay.com, www.priceline.com and www.freemarkets.com) show how the Internet shapes the prices paid for goods and services. According to Jupiter Communications (www.jup.com), the number of online auction purchases in the USA increased from 1.2 million in 1998 to an estimated 6.2 million in 2002, representing 11 per cent of total online shopping. Online auctions can be broken down into three segments as follows:

- *Person to person*: auction sites that provide sellers and buyers with a public marketplace to trade online (e.g. www.ebay.com).

- *Business to person*: auction sites that not only provide a digital marketplace for business suppliers to sell excess inventories, but also operate as retailers for the distribution of auctioned items (e.g. www.ubid.com, www.onsale.com).

Table 11.1	Basic e-Commerce	Integrated b2b e-hub
Web site versus e-hub	Sporadic, opportunistic usage	Deeply entrenched, habitual channel for business activities; becomes an integral part of a user's daily activities.
	Limited benefits	Compelling value proposition; significant reduction in transaction costs.
	Low margin commodity	Differentiated services; barriers to entry for competing hubs.
	Singular focus on procurement process	Multiple complementary business processes are integrated and optimized.
	Limited user retention	Barrier to exit and high switching costs for users; customer lock-in.

Source: Deutsche Banc Alex Brown (2000)

- *Business to business*: both sellers and buyers are business units and the auction is for resale to customers of procurement goods (e.g. www.comauction.com, www.tradeout.com).

Auction types can be divided into:

- *English/yankee*: with transparent and increasing bids.
- *Dutch*: price starts off at a high level and is continuously discounted until item is sold.
- *Vickrey*: sealed bid auction where the winner pays only the second highest bidder's price.

Figure 11.4 shows various e-procurement methods to address different supply characteristics.

In addition to auctions, there are: the e-marketplace (buyers use commodity exchanges to create a market that is focused on an industry or group of products); the e-catalogue (describes seller's lines and allows the buyer quickly to search for alternative sources); e-search (provides product information, detail of new technologies, suppliers and channels – useful in cases where the market is fragmented).

Syndication

This increasingly popular form of Internet distribution has its origin in the entertainment world but is now expanding into other areas of e-business. A new breed of entrepreneurs has built on the traditional syndication model to distribute video, audio, text and images through digital networks. Like their offline predecessors, online syndicators provide content that reaches new audiences via new media that include B2B and B2C web sites, corporate intranets and extranets and in some cases wireless Internet devices. According to Pack (2000: 31–8), there has been a boom in online syndication over the last three

Figure 11.4			
Four different e-procurement tools that address different supply characteristics	Fragmented	**E-auction**	**E-search**
	INDUSTRY		
	Consolidated	**E-catalog**	**E-marketplace**
		Standard **PRODUCTS** Custom	

Source: Based on Chen and Wilson (2000)

years due to a pressing need for site owners and network managers more efficiently to supply third party content to their end users. Their offerings range from end-to-end solutions that supply content to thousands of publications to do-it-yourself syndication software. Syndication suits the web because it only works with information goods. Because information is never consumed, infinite numbers of people can use the same information. Syndication also suits the web because a syndicated good does not usually constitute an entire product and reflects modularity (e.g. a comic strip does not make up an entire newspaper). This modularity is typical of the web. Third, syndication suits the web because it requires many independent distributors. With the Internet, information goods, modularity and fragmented distribution are all possible and often essential.

Syndication is rarely used by Internet companies to describe what they do. In reality, whilst the online brokerage firm E*Trade offers its customers a rich variety of information, including financial news, stock quotes, charts and research, it would be very expensive to provide such information from its own resources and would distract from its core business. Therefore, the firm purchases most of this material from outside providers.

On the web, commerce can also be syndicated. E-tailers often do this with shopping cart ordering and payments. It is through syndicating component activities that virtual companies can become a reality. Whereas in traditional companies connections are between firms in simple linear chains running from raw material producers to retailers, within a syndication network you can have originators, who create the original content, syndicators who package that content for distribution, often integrating it with content from other originators and distributors who deliver the content to customers. Therefore, business in a syndicated world bears little resemblance to its industrial predecessor. To succeed, executives need to change the ways they think about nearly every aspect of strategy and management. Table 11.2 contrasts traditional with syndicated business.

Table 11.2		Traditional business	Syndication
Everything changes	**Structure of relationships**	Linear supply and demand chains	Loose, weblike networks
	Corporate roles	Fixed	Continually shifting
	Value added	Dominated by physical distribution	Dominated by information manipulation
	Strategic focus	Control scarce resources	Leverage abundance
	Role of corporate capabilities	Sources of advantage to protect	Products to sell
	Role of outsourcing	Gain efficiency	Assemble virtual corporations

Source: Werbach (2000: 90)

Distribution channels in marketspace

Multiple channels

The use of multiple channels is now becoming the norm in international marketing. Internet channels coexist alongside marketplace channels. However, whilst the addition of an Internet channel potentially adds value for the firm and increases the firm's penetration level, it can have the negative side effect of intra-channel conflict with the marketplace channel and dilute support for this traditional channel. Value creation from the Internet can arise from:

- *Market expansion*: this involves reaching and attracting new segments of customers who buy via this channel. It also results in an increase in traffic in existing channels as the product receives extra exposure via the Internet among customers who then buy through their old channel.
- *Ex ante-transaction costs*: costs of drafting and negotiating agreements are significantly reduced in the Internet channel as companies can deal direct with their customers.

Value destruction via the Internet can arise from:

- *Cannibalization*: adding the Internet channel may shift existing customers from one channel to another catered for by the firm (internal competition for the ownership of the same customers).
- *Ex post-transaction costs*: may create intra-channel conflicts leading to lower levels of support for traditional channels. When this happens, transaction costs of monitoring existing channels will increase.

The advantages and disadvantages of adding an Internet channel are summarized in Table 11.3.

The B2B marketplace is alleged to offer a greater choice of merchandise from more suppliers, greater price competition by pitting this wider universe of suppliers against each other and genuine one-stop shopping. However, although there is much hype about B2B marketplaces and their ability to operate on a global basis, none is actually up and running as yet. Such marketplaces are supposed to rid the supply chain of a host of inefficiencies and provide more competitive prices. This is because they are in an early stage of

Table 11.3   The value-creating versus value-destroying capacity of an additional Internet channel in international B2B

	Value creation	*Value destruction*
Revenues	1. Market expansion	2. Cannibalization
Costs	3. Ex ante-transaction costs	4. Ex post-transaction costs

Source: Geyskens, Gielens and DeKimpe (2000)

development. The technology standards needed to connect buyers and sellers such as XML (enhanced World Wide Web language) are still in development. In addition, payment systems that ensure timely and secure settlement must be created, and logistics systems must ensure that the goods ordered arrive at the right place and time.

B2B marketplaces are horizontal or vertical. The horizontal marketplace deals in goods required in many industries (e.g. office supplies), whereas the vertical deals in goods that are particular to a specific type of industry. As such, they are the electronic version of the centuries old trading bazaars.

Some intermediary has to set up, own and run the online marketplace as with the offline marketplace. They generate revenue either by charging subscriptions based on expected volume or a fee for each transaction. Table 11.4 shows examples of various B2B global exchanges.

B2B in Asia

Asia provides an illustration of some of the distribution problems encountered in B2B when going international. According to Gartner, online transactions in the Asia Pacific by the end of 2003 will be worth US$270 million or 20 per cent of the world total. However, sources of perceived value for Asian buyers from the Internet are not the same as in the West because business environments are different. Whereas in the West additional services such as help with logistics are extras, in Asia these will need to be provided as part of the package to get firms started using the Internet. Experience in the West has shown that B2B marketplaces launched by big industrial insiders have the best chances of success. The same is likely to apply in Asia, particularly for industries with only a few large buyers or suppliers.

Large firms in Asia have the advantage of extensive networks of relationships (both formal and informal), made up of customers, suppliers, regulatory authorities, technology providers and investment banks, etc. Such networks are critical to the building of alliances for winning B2B markets. Companies that want to build online operations in Asia will need to take the following into account:

1. *Manufacturing dominates.* More than half the world's manufacturing takes place in Asia. Manufacturers buy more direct goods (80 per cent,

Table 11.4	*Industry*	*Participants*
Trading partners	Aerospace, defence	BAE Systems, Boeing, Lockheed Martin Raytheon
	Airline	Air France, America Airlines, British Airways, Continental Airlines, Delta Airlines, United Airlines
	Automotive	Ford, General Motors, DaimlerChrysler
	Energy, petrochemical	BP Amoco, Dow Chemical, Royal Dutch Shell Group, 11 others
	Grocery products	Procter & Gamble, Nestlé, Unilever, 50 others
	Pulp and paper	Georgia Pacific, International Paper, Weyerhaeuser

Source: *BRW* (2000c: 106)

i.e. used in production) than indirect goods (20 per cent, e.g. office supplies). US experience suggests that trade in direct goods is harder to move online than trade in indirect goods.

2. *Supply chains are less efficient.* Distribution and logistics account for 12 per cent of FOB value in Asia compared with 4 per cent in Europe, due to supply chains in Asia being less efficient and more fragmented. Whereas there are on average three to four intermediaries between buyer and seller in Asia, there are only one to two in Europe and the USA.

3. *Infrastructure is less well developed.* This lags behind the USA and Europe as Asian countries lack an efficient online payment system. In addition, there are few established third-party logistics providers and information on companies is scarce. Payments in Asia still have to go through the secure but complex letter of credit (LC) route. For example, in India issuing a letter of credit can involve up to seven banks and government agencies.

4. *Markets are smaller.* B2B markets targetting any single Asian country may have too little home demand to achieve sufficient scale. To improve communications, marketplaces must connect every buyer and seller in the supply chain by using technology compatible with different technology systems. No B2B marketplace in Asia as yet has such technology. Expanding B2B markets across Asia to achieve scale economies will be difficult as some elements of the marketplace will remain different from country to country to accommodate local differences in regulations, taxes and languages.

Example	Ford

Using the Internet, Ford hopes to change the marketing approach from a push to a pull strategy. The consumer stimulated by advertising and promotion will pull through the supply chain a product that reflects the consumer's exact specifications. Ford's capital requirements will reduce as it outsources and shares buying activities with other car manufacturers. It has established a new venture for this purpose – Covisint – which will be the world's largest B2B exchange connecting more than 50,000 suppliers to member companies. Whereas a typical purchase order costs US$150, a real-time order will cost about US$15. Additional savings will come from the need to maintain considerably reduced inventories when buying via the Internet.

International B2C

With e-business, it is possible to offer a much greater variety of products that can be offered via traditional retail outlets. However, with traditional retail outlets speed of delivery is only a problem if the item is out of stock. With e-commerce, orders are prepared for shipment only after the order has been placed. Therefore, speed of delivery can be a problem if the configuration and operation of the company's distribution value chain is not 'up to scratch'.

E-tailing

Providing the facility to shop electronically via the Internet enables e-tailers to offer better customer service than their bricks and mortar counterparts. They can personalize sites, create opportunities for customization and treat customers as individuals instead of segments. As they can exceed customer's expectations, they have the potential to create customer loyalty. Traditional retailers need to rethink their strategies so as to leverage their physical marketplace strengths as they participate in e-tailing.

Monnier (1999) has prepared a comparison of marketplace and marketspace retail operations (Table 11.5). In many ways, e-tailing is a modern day equivalent of traditional home shopping techniques such as mail order. Both combine ease of shopping from home with one-to-one marketing techniques. They both sell merchandise via pictures with descriptions, take orders electronically (e.g. by phone or fax in the case of mail order and by the Internet in the case of e-tailing), and deliver merchandise to the door.

Table 11.5   Different retail platforms

Real world (for comparison purposes)	Equivalent in the net	Comments	Examples
Own boutiques or shops	Virtual solo storefront	This strategy entails that it is up to the publisher of the storefront to attract 'qualified' users to the site.	www.levi.com
Own boutiques or shops but located within a shopping centre	Non-integrated cybermall	Usually these non-integrated cybermalls provide a simple link to many commercial web sites. These cybermalls often attract traffic using advertisement, editorial content, etc. By extension, most portal sites (Netscape, Geocities, Alta Vista) now have a shopping section and they can be considered as non-integrated cybermalls.	www.altavista.com
Specific department within a department store	Integrated cybermall	These platforms typically offer an array of services: traffic generation, virtual shop building software, secure payment platform, etc. Normally, these cybermalls offer a reduced graphical flexibility, but they allow easy and low-cost first steps in e-commerce.	Cybershop.com.sg Store.yahoo.com www.e-comptoir.com www.justnet.ne.jp
Full integration within a supermarket	Virtual supermarket	This option is the same as the 'virtual solo storefront', with the difference that the e-merchant is not a manufacturer but a middleman.	www.amazon.com www.onlineties.com

Source: Monnier (1999: 62)

The critical difference is that one uses print while the other uses the Internet. Another difference is that with mail order opportunities for personalization are much more limited and the print media employed is neither interactive nor as timely. The e-tailer learns about the customer and this serves as the basis for dialogue in the future and relationship creation so as to convert the browser into a buyer. This learning takes three forms:

- basic, personal information provided on registration or via self-completion questionnaires
- purchasing habits
- clickstreams or site navigation (the way the consumer behaves when using the Internet and what interests the consumer). This can be used to measure the effectiveness of the site, the ease with which customer can navigate it and the effectiveness of any advertising shown. Collectively, these provide a more detailed picture of each customer.

E-tailers are open around the clock and usually a 'help desk' person is available to assist at any hour. In addition, the capacity of the e-tailer to carry out constant dialogue is part of the personalization process. Products sold via the web have the advantage of being handled only three times compared with an average of ten times for goods sold through supermarkets (Ross, 2000: 63–4). Australian buyers have been enthusiastic about e-grocery. However, although it has the highest level of repeat transactions of any online service, it still only involves a small specific demographic segment of the population. US experience indicates that it takes between five and seven purchases before online customers are converted. However, e-tailing is not without order fulfilment problems and a recent US survey found that only 37 per cent of online shoppers encountered no difficulty. Table 11.6 shows the types of difficulty encountered in online shopping.

Although traditional retailers are frightened of going online because of cannibalization of sales, failure to do so removes first mover advantage and will see erosion of market share in the future.

Table 11.6		%
Online shoppers having difficulty	No difficulties	37
	Out of stock items	31
	Site temporarily down	23
	Couldn't find item	21
	Received item late	14
	Didn't receive item	6
	Poor customer services	6
	Site out of business	5

Source: NPD, cited in CyberAtlas (2001)

Types of Internet shopper

There are five types of Internet shopper:

1. *Traditionalists.* These are most of the population. They are mainly non-working, middle-class women with families. They shop several times a week and are not excited by new technology. Few of them have computer or Internet access. They are not interested in e-grocers because they cannot see the products and would miss the social aspect of shopping.

2. *Passive shoppers.* They are excited about technology but hate grocery shopping. They tend to use convenience stores and smaller supermarkets. They are brand loyal and see e-grocers as a more relaxed way of shopping.

3. *Value seekers.* They tend to be younger people who shop around. They are not satisfied with current shopping experience and have not found a place that suits their needs. They are more excited by digital TV, digital cameras and mobile phones than getting a computer or access to the Internet at home. They are sceptical about e-grocers but interested in how they work.

4. *Modern responsibles.* They are excited by new technology and most have a home computer and pay TV. They work full time and like to spend time with the family. They have a high monthly grocery expenditure and access to the Internet and they like to browse for hours. They find e-grocers appealing.

5. *Time starved.* They come from a higher socioeconomic group. They feel they never have enough time to get things done. They have high weekly grocery bills and a great dislike of grocery shopping. They are excited by technology and have access to the Internet. Finally, they view e-grocers as a viable alternative to traditional shopping.

Example	*Three Australian retail cases*

Coles-Myer

E.colesmyer is the new e-commerce division of Australia's largest retailer. This includes Myer Direct (a catalogue business that is being reborn as an internet-based retailer), Coles Online (the supermarket home shopping experiment), and other new businesses related to the electronic environment.

It will have four divisions. These are (1) e-tailing (Myer Direct, Coles Online and an expanded

Coles Myer portal); (2) e-trading (services for the retailer's 65,000 local suppliers), (3) e-services (data processing and market research activities); (4) e-commerce business development (create new e-commerce projects and handle stock market floats).

One major problem is fulfilment as Boston Consulting Group found that 20 per cent of products ordered online in Australia were never delivered. Advantages include buying power which compensated for lack of flexibility

▶

compared with online retail start-ups. Another advantage is its having access to the largest retail database in Australia through its parent (*BRW*, 7 April, 2000).

Wine Planet

Wine e-tailer, Wine Planet has increased sales from A$25,000 in March 1999 to A$670,000 six months later. This, according to co-founder Rob Walters, is because wine is a perfect example of a product suitable for enriched consumption due to the wealth of information e-tailers can make available on the Internet. This empowers consumers to make knowledge-based rather than label-based purchasing decisions. As of June 2000, it has a staff of 100 of whom 30 are in Britain. It markets its brand, not those of the wines it sells, and it aims to be the number one brand for a wine web site in the world. Such has been their success that they have been acquired by Foster's as part of that firm's expansion into the wine business, and will now become the Internet arm of that marketplace operator. However subsequently, *BRW* (15 June 2001) reported that Foster's closed the WWW.Wine Planet site. Despite its being Australia's third most popular site, its losses continued causing Foster's to abandon its A$92 million investment.

Skates

Bont Skates of Campsie in Sydney (www.bont.com) uses global web site promotion to sell its ice skates and in-line speed skates all over the world. Its site, set up five years ago, receives about 5000 hits a day. The success of this 'international front window' is attributed to:

- choosing a simple name to attract hits driven by search engines
- minimizing the links on the web site (because we want people to stay on our page)
- Sending out URLs and logos for others to link to Bont (because very few take us to task about reciprocating – they just link us up)
- having a relevant and interesting news page
- sending out news to key sporting web sites which mount Bont banner ads in return.

The firm has a synergistic relationship with FedEx to ensure superior manufacturing flows through to the delivery of the goods. Through this relationship they can send skates overnight to 17 Asian countries. Coupled with an ability to customize to personal requirements, this has caused the Internet side of the business to become the fastest growing element (the *Logistics Buyer*, March 2000).

Artificial shopping agencies

Artificial shopping agents (variously known as external agents, autonomous agents or shopping bots) have the potential to change current market relationships because they work on behalf of individual consumers rather than offer advice to consumers on behalf of retailers. Visits by individuals to web sites to undertake transactions may give way instead to visits by software agents on behalf of the individual. The tasks performed by these agents can include product or service search and evaluation, retailer search and evaluation, selection, negotiation, payment and delivery arrangements. This is possible because the web, being computer based, is not only information oriented but structured around computational machines.

International logistics issues and e-business

General issues

A substantial volume of traditional trade will be influenced by the Internet and made more efficient through speedier delivery using Internet-based transport, logistics and border crossing procedures. Some estimate that Internet trade across borders could amount to 20–30 per cent for many products as the Internet reduces traditional barriers to trade of distance, time and language by providing a standardized way for business to communicate (Commonwealth of Australia 1999). An increasing number of international business transactions have the potential to be handled via the Internet, and this number will increase as institutional financial markets move to an Internet base.

Whereas for bricks and mortar businesses the value chain involves inbound logistics (shipping product from manufacturer/wholesaler to distribution centres) and outbound logistics (shipping product from distribution centres to retail stores, sales and marketing), with e-commerce, the distribution value chain can differ widely depending on the configuration of the value chain and the level of outsourcing. Specific areas of difference are that e-commerce companies may ship small shipments to individual customers, warehousing and consolidation operations may not be required and shipment sizes are likely to be smaller.

Electronic data interchange (EDI)

This was one of the earliest applications of electronic commerce and was driven by the explicit goal of lowering purchasing costs. The laborious matching of paper documents for international shipments was replaced by a system where the necessary paper documents were consolidated in digital form on a central server. There the matching took place with greater speed, fewer errors and a reduction in labour costs.

Logistics hubs

A major drawback of B2B Internet exchanges is the lack of an electronic logistical component. Just because it is possible to buy or sell a product on the web, this does not mean that you can deliver it cheaply. This is particularly important in international marketing, as buyers need to know the landed price in their factory (CIF), not the price in the supplier's warehouse or FOB. Therefore, many B2B hubs are building in logistical platforms to provide in addition to pricing, delivery costs, and fulfillment details and tracking services. This may also be achieved by an alliance between the B2B hub operator and a logistics company (e.g. that between PlasticsNet.com, a trading exchange for firms in the plastics industry, and Schneider Logistics, a Wisconsin based trucking and logistics company).

Transborder movement issues

The Internet in particular and the electronic environment in general have the potential to cause:

- an increase in the volume of cross-border transactions due to its impact on warehousing, transport and border facilitation
- promotion of more efficient communications between firms and intermediaries including government agencies
- reduction in costs of border delays and preparing and handling documentation to move goods across borders; in the past this added several percentage points to landed prices
- elimination of complex documentation which can be intimidating and discourage small firms from undertaking international business
- facilitation of quick rate quotations enables small shippers to compete more effectively with larger ones.

However, although paperless international trade is a reality, it is still not all encompassing and does not address the problems of customs clearance, especially in the developing world. Despite this, it is likely that electronic trade facilitation could add considerably to GNP in Asia Pacific. Singapore Customs and Excise Department estimates costs of processing goods entering/exiting Singapore at 70 per cent less if online technologies are used. In Hong Kong SAR, the government created Tradelink Electronic Commerce Limited to provide online trade administration services to Hong Kong traders and funded this body with HK$425 million (A$106 million). In Hong Kong, hard copy trade declarations and quota documents are no longer possible.

Cost issues

Costs most likely to be affected by differences in the configuration of the value chain between bricks and mortar and e-business companies are inventory costs, order handling costs and transportation costs. The specific impacts are as follows.

Inventory costs

While with bricks and mortar companies some inventory needs to be located at a physical store location, e-commerce companies can hold all inventory at a more centralized location, or not even take possession of the goods until the order arrives. This degree of centralization versus decentralization has impact on costs, especially as the former requires a firm to hold lower levels of inventory overall. Furthermore:

- some inventory held in retail stores is for information purposes (floor models) whereas with e-commerce such information is provided through the web site
- web sites provide superior customer and sales information that leads to lower inventory levels by comparison with bricks and mortar venues
- e-commerce firms can maintain a virtual inventory as they do not have to place an order on the supplier or factory until the order is received from the customer
- separation of physical inventory from the retail location allows e-commerce firms to outsource the holding of inventory.

On a global basis, opportunities for centralization are limited by differences in product varieties and product packaging required by different country markets. For products with high levels of global standardization (e.g. chemicals), opportunities for centralization of inventories on a global or regional basis will be higher than for nationally differentiated products such as food.

Order handling costs

As bricks and mortar firms ship larger quantities to fewer distribution centres and are not involved in picking items for dispatch to customers direct, their order handling costs are likely to be less than for e-commerce firms. Because such firms offer a wider variety to choose from, order costs will also be greater than for bricks and mortar firms. As the handling of individual customer orders is very labour intensive, e-commerce firms may shift their distribution centres to low labour cost countries.

Transportation costs

Whereas for the bricks and mortar firm these involve shipping goods from manufacturing facility to physical storefront, for the e-commerce firm they involve delivering product from manufacturing facility to the customer (including clearance through customs when borders are transited). Often, however, people begin to place an order via the Internet and abandon it when they see how much distribution costs add to the total purchase price.

Once the order is entered, there is no certainty that the order will be clicked through. Often the buyer is disillusioned when shipment costs are added and does not click through the purchase. Surveys have shown that this abandonment of shopping carts averages 40 per cent to 45 per cent in most countries.

Location issues

The Internet involves a delinking of value creation from location and effects the motivation to locate value-added activities in different parts of the world. Such motivations include access to expanded markets, access to specialized resources, factor cost advantages, exposure to the latest ideas and keeping competition at bay (Zaheer and Manrakhan, 2000). Two elements of the Internet impact on choice of location:

- digitization of value adding content and delivery
- the ability of the Internet at low cost to form an electronic network that connects various corners of the world.

Many of the factors in the marketplace that mandate physical co-location with customers, such as tariff barriers, face-to-face relationship building and proximity so as to provide after sales service, do not apply in marketspace. This is because the Internet enables many of these factors to become 'disembedded' from a particular location. Zaheer and Manrakhan (2000) argue that the higher the digitization of content and delivery, the greater the possibility of remotely accessing the elements that need physical co-location in the marketplace.

Value chain configuration decisions in e-business distribution

Because distribution value chain configuration for an e-commerce firm is not bound by physical location of retail outlets, e-commerce firms have the opportunity to create optimal value for the customer at minimum cost. Critical decisions in this connection interact and are illustrated in Figure 11.5.

The five key decisions are as follows:

1. *What level of customer service should be offered?* The optimal level of customer service differs across countries and industries due to the differences in the valuation of these service attributes by customers in different countries. Influencing this will be whether firms deal with global or multi-domestic customers who may expect the same level of service across countries.

2. *Which parts of the value chain should be performed internally and which parts should be outsourced?* Outsourcing involves loss of control, which may reduce customer service levels. In the international context, outsourcing becomes more risky as control of distant subcontractors is more difficult than control of local subcontractors, thus increasing transaction costs.

Figure 11.5

Value chain configuration: key decisions

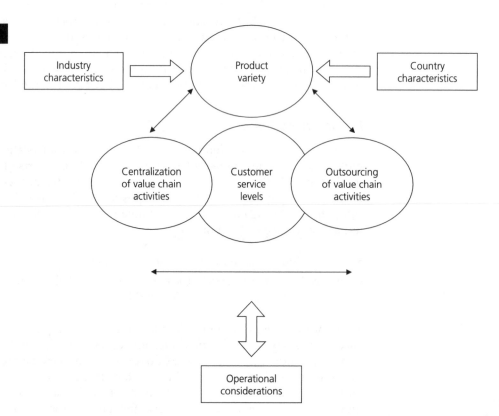

Source: Christmann and Kaslow (2000)

3. *What should be the level of centralization or decentralization of the distribution value chain and where should distribution centres be located?* Having a number of decentralized distribution centres may reduce the transportation costs to individual customers and allow for faster delivery. Demographic and geographic aspects of location as well as other country specific aspects primarily affect such a decision. These are proximity to customers, availability of low cost labour and transportation infrastructure surrounding the distribution centre location.

4. *What should the variety of the product mix offered be?* The variety offered is an important determinant of inventory and handling costs.

5. *Significance of country characteristics.* These affect expectations on the part of consumers. Infrastructure is especially important. The speed of local Internet services affects both the cost and effectiveness of this channel. Many developing countries employ cellular phone technology because of the high cost of installing and maintaining physical cable systems. In such regions, Internet services may not be available until someone provides a wireless connection. Other countries may have access to the Internet but it is neither of sufficient speed nor availability to warrant investment at this time. Internet shopping is only feasible when the item

Figure 11.6 Third party logistics (TPL) firms

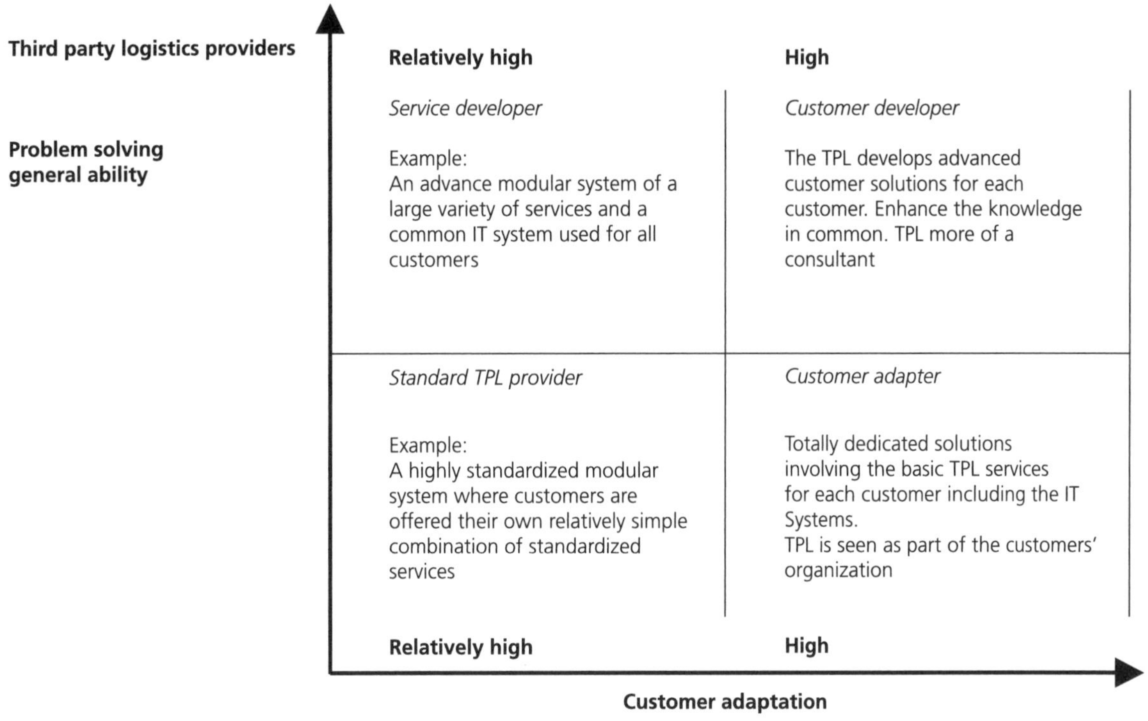

Third party logistics providers	Relatively high	High
	Service developer	*Customer developer*
Problem solving general ability	Example: An advance modular system of a large variety of services and a common IT system used for all customers	The TPL develops advanced customer solutions for each customer. Enhance the knowledge in common. TPL more of a consultant
	Standard TPL provider	*Customer adapter*
	Example: A highly standardized modular system where customers are offered their own relatively simple combination of standardized services	Totally dedicated solutions involving the basic TPL services for each customer including the IT Systems. TPL is seen as part of the customers' organization
	Relatively high	**High**

Customer adaptation

Source: Alfredsson and Hertz (2000)

is a standard reorder or the customer is able to access information on a timely basis to support the purchasing decision. In countries where infrastructure services are provided by government, these may be limited and may not provide complete coverage of the country. Such infrastructure shortcomings may inhibit B2C delivery to the customer's door.

As can be seen from Figure 11.6 above, third party logistics (TPL) providers can be categorized as service developers, customer developers, standard TPL providers and customer adapters, depending on their problem solving ability on the one hand and their willingness to adapt to customer needs on the other.

Questions

1. Why does the Internet facilitate outsourcing in international marketing?
2. In what ways are the international intermediaries in marketspace likely to differ from those in the traditional marketplace?
3. To what extent are B2C transactions in marketspace different from direct mail business across national borders?
4. Under what circumstances should global distribution involve a blend of marketspace and marketplace approaches?
5. The Internet increases some physical distribution costs on the one hand while reducing some physical distribution costs on the other. Under what circumstances is there a net benefit in international marketing?

References

Alfredsson, M. and Hertz, S. (2000) 'Strategic development of TPL providers', *Proceedings of the 16th Annual IMP Conference*, 7–9 September, Bath: University of Bath.

Bulletin (2001–2) 19 December–2 January: 62–3.

BRW (2000a) 7 April.

BRW (2000b) 15 June: 94.

BRW (2000c) 27 October: 106.

Chen, H. Y. and Wilson, D. T. (2000) 'Online auctions: Are relationships doomed?', *Proceedings of the 16th Annual IMP Conference*, 7–9 September, Bath: University of Bath.

Christmann, P. and Kaslow, G. A. (2000) 'Global e-commerce companies versus brick and mortar companies: Decomposing the distribution value chain', unpublished article, University of Virginia.

Commonwealth of Australia (1999) *Creating a Clearway on the New Silk Road: International Business and Policy Trends in Internet Commerce*, Canberra: Australian Government Publishing Service.

Craig, C. P., Douglas, S. P. and Flaherty, T. B. (2000) 'Information access and interpretation: The internet and consumer behaviour in international markets', *Proceedings of the eCommerce and Global Business Forum*, 17–19 May, Santa Cruz, CA: Accenture Institute for Strategic Change.

Cyber Atlas (2001) www.cyberatlas.com.

Deutsche Banc Alex Brown (2000) 'Revolution 2.0: The rise of the B2B e-hub', *North American Equity Research* 1 March.

Forrester Research (1999) 'Net marketplaces grow up', December, www.forrester.com/er/print/research/report/0,1338,8774,ff.html.

Geyskens, I., Gielens, K. and Dekimpe, M. G. (2000) 'Establishing the internet channel: Short term pain buy long term gain?', *Proceedings of the 29th EMAC Conference* 23–26 May, Rotterdam: Erasmus University.

Hollensen, S. (2001) *Global Marketing – A Market Responsive Approach*, 2nd edn, Harlow: Prentice Hall.

Howarth, B. (2001) 'E-business 2006', *BRW*, 9 February: 60–65.

Klein, L. R. and Quelch, J. A. (1997) 'Business to business market making on the internet', *International Marketing Review*, 14 (5): 345–61.

Logistics Buyer (2000) March: 4.

Lynch. P. and Beck, J. C. (2000) 'Profiles of global internet buyers: Evidence supporting region specific strategies', *Proceedings of the eCommerce and Global Business Forum*, 17–19 May, Santa Cruz, CA: Accenture Institute for Strategic Change.

Monnier, P. D. (1999) *Cybermarketing: A Guide for Managers in Developing Countries*, Geneva: International Trade Centre.

Pack, T. (2000), 'Syndication: Content hits the distribution jackpot', *Econtent* 24(1): 36–40.

Quelch, J. A. and Klein, L. R. (1996) 'The internet and international marketing', *Sloan Management Review*, spring: 60–75.

Ross, E. (2000) 'Shoppers are yet to check with grocers', *BRW* 4 August: 63–4.

Samiee, S. (1998) 'Exporting and the internet: A conceptual perspective', *International Marketing Review*, 15 (5): 413–26.

Sarkar, M. (2000) 'Show me the money: Cybermediation in global eMarkets', *Proceedings of the eCommerce and Global Business Forum*, 17–19 May, Santa Cruz, CA: Accenture Institute for Strategic Change.

Strutton, D., Srivastava, R. and Pelton, L. E. (2000) *Intermediaries, Extramediaries and Metamediaries in the global economy*, html/strutton-srivastava-pelton.html.

Walsh, J. and Godfrey, S. (2000) 'The internet: A new era in customer service', *European Management Journal* 18 (1): 83–92.

Zaheer, S. and Manrakhan, S. (2000) 'Location and value creation in a digitized and networked world', *Proceedings of the Conference of the Academy of International Business*, November.

Case Study 11 *The automobile industry's virtual marketplace: Covisint implementation issues*[1]
Francine Schlosser

The Introduction of a virtual marketplace

In February 2000, the big three North American automakers, DaimlerChrysler, General Motors and Ford Motor Company jointly announced a combined B2B integrated supplier exchange, or vertical marketplace, through a single global portal. This portal, originally called NewCo, evolved into the Covisint virtual marketplace of today. Heralded as the world's largest internet-based virtual marketplace, its founders envisioned open participation of suppliers and original equipment manufacturers (OEMs). Optimism and high expectations accompanied this cooperative venture. For example, the Chief Executive Officers of DaimlerChrysler, Ford and General

Motors publicly supported the Covisint launch. Juergen Schrempp, Chairman of DaimlerChrysler, was optimistic:

> DaimlerChrysler's plan for a separate exchange came together with Ford's and GM's. We bring a global presence, large volume and excellent supplier relationships to the new venture. (DaimlerChrysler, 2000a)

Jacques Nasser, President and CEO of Ford, discussed the attractiveness of the venture for all industry participants:

> Today's announcement is another example of how the Internet is transforming every piece of our company and our industry.

▶

It's exciting, it's dramatic, and it's only going to accelerate. We'll push this transformation even further to bring sustainable benefits to our customers, our suppliers, and our dealers.
(DaimlerChrysler, 2000a)

G. Richard Wagoner, Jr, President and CEO of General Motors, described the cooperative effort involved in the Covisint venture:

As we continued to build our separate exchange sites, we quickly realized traditional, individual stand-alone models weren't the winning strategy for us, our industry, our suppliers, and ultimately our customers. By joining together, we can further increase the pace of implementation, thereby accelerating the benefits to everyone involved. We are excited about the opportunity to build on what each of us started separately, and create the best trading exchange in the world. (DaimlerChrysler, 2000a)

Structure of the virtual exchange

Covisint is a multi-member joint venture with DaimlerChrysler AG, Ford Motor Company, General Motors, Nissan and Renault, with technology partners, Commerce One and Oracle. In December 2000, Covisint became a legal entity (Covisint, 2003) Over the next three years, the new venture experienced significant levels of turnover, most strongly characterized by annual turnover in the chairman and CEO executive positions. In 2001, European and Asia Pacific offices were opened.

Covisint represents a dynamic alternative to the traditionally static bidding process. OEMs and earlier tier suppliers invite later tier suppliers to sign up with Covisint for online auction participation. This registration entails disclosure of information about the supplier. Originally the auction was run as a reverse auction, where a maximum price is set by the customer and, depending upon the number of participating suppliers, the price declines in the

bidding process. During bidding the customer can view supplier identity and bids. This process reflected a push by the OEMs for lower prices. More recently, the trend has reverted to a one-bid auction, where the supplier receives an request for proposal (RFP) from a customer with a five-day respond and return election. In this way, Covisint has become more of a medium between customers and suppliers to electronically receive and submit RFPs.

This aggregation of demand was also billed as a benefit to suppliers, who could now supply materials under one standard set of terms, using a supported and standardized technology, thereby reducing their own marketing and administration costs.

During its expansion, Covisint became more strongly allied with DaimlerChrysler, who developed a process called DCXNET to address the entire bidding process. DCXNET also includes consideration of technical service, production guarantees, flexibility and commitment. Recently DCXNET has been augmented by a new quality management system that offers real-time tracking of specific party quality measurement available to both the OEM and its suppliers.

Pressures on OEMs

The use of online auctions facilitated Daimler-Chrysler's desire for lower prices and pushed the responsibility for cost cutting further up the supply chain. This was evidenced in an excerpt from the section on Global Procurement & Supply in DaimlerChrysler's (2001) Annual Report:

The short term unit-cost reductions set out for 2001 in the Chrysler group turnaround plan for 2001 were surpassed. This achievement was due to Chrysler Procurement's ability to obtain significant cost reductions from suppliers.
(DaimlerChrysler, 2001: p. 48)

This report noted that during Covisint's first operating year, Chrysler reported a 17 per cent savings in material costs of parts purchased in 27 online auctions. Additionally, Covisint also enabled a 92 per cent reduction in the amount of leadtime Chrysler took to send production programme information to suppliers. This created a situation where information could be made available to the whole supply chain simultaneously, instead of requiring sequential communication (DaimlerChrysler, 2000b).

Pressures on suppliers

The introduction of a virtual marketplace was met with mixed reviews. Although the OEMs strongly supported its use, their suppliers were less than enthusiastic. Interviews with representatives of Tier 2 and 3 automobile suppliers were flavoured with scepticism. For example, Tom Horvath, the Sales Manager at a Tier 2 plastics supplier, discussed why he did not intend to use the system. He had just met with an OEM who wondered why Tom wasn't using Covisint. Tom described the first time he was instructed to use the system by one of his customers (OEM):

> When we entered the online auction, I sat in front of my computer for 3 hours and watched the bidding. It went from a $3 million dollar order to a half-million dollar order. Now, how could anyone move down that far? There were forty bidders instead of the normal five or six. One of the original bidders ended up getting the bid so it says something about his pricing at the start. We didn't bid at all. I had my $2.5 million bid, sitting beside me, but I wanted to see how it would play out. The next day the customer called me up and said, why didn't you bid? I said, I'm not bidding in that – how can anyone make money at $1/2 million dollars? I'm not playing ball – in fact, I'm taking my ball and going home! Then, it turns out that the company that got the bid was an Indian company that was sourcing the work in China, and had to make arrangements to

> get the parts in on time. When the customer checked them out (they do an on-site visit), it didn't look very reliable.

Tom believed that, after these auctions, the work was often awarded to his company, because customers knew who they were and already had a good relationship with them. More importantly, the OEM customers knew his company was reliable.

Similarly, another interviewee, Bob Fowler, the Vice President, Marketing and Sales, at a Tier 2 metals supplier confirmed that his company had participated in few online bids. Although the OEMs initially pushed Covisint, he found that most of his sales were done on a face-to-face basis and through a single bid tender. He voiced his concerns with the Covisint system:

> The senior people in the customer companies are pushing buyers to get the lowest price, but the buyers want to source based on price, quality, on-time delivery and the fact that you're local. Being local is important for lead times. If you buy offshore, then the supplier has to keep a safety stock in North America in case the ship sinks or there's a port strike. This means the supplier is carrying more inventory, not the customer. Even if you ship the part to the customer, the customer doesn't recognize it in his warehouse for five days or until he uses it. There is an opportunity for North American suppliers to expand internationally, but we generally deal with the Big Three in North America. This is partly because we're based here, but also we have no physical facilities in Europe and the Far East, and when you're supplying overseas, at the very least, you need to have a warehouse over there. Overall, our profits are much less using online auctions than if we bid in the traditional way.

Bob's issues seemed to discount the notion of shared cost savings throughout the industry, as well as the facilitation of global commerce lauded by the Covisint proponents. Interestingly, Bob discussed how suppliers and OEMs often used Covisint as an information medium. For example, his company was participating in a pilot quality project with Covisint. The project required online reporting of incidents and how they were resolved by the supplier.

Jean Dubai, Sales Engineer at a Tier 2 metals supplier, confirmed the importance of quality in supplier selection, an attribute that might not be present in the lowest bid. He suggested that it was very important for marketing and sales representatives to know the costing structure of their own products or, in the heat of the moment, they could commit the company to a contract that was not profitable. He discussed the potential for fraud inherent in the online auction process.

> The process is rigged. You don't know who the other bidders are, so they might be ghost bids where the customer is trying to bring down the price. Or, suppliers can fix the auction by not going below the price. Each time a customer changes a supplier, they have to go through an engineering quality test program to validate the component and ensure it is up to standard. This test has to occur at all levels of supply, so if it's a new Tier 3 supplier, then the Tier 3 supplier has to be tested, plus the Tier 2 and Tier 1 suppliers. Each test costs $300,000–$400,000, which might equate to two to three years worth of components. So suppliers may say we're going to stay within half a cent so that it isn't worth it for a customer to switch. This keeps the pie the same, with all suppliers retaining their market share.

These quotes show a markedly different perspective than the optimistic ones earlier voiced by the OEMs. This reluctance to use the online auction process became clear to Covisint and a new strategy was developed.

Covisint's latest strategy

In response to the scepticism and disinterest displayed by the suppliers, Covisint began to formulate a new strategy. This strategy would require the participation of all industry players to ensure its success. It was kick-started during a recent presentation to the 2003 Automotive News World Congress. Bruce Swift, President and CEO of Covisint, suggested:

> There is a call to action to build bridges where suppliers and OEMs join together to implement standard processes, with a focus on the development of new processes not the technology. (Swift, 2003)

This heralded the start of a bright new era for Covisint – or did it?

Questions

1. All three automakers imply the participation of all industry stakeholders in the development of the exchange. They describe a win–win situation for suppliers, customers and dealers. Is this what happened? What steps might they take to ensure industry buy-in?

2. How and why has the use of Covisint changed? Is this a problem? For whom?

3. How does industry reliance upon relationship development influence the success/failure of an electronic trading place? In such an industry, is a virtual marketplace competence enhancing or competence destroying?

4. How does the structure of the industry (i.e. monopoly, oligopoly, perfect competition) influence the success of a virtual marketplace? How did it impact the introduction of Covisint in the autoindustry?

5. Are supplier resources optimized? One employee must be dedicated to watch the bidding process and must already know their own lowest possible bid. Is this truly a dynamic process for the suppliers and the customers?

6. Will an increased set of supply alternatives, including international bids, lead to lower costs for customers? What types of process considerations might influence the success of a technological implementation?

Note

1 This case is based upon interviews with anonymous industry participants and statements available publicly on the WWW.

References

Covisint (2003) *Historical Milestones*. Retrieved 29 July 2003, from source: www.covisint.com

DaimlerChrysler (2000a) *World's Largest Internet-based Virtual Marketplace Detroit, February 25, 2000*. Retrieved 31 July 2003, from source: www.daimler chrysler.de/news/top/2000

DaimlerChrysler (2000b). *DaimlerChrysler Reduces Costs Through Online Purchasing. Stuttgart/Auburn Hills, MI, December 22, 2000*. Retrieved 31 July 2003, from source: www.daimlerchrysler.de/news/top/2000

DaimlerChrysler (2001) DaimlerChrysler 2001 Annual Report. Retrieved 31 July 2003, from source: www.daimler.chrysler.de/investor/reports/annual01/download/procure_e.pdf

Magid, L. J. (2000) 'B2B marketplaces are becoming big business'. *Los Angeles Times* 22 March. Retrieved 31 July 2003, from source: www.larrysworld.com/articles/sb_b2bvirtual.htm.

Swift, B. (2003) 'Bridging the gap', presented to the 2003 Automotive News World Congress, 14 January. July 31 Retrieved 2003, from source: www.covisint.com

12 Effective international promotion strategies using the Internet

Learning objectives

After studying this chapter, you should be able to:

- Recognize ways in which the traditional communications model needs modification in marketspace.

- Create an international promotion strategy using the web.

- Develop techniques for creating buyer loyalty via the Internet.

- Devise approaches for promoting your web site across national boundaries.

- Appreciate how each promotional technique in the marketplace needs modification when applied in marketspace.

Introduction

The Internet is considered to be a global channel of communication, but the online messages are perceived in the local cultural context of the user. Herein lies the dilemma that often causes the results from Internet promotion to be less than anticipated. In some cases this is due to management assuming that the medium will guarantee the message response. Effective Internet promotion requires that the medium not be taken for granted:

Business managers that use the Internet as a major component of their international marketing communications strategy face great challenges. The popularity of the Internet with consumers and businesses drives thousands of firms to promote their products and services using World Wide Web sites. Technology has created a competitive arena that enables exposure to consumers worldwide, who can now easily communicate with each other. This potential for exposure has dramatic implications for any business considering the Internet as a promotional vehicle. The growing popularity of Internet sites, where users may discuss their feelings about companies and products, allows an increased scrutiny of all aspects of business. If companies do not deal effectively with this scrutiny, brand equity is vulnerable to erosion. Therefore, all contingencies inherent in promotional efforts on the Internet must be weighed carefully. Businesses which examine the ramifications of online exposure are better able to create and maintain a positive Internet strategy which facilitates effective international promotion via web sites. (Van Doren, Fechner and Green-Adelsberger, 2000: 21)

A survey by the *Economist* in 1997 revealed that 75 per cent of customers who shopped on the Internet went on to purchase their goods or services through traditional channels. This suggests that the Internet plays a more important role as a worldwide advertising and promotional vehicle than it does as a selling tool. Compared with other media, the spread of the Internet has been much faster. Whereas it took 38 years for radio to reach 50 million homes, TV 13 years, cable 10 years, it took only 5 years for the Internet to reach 50 million homes (McCann-Erickson, Paul Kagan Associates and Morgan Stanley Technical Research, cited in Westland and Clark, 1999: 453).

Jupiter Communications predicted that by 2002 Internet advertising revenues would approach US$8 billion and account for some 4.1 per cent of advertising spending. Its increasing appeal as a promotional vehicle is because it is able to target specific customer segments and is both interactive and consumer driven, offering the potential for marketers and consumers to communicate directly with each other (Van Doren, Fechner and Green-Adelsberger, 2000: 27).

Table 12.1 (p. 269) shows how the web compares with other media as a promotional medium in terms of its attributes.

Communication models in marketspace

Infrastructure issues

All media require a degree of investment in infrastructure so that the message can be received. In some cases, the majority of the cost is met by the owner of the medium (e.g. the billboard) and in others by the recipient of the message (e.g. the television set). In international marketing, affordability of infrastructure can be an issue in both utility of the medium and whether the message will be received by the target audience.

Example	*China prepares for e-business*

As part of its redevelopment, China has invested US$25 billion in telecommunications infrastructure in the last year (2000). As a result, urban phone penetration has increased to 29 per cent compared with 16 per cent nationwide according to the US Department of State. This is evidence that the government is putting in place the building blocks for additional online activities. As the number of online users in China increases, so will the use by the advertising industry of the Internet as a viable, cost-effective promotional medium. Through it the industry will be able to

▶

reach consumers and provide customized messages according to region and mindset.

From 1999 to 2000, the number of Internet users in China increased from 8.9 million to an estimated 20 million, with estimates for 2005 being 37 million. While this last figure still only represents a 3 per cent penetration rate, the numbers are still significant from an advertising perspective. Additionally, the use of online provides advertisers with a medium that is more accountable than traditional media as the advertiser is able to monitor the exact number of times that their advertisement has been seen.

As with Internet penetration rates, the take-up of online as an advertising vehicle has been relatively slow to date. In 1999, total online advertising revenue was only US$12 million. However, Forrester Research predicts this will grow to US$100 million by 2002 and to US$440 million by 2004.

Source: Hachigian in *Foreign Affairs* (March, 2001); US Department of State *Country Commercial Guide* (2000: 27; Forrester Research, DCMA Presentation, Singapore (2000)

Unlike most forms of media, advertising has not been a major factor driving and funding the growth of the Internet. This is because web users directly pay for 99 per cent of the cost of equipment and content including subscription fees for many services. As advertising revenues on the web increase, the percentage of total costs of services provided will shift from the current user-fee model to the more traditional advertising supported model. This may change the utility of the medium as a vehicle for international marketing.

Application of traditional communications model

Traditional media have two capabilities – building brands and direct marketing. In general, most promotional forms are useful for one or the other. The Internet, however, has the characteristics of both broadcast mass media and direct response advertising. It is more like newspapers than TV on the one hand, but the medium and response convenience elements are closer to TV than newspapers from the perspective of impact on consumers. Figure 12.1 (p. 270) shows a traditional communications model.

In the traditional model of communications in the marketplace, there are clear distinctions between the sender, the message and the recipient, and control of the message is with the sender. In marketspace, control of the message is shared between sender and receiver because of the interactivity of the medium, the ability of the medium to carry a message back in reply to that sent, and the impact of the information technology on time, space and communication. The above impacts on the feedback loop which is inbuilt into the Internet and on the aspect of interference. In general, interference is more likely to be from Internet clutter and less from external sources. Figure 12.2 (p. 270) illustrates how interactivity affects the communications model.

Promotional strategy using the web

The web represents a change away from a push strategy in international promotion, where a producer focuses on convincing an agent to represent the

Table 12.1 Comparison between the web and other media

	WWW	Phone	Fax	Video-text	Teletex	TV (analogue)	Radio	Letter	Newspapers	EDI*
Multimedia	Yes	No (voice)	No (image, text)	No (image, text)	No (text)	Yes	No (voice)	No (image/text)	No (image/text)	Yes (potentially)
Interactive	Yes	Yes	Yes (not in real time)	Yes	No	No (yes if digital)	No	Yes (not in real time)	No	Yes
Data area downloadable and editable	Yes	No	No	Yes (more or less)	No	No	Not really	No	No	Yes
Worldwide	Yes	Yes	Yes	No	No	Rarely	Rarely	Yes	Rarely	Rarely
Multi-platform	Yes	NA	NA	No	No	No	NA	NA	NA	No
Access is fully or selectively open	Yes	Yes	Yes	Open	Open	Open	Open	NA	Usually open	Usually proprietary
Permanently open	Yes	Yes	Yes	Yes	Yes	Yes	Yes	NA	NA	Yes
Cheap access	Yes	Local communication only	Local communication only	Yes	Yes	Yes	Yes	Only if locally	Yes	Set-up is extensive
Easily updateable/immediate effects	Yes	NA	NA	Yes	Yes	NA	NA	NA	NA	Yes
Some information about readers can be collected	Yes	NA	NA	Yes	No	No (unless digital)	No	NA	Yes (if subscription)	Yes
Take legacy systems	Yes	NA	NA	Rare	Rare	NA	NA	NA	NA	Difficult
Personalizable	Yes	NA	NA	No	No	No	No	NA	No	Yes
'Information pull'	Yes	NA	NA	Yes	Yes	No	No	No	No	Yes/no
Reliability	Not yet	Yes	Yes	Some	Yes	Yes	Yes	Yes	Yes	Often
Fast access	Not yet	NA	NA	Yes	Yes	NA	NA	NA	NA	Often
Accessible by a large audience	Not yet	Yes	Yes	Not really	Yes	Yes	Yes	Yes	Yes	No
Safety	Not completely yet	No	No	Yes	NA	NA	NA	Yes	NA	Often

(NA = not applicable or not compatible; Shadowed cells point out clearly positive points.)

*EDI (electronic data interchange) refer to the exchange of data between private networks of computers using a proprietary technology.

Source: Monnier (1999: 21)

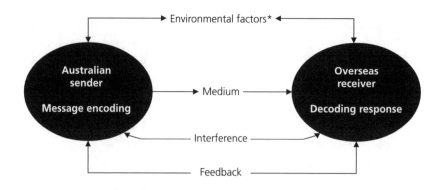

Figure 12.1

Typical
communications
model

* Differences in culture, politics, laws/regulations, economic development,
   competition, education, infrastructure and technology.

Source: Griffin (1993: 11)

Figure 12.2

Summary of
communications
models for
(a) traditional media
(b) new media

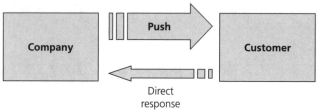

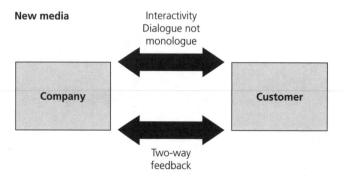

Source: Chaffey (2000: 41)

products or services or a distributor to stock its goods, towards a pull strategy in
which the producer communicates directly with the customer and promotional
costs are reduced in the process. The differentiating feature of the Internet from
other promotional vehicles is that of interactivity and this results in the Internet
combining the attributes of both selling and advertising. Interactivity facilitates

a completely new approach to reaching potential customers. Unlike television, for example, where the consumer passively observes, with the web there is an active intent to go onto the Internet and a greater degree of attention to content as a result.

Advertising models developed in the marketplace environment offer three principal effects of advertising: the cognition, which is the thinking dimension of a person's response; the affect, which is the feeling dimension of the response; and the experience effect, which is the unconscious memory of purchasing and usage. This is the high involvement approach to advertising. By contrast, there are also low involvement approaches in which advertising reinforces behaviour, rather than causing it. In this case, advertising has a cognition element in that it creates awareness, but the experience of the product causes the affect element or decision to prefer or purchase the brand. In order to see how advertising on the web differed from traditional forms of advertising, Kennedy (2000) applied the Vakratsas and Ambler taxonomy (1999), to various forms of media. The outcome is shown in Table 12.2, where 1 = 'does not work in this way' to 5 = 'does work in this way'.

Table 12.2 indicates that the web, in comparison with other forms of advertising, tends to be high on information, low on generating an emotional response and not as good at reinforcing existing behaviour.

Sutherland (2000) suggests that the web is a very different medium. It operates in a very different environment and one in which a continual stream of decisions is demanded from the user. Each click represents a decision and therefore the web is a very high involvement medium. In addition, unlike traditional media, the web is a medium by which the user can click through and obtain more information or actually purchase the product. Web advertisements can and are often targeted to a user profile that in turn affects the way the message will be received. Increasingly, the ads displayed on the web are specific to user interests and appear as these interests are revealed while the user navigates the web.

In order to provide value to the potential international customer and hold interest, the web site must be attractive and user friendly. This involves an appealing design, being available in the buyer's language (or one with which the buyer is likely to be familiar) and be aesthetic in terms of colour and background (taking into account buyer's cultural norms). It should be easy to navigate, contain the information that the buyer is likely to want and be easy to access.

The most common form of advertising on the web (as opposed to advertising the existence of the web site) is banners across the top of commercial sites.

Table 12.2	Model	Code	TV	Print	Billboards	www
Vakratas and Ambler taxonomy applied to media	Information	C	4	5	3	5
	Emotions, feelings or likeable	A	4	2	2	2
	Persuasion (hierarchy of effects)	CA	2	2	1	2
	Reinforce existing behaviour	CEA	4	4	4	3

Source: Kennedy (2000: 650)

Advertisers pay according to the number of 'impressions' an ad gets (i.e. how many people see the ad regardless of whether they click on to it). Charges vary from US$120 per thousand impressions to as little as US$6 for the same number. Banner ads are interactive as clicking on them opens up a new web page and ways of making the actual purchase.

Unlike television, with the Internet consumers are more in charge of what they see. It has been found that banner ads and interstitial pop-up advertisements are less effective than formerly as TV tactics do not work as well on the Internet. Razzouk and Seitz (2001) report research to the effect that only 8 per cent correctly identified the presence of one banner ad. Of those, 50 per cent incorrectly identified the product or could not identify the product at all. Sixty-two per cent saw no banner ad but 70 per cent correctly identified the web site on which the ads were placed. The most effective tactics appear to be brand marketing with something given in exchange for information such as a free sample or a timesaving hint (Van Doren, Fechner and Green-Adelsberger, 2000: 26).

Building buyer loyalty

Using the web as a vehicle for building loyalty on the part of international buyers involves a number of different stages:

1. *Attract*: attracting clients to visit the web site. They do so on a voluntary basis and will not come simply because a site has been created. To create awareness of the site, it is necessary to use banner ads and links to other sites

2. *Engage*: engaging visitor's attention. This is necessary in order to get the visitor to the site to participate and encourage interaction. Most sites fail as promotional mediums because they are boring and have poorly presented material. In this connection, the content of the site is most important.

3. *Retain*: retain the visitor's interest in your site. This is important to ensure repeat visits to the site and the creation of a 'one-to-one 'relationship between the firm and its potential overseas customer. One way of achieving this is by persuading the customer to provide information on their requirements so that the firm can customize its offering and thereby increase switching costs.

4. *Learn*: learn about the client and their preferences. This is enabled by providing on the site a facility for easy feedback and comment. The use of cookies can assist.

5. *Relate*: adopt a deliberate policy of building relationships with site visitors. This is achieved by providing value added content, by tailoring the product/service to the needs of each customer and promising customized delivery.

McKinsey's ePerformance Scorecard (BRW, 2000: 63) shows that only 4.5 per cent of web site visits result in a sale, and only 1.3 per cent of web site visitors are repeat buyers. Given the costs of creating a web site and attracting people to visit it, unless visitors keep returning to the site and initial purchasers via the site become repeat purchasers, then the site development costs are unlikely to be amortized and profits will remain elusive. This is what has happened to date with many dot.coms, especially in the B2C sector. Many such firms that have encountered problems have failed to pursue a deliberate policy of creating buyer loyalty. McKinsey and Company found that the typical offline firm spends three to five times more on customer retention than its online competitors (BRW 2000: 63). Such loyalty is just as important in marketspace as it is in the marketplace. According to Reichheld and Schefter (2000: 106), 'without the glue of loyalty, even the best designed e-business model will collapse'. Their research has shown that, contrary to popular conceptions, the web is a very sticky place in both B2C and B2B marketing. They found that most online customers are loyal and that web technologies, if used correctly, reinforce inherent loyalty. Failure to create such loyalty leaves the online firm at the mercy of only the most price-sensitive buyers who are unlikely to be as profitable. They found that increasing customer retention rates on the web by 5 per cent increases profits by 25 to 30 per cent.

At the beginning of a relationship, the outlays to acquire customers are usually much higher in e-business than in traditional channels. In apparel e-tailing, new customers cost 20 to 40 per cent more for Internet companies than for traditional retailers. However, evidence suggests that web customers tend to consolidate their purchasers with one primary supplier to the extent that purchasing from the supplier's site becomes a regular routine. This is particularly the case in B2B. Reicheld and Schedffer (2000: 106) found that in apparel e-tailing, repeat customers spend more than twice as much in months 24 to 30 of their relationship than they do in the first six months, thus reinforcing the need to actively create customer loyalty on the web. Figure 12.3 illustrates this.

Figure 12.3	
Customer life-cycle economics in e-commerce	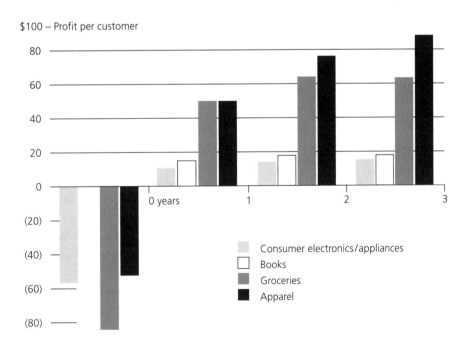

Source: Bain & Company and Mainspring, as cited in Reichheld and Schefter (2000: 107)

Loyal customers also refer new customers to a web supplier they are happy with. While referrals are lucrative in traditional commerce, the effect is amplified on the web since word of mouse spreads faster than word of mouth. One of the difficulties in creating buyer loyalty on the web is that of building trust in a situation where business is conducted at a distance and risks and uncertainties are often greater, or perceived to be greater, than in the international marketplace. Promotional activities in the marketplace show faces and usually faces do not lie, despite what words are uttered. It is difficult to be deceptive as body language will give you away and create inconsistencies between the perception of what you say and what you really mean. Because online customers cannot look the sales person in the eye and read the body language, because they cannot evaluate the credibility of the firm by its physical space or office location, and because they cannot touch or feel the product on offer, they have to rely on images and promises as conveyed by the site. Because of these factors, the site must conform to the notion of being 'a site I know and can trust'. The above research found that price does not rule the web, trust does.

Amazon.com has come to dominate the online book market by creating the most reliable and trustworthy site in the business. Millions of customers are comfortable letting Amazon store their names, addresses and credit card details in their system. As a result of this trust, Amazon's customers can make repeat purchases with just one click and customers keep coming back, not only for books but also for videos, CDs and other products. (Reichheld and Schefter, 2000: 108)

Effective web sites

The creation of loyalty requires a focused web site. This means that it should be designed simply, fast to load and easy to use. The key ingredients of an effective web site are as follows:

- *Generates confidence* – needs to refer to tangible or marketplace elements such as known logos, company premises and postal address.
- *Fast and user friendly* – should avoid fancy graphics that take time to download and the bells and whistles that demonstrate the skill of the web master.
- *Focus on communication* – not decoration, and be well thought out in terms of conveying information in a user friendly way.
- *Easy to update and scale-up* – so that a novice can update rather than a skilled (and expensive) professional web master.
- *Permanently operational* – 7 days a week, 24 hours a day, which means minimizing down time by choosing a reliable web presence provider.
- *Hacker proof* – although no site is immune it should be designed so as to make hacking as difficult as possible (Monnier, 1999).

Many firms lose loyalty by cramming too many offerings or products on their sites and trying to include all levels of technical expertise, all service requirements and all degrees of brand preference. When this occurs, the site becomes slower to load and more complicated to use. Its utility as a promotional medium disappears and customers give up and fail to return. This problem can be minimized by reducing the byte size. Ways of doing this are:

- minimal use of graphics (or at least attempt to edit their size)
- link to pictures where possible
- warn user about file size
- simple layout
- judicious use of HTML (cull obsolete code)
- avoid the use of Java and other modern cope applications
- avoid the use of frames.

Unfortunately, too many web companies spend their e-marketing dollars on indiscriminate banner ads and online coupons and too little on building communities and promoting referrals. Whereas in the marketplace customers leave no record of their behaviour unless they buy something, and even then the data is limited, in marketspace every move they make can be documented electronically, click by click. If a customer exits when a price screen appears, it is likely he/she is price sensitive. If the customer jumps from page to page without initiating a transaction, then it is likely that the customer is frustrated at being unable to find what is wanted, or is using the web for comparison shopping with a view to eventual marketplace purchase. Few firms adequately treat this data as a source of market research information about the effectiveness of their site as an international promotional medium.

This suggests that much more care needs to be taken as to both the content and presentation of the Internet site. The Internet will not be a truly international promotional medium until it ceases to be a reflection of Anglo-Saxon culture. Dowling (1999) points out that in the next few years, despite censorship, the number of Internet users in China will exceed the number in the USA. Therefore, to tap these users a Mandarin translation of one's web site will be essential. Translation is the first step in localizing the appeal of most products promoted via the Internet. As in marketplace, in marketspace research has shown that second language English speakers prefer a localized product to a lower priced English language product and respond to diverse national, local and community considerations. The extension of the multi-cultural process via the Internet involves specifically creating sites that reflect regard for the history of the country, appreciation of diversity, being comfortable with change, an open and flexible mind and sensitivity to cultural differences. Unless this is achieved, it will be difficult for business to capitalize on the unique advantage of the Internet – that of customizing offerings to buyers' specific needs, i.e. exploiting the profiles of their customers. Ways of localizing the web site to enhance its appeal in developing countries are:

- use of local language
- use of local symbols and logos

- utilize established branding (co-brand with an existing brand)
- incorporate local content (shows transparent understanding of the issues faced by the people)
- incorporate a local contact in the 'contact details'.

Another issue in Internet promotion is to what extent should promotion via the Internet replace other forms of promotion. This requires an appreciation of what activities the Internet replaces that were previously used for promotion via marketplace media. Forrester Research surveyed Internet users in the USA and asked them what activities they had given up in order to spend more time on their computers.

Promoting the web site

Having a web site is not enough in itself to attract 'hits' from international buyers. It is necessary to promote the site by both traditional and electronic means. For many e-tailers this means multimillion advertising campaigns to build awareness of their site. Various techniques are to feature URL addresses on all correspondence, traditional advertisements and other marketplace forms of promotion. Direct print or broadcast media can also be effective in directing repeat users to a web site, often at a much lower cost than that applicable to portal advertising. This is particularly the case in Asia where to date Asian web sites prefer to advertise offline rather than on the net.

The promotion of web sites is intended to generate 'qualified' traffic (i.e. potential or probable clients). Promotional methods can be divided into online and offline methods.

Online methods

- *Search tools* – often specialized and relate to a specific area of activity.
- *Advertising banners* – these are hyperlinked to the web site of the advertiser.
- *Sponsoring* – a site is sponsored in a similar way that a sporting event is sponsored.
- *Interstitials* – these are advertisements that appear for a few seconds before another page is downloaded.
- *Discussion groups* – can be used to promote a site on an indirect basis.
- *Mass e-mailing* – particularly effective when the firm creates its own list rather than relying on a more broadly-based commercial list.
- *Associate programs* – associate sites refer to a main site for a commission.

Offline methods

- *Traditional mass mailing* – this is effective if well targeted but it is expensive.

- *Advertising* the site in fairs, on billboards and on other signage such as shopping trolleys can be very effective.
- *Use of existing infrastructure* – shops, newsletters, etc. to promote the existence of the web site.

Maddox and Mehta (1997) studied the impact of inclusion of web addresses in traditional advertisements. They found that both Internet and non-Internet users noted the inclusion of such URLs and that advertisers with web addresses were perceived as being more customer focused, more sophisticated and more likely to stay in business longer. E-mail campaigns to draw attention to the site are another technique. Featuring the site on search engines and banner advertisements on other sites can also draw attention to the site. Finally, cyber cafés and links to other sites are additional means of creating an awareness of the site.

The cost of creating promotional strategies to attract visitors to the web site, to interest them in making purchases and persuade them to frequently revisit the site can be expensive. One technique of promoting the site is to register it with a search engine. There are large repositories of URLs and whenever the search is for a product in your category, reference is made to your web site. This involves the firm buying a keyword from the search engine operator. It is necessary, if search engines are to be effective international promotional vehicles, that the information provided to the search engine operator be regularly updated.

A second frequently used technique is that of banners. Banners are graphic images with HTML codes that link to another web site. Banners can be considered as the 'billboards of cyberspace'. They can appear anywhere on a web page and can transport the visitor from one web page to another by clicking on the banner. Advertisers try to place their banner strategically in case the online user wishes to obtain additional information about the content of the advertisement in the banner. Briggs and Hollis (1997) studied the effect of banners. They found that banners helped increase brand awareness, reminded consumers of a brand's existence, stimulated latent brand associations, affected attitude towards the brand and ultimately increased the likelihood of purchase. A similar method of promoting a web site is to place a hyperlink for your business site on the web site of another business. Some businesses, especially those whose activities are complementary, provide this facility to each other on a reciprocal basis. Another means of promoting the web site is inclusion in an Internet Yellow Pages service where these exist. Costs of listing range from free to inexpensive.

E-businesses with low rates of customer churn tend to market themselves more selectively. They use web sites that have highly targetted demographics or special interest areas (e.g. sports). These sites tend to draw the largest number of potential heavy users who are 14 times more likely to click through ads to real purchase screens. In contrast, banner ads on Internet portals such as Yahoo! or America Online tend to attract browsers. However, banner ads on portal sites have a role in building cumulative mindshare (BRW, 2000: 63).

It is necessary to establish well in advance what the purpose of the site is to be if it is to be an effective promotional medium for the company. Van Doren, Fechner and Green-Adelsberger (2000) argue that there are four possible scenarios for web sites as promotional vehicles. These are illustrated in Figure 12.4.

Figure 12.4		
Four possible scenarios for promoting on the Internet		

1	☐	➤ Web site only/information ➤ No interactivity ➤ Mass market approach/no focus ➤ No measurability of web site effectiveness
2	☐	➤ Web site for limited interactivity ➤ E-mail set-up for customer inquiry ➤ Minimal market research ➤ Limited measurability of WWW site effectiveness
3	☐	➤ Full interaction capabilities ➤ Off-line transactions ➤ Banners, buttons and other enhancements ➤ Focused market research capabilities ➤ High measurability of web site effectiveness
4	☐	➤ Extensive interaction ➤ Videoconferencing ➤ Full on-line transaction and distribution channel capabilities ➤ Optimal focused market research capabilities with leverage ➤ Optimal measurability of web site effectiveness

Source: Van Doren, Fechner and Green-Adelsberger (2000: 24)

Scenario 1

This involves the establishment of a simple web site (one or two pages). This is the first step for a business that has decided to promote via the Internet. It is suitable in cases where the business wants enhanced name recognition but does not wish to interact with users, or wishes to create awareness of how to obtain its products through traditional channels. Used in this way the Internet is a mass advertisement without a mechanism for users to interact. This form of web site is low risk, low cost and low payoff.

Scenario 2

This appeals to the firm that not only wants to establish a presence on the Internet, but also to create user interest so that the user returns to the site. It does not want to sell its products/services online, but wants users to respond to its promotions. By getting users to respond, the firm can gather valuable data that will assist its future promotional approaches. Unlike Scenario 1, this scenario does involve some form of interaction. This type of site can range from inexpensive to expensive depending on actual promotional techniques used and the complexity of the site.

Scenario 3

This offers detailed customer service tools such as online help, product instructions, warranty information, online customer feedback forms and other forms of interaction with customers such as chat groups. Promotional techniques can range from simple banners to interactive games. The greater interaction enables the obtaining of greater levels of information that can be used to build customer loyalty. This provides a greater level of measurability of web site effectiveness as it is fully interactive.

Scenario 4

This involves expanding the use of the site to include online ordering. This extends the site from a promotional vehicle to a distribution vehicle in two ways. First, it serves as a direct channel where digital products (e.g. music) are sent from the producer to the online user. Second, it operates as an indirect distribution channel (as with cybermalls and shopping centres). In this case, often the customers, have an input into what they receive and the opportunity to mix and match products. In this scenario, multimedia can be used to interact with users (e.g. show video clips) and the interaction time between marketers and consumers is extended, allowing for deeper relationship development. Sites requiring interactivity are costly. As an example:

> Eddie Bauer is a US clothing company specializing in outdoors/casual clothing. It uses the approach of giving online shoppers hands-on experience by allowing them to combine garments online to see how they look before purchasing them. Users have to provide specific information in order to complete the online sale.

This scenario differs in the extent of interaction with the customer. It also differs in the degree to which the consumer is asked to provide information. *Marketing News* (1998) reported a survey by Yankelovich and Partners which showed: 76 per cent of online customers are willing to provide personal information if it will help them obtain a more customized product/service; 92 per cent are willing to talk about their hobbies or interests; 77 per cent are willing to complete short surveys; 73 per cent are willing to provide demographic information; 67 per cent are willing to give their names. These US-based statistics need interpretation in terms of cultural norms as far as other countries are concerned, especially in Asia where privacy is more protected, or in countries where a significant percentage of business passes through 'unofficial' channels.

Promotion on the web

Advertising on the web

Although still a small percentage of total advertising spend, Internet advertising is growing at five times the rate of non-Internet advertising. The break-up of Internet advertising by form in 1999 was:

- banner advertisements   56 per cent
- sponsorships   30 per cent
- interstitials (TV-like commercials)   5 per cent
- e-mail   1 per cent.

Banner ads

Although tracking mechanisms are in place, people are learning to ignore them and both revenue and prices charged are reducing as a result. Despite this, banners do build brand presence and this can be very important if the brand does not already exist in the marketplace. Offsetting this is the fact that the recall for the subject of the banner advertisement is usually very low.

Sponsorships

A sponsor pays to sponsor content such as a section of a web site. The sponsorship may include banners or buttons on the site and possibly a tag line.

Interstitials

Interstitials are ads that load in the space between a page being requested and a page being loaded. They can take two forms. The 'pop-up' usually opens as a page is loading, advertises a product or service and then closes itself. The 'inline' usually occurs in immersive environments that require long download times such as Java. They often provide game play information as well as advertising opportunities, while 'pop-ups' are typically intended for advertising alone. Interstitials often provoke a negative reaction by visitors to the site.

Webvertising has the potential to be truly international as it is a form of communication that the consumer controls by dictating both the direction and the speed of the communication. The traditional models of advertising effects are likely to be inadequate for explaining online processes in media that demand constant active evaluation as opposed to passive reception.

Direct marketing via the web

The Internet represents a shift towards more direct international marketing and in many respects is similar to direct mail. However, the response is immediate as opposed to direct mail where the response is delayed. In addition it commands the customer's attention, whereas many direct mail pieces go into the wastepaper basket. It also commands greater attention than direct mail because it is usually a response to a search for information. According to Stone (2000), response rates to e-mail can be three to five times better than for direct marketing.

E-mail by contrast is similar to direct mail in that the messages received may be both in response to a request and unsolicited. Customers can be encouraged to register their interest in receiving details of new offers by e-mail and to register for regular news information updates. Although e-mail may be a speedy low-cost alternative to postal mail (snail mail), there is still a need for identifying and compiling a list of potential customers for contact. Forrester Research claims that the market for e-mail marketing services will grow from US$156 million in 1999 to US$4.8 billion in 2004. Unsolicited e-mail (spam) is similar to the 'junk mail' category of direct mail, and creates an equally negative reaction. Table 12.3 contrasts mass marketing, direct marketing and Dell's form of direct marketing.

Direct marketing via the Internet is often referred to as permission marketing because when the Internet is involved in effect you are first asking customers if you can send them information. In the process you are establishing in advance whether the person in the other country is likely to be interested in your offering. When a customer visits the web site, they are asked whether they would like to hear from the site again about special offers, etc. If the response is positive and they 'opt in', this begins a relationship with the customer and is more likely to generate a positive response than direct mail. This technique is 5 times more cost effective than direct marketing and up to 20 times more effective than banner ads. Although a direct mail campaign might achieve a positive response rate of 2 per cent, permission marketing campaigns can achieve a rate of 60 per cent (BRW, 2000: 54). Contributing to its effectiveness is the power of the medium to solicit information about the customers and their requirements to ensure that they only receive relevant offers. Direct marketing on the Internet represents a return to dialogue marketing away from monologue marketing selling, and in the process marketing costs are falling and response rates are rising. Firms with experience in direct marketing are often well placed to make the transition to web-based marketing, as Table 12.3 illustrates.

Table 12.3 From mass marketing to Dell's direct marketing

	Mass marketing	Traditional direct marketing	Dell's direct marketing
Best outcome	Volume sales	Customer data	Customer data and relationships
Customer behaviour	Passive	Passive	Active
Market	High volume	Targetted goods	Targetted individuals
Nerve centre	Madison Ave.	Postal distribution centres	Cyberspace
Preferred media vehicle	TV, radio, magazine	Direct mail, catalogues, broadcast media, teleshopping, print media, telemarketing, electronic teleshopping	Use web site to replicate print media, catalogues, etc. Use e-mail to replicate direct mail
Preferred technology to get attention	Storyboards	Databases	Use online service to replicate telemarketing servers, onscreen navigators, the web permission marketing with respect and high response
Worst outcome	Channel surfing	Recycling bins	Log off

Source: Adapted from Moore (2001)

Example	Getting a leg up

The Stitching Horse Bootery (http://www.boots online.com.au) was established in 1977 to provide boots and outdoor wear of Australians. It operated as a retail outlet and mail order operation in Melbourne, and at the time specialized in products such as Frye Boots, R. M. Williams, Redwings and Timberland.

The store also received regular visits from tourists, who brought products to take home. This was often followed up by the consumer requesting additional information and merchandise for friends and relatives. In the late 1980s, major films such as *Crocodile Dundee* and *The Man from Snowy River* served to promote these goods to a wider audience.

The progression to online retailing was natural. Boots online now offer a wide range of outdoor gear, from the R. M. Willimas range to Akubra Hats, High Country Coats, and now to boat shoes and health footwear. The result is a service that rivals the local corner store. An average of 15 per cent of sales are now made online.

Ordering items is simple. The style, size, makes and colour are selected from the menus and added to the 'shopping cart'. Differences between countries, such as sizes and exchange rate information, are kept current with a link provided for daily exchange rate information. Payment can be made by any major credit card, and orders are logged online through mail order, fax or phone. As an additional service, for people who are unwilling to give credit details online, Boots Online will phone the customers anywhere in the world to obtain the information verbally.

Source: Commonwealth of Australia (1999: 29–30)

Viral marketing

The concept of viral marketing is based in the premise of creating a piece of marketing collateral that customers will want to pass on to their peers. The Internet forms an ideal medium through which viral messages can proliferate at high speed. To date, this technique has been used most effectively in gaining support for causes such as those associated with preserving the environment. The potential of the technique in international marketing is still to be realized. Viral marketing is often compared to word of mouth. It is different in that there is less ability to control word of mouth. Flemming, Jenkins and Main (2001) argue that viral marketing can be both voluntary (where participants are encouraged to pass on a communication to like-minded users) and involuntary (adding tags or attachments to free services).

Virtual communities as targets for international promotion

The Internet is creating communities of users that could not have been formed without the new ability to connect across extremely diverse and dispersed locations. Kozinets (2000) distinguishes between five types of virtual communities on the basis of structure.

- *boards* – these function as electronic bulletin boards
- *rings* – these bring together thematically linked web pages
- *lists* – these are e-mail lists united by a common topic or purpose

- *dungeons* – themed virtual locations in which interactions are structured by role-playing rules
- *chat rooms* – unthemed virtual locations loosely organized around common interests.

Whereas the first three use asynchronous, time-delayed communication and the content tends to be more information based, the last two use synchronous, real-time communication and the information has a greater recreational and social content.

From a marketing perspective, customers are starting to form their own virtual brand communities independent of the company, e.g. the newsgroup devoted to Harley-Davidson motorcycles. Anti-brand communities have also been established as with the 'Boycott Nike' sites.

International trade promotion and the web

The major form of international trade promotion is the trade show, which enables potential buyers to see the foreign product at first hand as well as to touch it, feel it and pull it apart. The Internet can never replace the 'hands on' advantage of the trade show. Effective trade show participation requires the use of supplementary promotional activities such as advertisements in trade journals, direct mail campaigns to let customers know that you will be participating, and public relations activities to focus attention on your participation. E-business promotion can replace or add to these supplementary activities.

While it is possible to operate a virtual trade show for your products on the web, such shows are more effective if used in conjunction with presence at a physical trade show because of the factors mentioned above. This helps firms exhibit their products before, during and after physical trade fairs. For firms unable to afford a presence at a physical trade show, the virtual trade show is a less expensive alternative and better than no show at all, despite its limitations.

Research by Firoz and Banta (2000) into features that will drive B2C commerce, involving 1200 US Internet users, included a number of trade promotion activities as indicated in Table 12.4. This table gives the percentage of Internet purchasers that are motivated by specific features of the Internet offering.

Table 12.4	Feature	Percentage of Internet purchasers
Features that will drive e-commerce (B2C)	Free product delivery	98
	On-time delivery guarantees	95
	No sales tax	91
	Coupons/promotions	83
	Toll-free customer assistance	68
	Live, online customer assistance	62

Source: Firoz and Banta (2000: 85)

Public relations and the web

Firms are becoming increasingly aware of the role of word of mouse in public relations activities. This is important because of referrals via the Internet and the shift in power with the Internet from producer or merchant to consumer. Corporations are increasingly monitoring news groups, mailing lists and chat sites to find out what consumers like and dislike about their company. One difference between word of mouse feedback as opposed to word of mouth feedback is that, because of the unregulated nature of the web, it is sometimes difficult to know if the former is true.

Market research and the web

Microprocessors make it possible to quantify the number of visits made by overseas persons to a web site by click-through rates, which measure not only visits but also the number of times an online user logs onto an advertisement for additional information. However, the problem lies in measuring the quality of the responses. While some firms only want a count of the number of hits on their web site each day, those interested in using the web for market research seek more meaningful information about visitors to the site such as demographics or psychographics. One danger of relying on the number of hits as a measure is that it does not discriminate between first time visitors to the site and repeat visitors. According to Van Doren, Fechner and Green-Adelsberger (2000: 33), effective market research on the Internet involves more than counting and has many other advantages if used to maximum effect. Some of these advantages include the elimination of interviewer bias and error, cleaner data editing, randomization of brands, speed in conducting surveys, and a lower cost for conducting surveys in marketspace compared with the marketplace.

An important issue facing managers is how data captured as a byproduct of existing online systems can be intelligently used to support relationship exchanges. The ability to do so is referred to as e-intelligence. E-intelligence is the adding of intelligence to electronic data. It can represent the creation of knowledge from the information flowing to the firm from its web-based and traditional systems. E-intelligence is an overarching concept that allows firms both to customize and enhance personal relationships with customers and suppliers and improve the effectiveness and profitability of business processes and operations via the Internet and traditional channels.

Internet-based surveys allow researchers greater control over the quality of data and secure broader customer feedback. As the Internet evolves, it is likely that clearer standards for evaluating the effectiveness of web sites will emerge. According to Hamill (1998: 434–5), secondary data sources on the Internet related to international marketing include:

- Small Business Administration's Office of International Trade Guide to Exporting (www.sbaonline.sba.gov/OIT/info/links.html)
- A Basic Guide to Exporting (www.maingate.net/us-exports)
- ExportTutor (web.miep.org/tutor/index.html)

- I-Trade Export Guide (www.i-trade.com/dir01/exprtgui/)
- Assist International (www.assist-intl.com)
- Serra International Import Export Directory (www.serraaintl.com/morelink.html).

Compared with traditional methods of primary data collection, the use of the web for this purpose offers a number of benefits. These include time saving, reduced cost, automation of the data and convenience. In addition, recent research indicates that online surveys elicit a quicker response and that responses to open ended questions are higher than in conventional postal surveys (Shu and Wong, 2001). Limitations of online surveys relate to the sampling frame as respondents to such surveys tend to come from the better educated, more affluent sectors of the population. The difference in PC ownership across different age, education and income groups also creates bias.

However, surveys via the web are becoming commonplace, despite the disadvantages associated with securing representative samples and the low response rates achieved. Often this is due to the structure of the questionnaire, which irritates the respondent by not allowing any question to go unanswered. Focus groups where participants engage in a discussion by e-mail are also increasing, although one of the key benefits of focus group discussion is lost – the synergy that arises from face-to-face discussion. In addition, there is an inability to capture the non-verbal aspects of group behaviour, which is a unique characteristic of face-to face focus groups.

There are a number of methodological limitations of online interviewing. These include the lack of paralinguistic cues, less control by the researcher over the conduct of the interview (as the interviewer cannot interrupt a response to seek clarification), and less spontaneity in participants' responses because of the asynchronous nature of the situation (Catterall and Maclaran, 2001). However, the removal of spatial location in online research facilitates the conduct of simultaneous research across national boundaries.

Other issues

Branding

In the physical world, marketers know that a brand is the sum in the consumer's mind of the personality, the presence and the performance of the product/service. The same applies in the digital world. In addition, in this world, the digital marketer will need to manage the customer's online experience of the offering from first encounter to purchase to delivery and beyond, as on the web experience is the brand.

However, because of the relative newness of the Internet, there are few established Internet brands (some exceptions being Amazon, Priceline, eBay, E*Trade and Dell Computer). For this reason, people are more likely to click onto brands they know from reputation established in the marketplace. However, because of its borderless nature the Internet has the capacity to create a spillover effect of brands from country to country, and to promote brand association with both company and country of manufacture. Because of its interactive nature, the Internet enables the consumer to interact with the brand before purchase by facilitating the acquisition of information about the brand, alternative models, associated financial packages and available options.

Limitations on using the Internet to build brand recognition lie in the nature of the medium itself. The medium at present suffers from limited bandwidth and limited usage time. Until interactive multimedia services are commercialized to be able to provide video of similar quality to that of TV, the web will not be able to provide the same emotional intensity and image building as TV or cable advertising. Furthermore, average e-time spent on the Internet approximates 2 per cent of time spent watching broadcast and cable TV. The only exception to the above would be use of the Internet to create brand recognition by web retailers and content providers, as they are marketing to potential customers already using web services. Figure 12.5 illustrates the elements of a strong Internet brand.

Country of origin

The country of origin effect is that stereotypical perceptions attach to products originating in specific countries, and these perceptions influence both purchase intention and purchase behaviour. Research by Ellerman (2000) found that because of its global characteristics the Internet caused a modification in country of origin effect. Comparing purchase intention with products offered for sale via conventional channels on the one hand and via Internet channels on the other, Ellerman (2000) found that country of origin effect was less when goods were marketed via the Internet.

Legal issues

Advertising and promotion on the Internet may be subject to the laws of the country in which the message is received. It cannot be assumed that because the

Figure 12.5

Elements of a strong Internet brand

Source: Chaffey (2000: 47)

web advertisement has been cleared as complying with the law in Australia, for example, it will be acceptable in other countries. Even within countries, laws as to advertising and promotion vary between states. Therefore, the advertisement may be acceptable in some states in an overseas country but not in others. One area where problems arise is with coupons in Internet advertisements as legislation with respect to coupons varies substantially between countries and between states. A reasonable approach is to pick the key overseas markets for the product to be promoted and seek clearance for the advertising or promotional materials in those markets. The costs of so doing are likely to be more than offset by the lower cost of web as opposed to conventional forms of promotion.

Another legal aspect relating to promotion is the possibility if infringing someone else's intellectual property rights when promotion is via the Internet. The brand name, patent or copyright may be held by another person in the other country. When your ad is downloaded there, it is possible you could be deemed to have breached the another party's intellectual property. The only way around the problem is to check and seek clearances in major overseas markets where your promotional message is likely to be received.

Another digital promotional vehicle

Internet radio stations are emerging at a fast pace in developed countries. They are linked through Internet service providers to listeners' computers and mobile phones, providing a greater choice of music than that normally available from other radio stations. Digital One, for example, has ten audio streams pitched to specific tastes. Unlike conventional stations that pay for broadcasting licences and must abide by regulatory standards, Internet stations have virtually no restrictions and are cheap to set up (*BRW*, 13 October 2000: 96). To date their advertising revenue has been small, but this could change as these stations can readily identify their listeners and attract niche advertisers. Revenue potential lies in subscriptions, banner advertisements and linking to web sites selling the product being promoted.

Government promotion of export consciousness via the Internet

Government trade promotion agencies are increasingly using the Internet to assist their national firms to promote overseas, to bring overseas opportunities to the attention of firms and to educate firms on government policies and assistance programmes related to export. An analysis of Internet use by various export promotion agencies (www.seve.co.uk/edit6.html) revealed that its application was in three areas: a communications tool supporting network relationships, a low cost export market research resource; and a vehicle for global promotion through the design, development and effective marketing of company web sites. The five sites analysed (British Exports Interactive, Scottish Exporters Virtual Community, Austrade World Direct, Export Canada and German Export) are all in developed countries. However, recent studies by the International Trade Centre in Geneva have shown an uneven pattern of Internet use by export promotion agencies in developing and transition economies. Less than half of the 51 agencies surveyed had any specific e-trade component in their national export development strategies. Among those that had an e-trade strategy, few had an integrated approach for ensuring that there was an appropriate environment for e-trade growth, and even fewer had established e-trade support programmes for their business sector.

Conclusion

Consumers are unlikely to forget the difference between speaking to a person and tapping into a computer. They will need both services, which means that promotion in marketspace will go hand in hand with promotion in the marketplace. The web is a tool for promotion, not a strategy, and its unique capabilities are used to improve communication. The Internet is not a substitute for marketplace promotion but a complement to it.

Questions

1. How can Internet promotion be used to convert Internet browsers into Internet shoppers?
2. Why are infrastructure limitations in marketspace greater than such limitations in the international marketplace?
3. Develop a strategy for building international buyer loyalty on the web for a product with which you are familiar.
4. What are the common failings of Internet sites as vehicles for international promotion?
5. Do you consider the Internet is better suited for international selling, international advertising, or international trade promotion?

References

Briggs, R. and Hollis, N. (1997) 'advertising on the web: Is there response before click-through?', *Journal of Advertising Research*, 37(2): 33–45.

BRW (2000) 20 April; 7 July; 13 October; 20 October.

Catterall, M. and Maclaran, P. (2001) 'A cyberspace odyssey: Researching virtual communities using online ethnography', *Proceedings of the Academy of Marketing Conference*, 1–4 July, Cardiff: University of Cardiff.

Chaffey, D. (2000) 'Achieving Internet Marketing Success', *Marketing Review* 1(1): 35–9.

Commonwealth of Ausrtralia (1999) *Creating a Clearway on the New Silk Road – International Business and Policy Trends in Internet Commerce.* Canberra: AGPS.

Dowling, R. J. (1999) 'Covering the world's e-Revolution', *Business Week* 3640: 1.

Ellerman, S. (2000) 'Modification of the country of origin effect when purchase selection occurs over the internet', unpublished research report, Master of Marketing Program, University of South Australia.

Firoz, N. M. and Banta, C. (2000) 'Business in the age of the internet – strategy for success on the e-playing field', *Proceedings of the 5th International Conference on Global Business & Economic Development, 'Managing Global Business in the Internet Age'*, 4, 21–24 June, Beijing: University of International Business and Economics, 81–91.

Flemming, W., Jenkins, L. and Main (2001) 'Viral marketing – is it word of mouth?', *Proceedings of the Academy of Marketing Conference*, 1–4 July, Cardiff: University of Cardiff.

Griffin, T. (1993) *International Marketing Communications*, Oxford: Butterworth-Heinemann.

Hachigan, A. (2001) *Foreign Affairs*, March.

Hamill, J. (1998) 'Export Guides on the Net', *International Marketing Review* 15(5): 434–6.

Kennedy, R. (2000) 'The forms that www ads take', *Proceedings of the ANZMAC 2000 Conference – Visionary Marketing for the 21st Century: Facing the Challenge*, Griffith University, 648–52.

Kozinets, R. V. (2000) 'The field behind the screen: Using the method of netnography to research market-oriented virtual communities', www.kellog.nwu.edu/faculty.

Maddox, L. M. and Mehta, D. (1997) 'The role and effect of web addresses in advertising', *Journal of Advertising Research* 37(2): 47–59.

Marketing News (1998) 'Interactive marketing', *Marketing News* 14 September: 9.

Monnier, P. D. (1999) *Cybermarketing: A Guide for Managers in Developing Countries*, Geneva: International Trade Centre.

Moore, P. (2001) 'A new business model – the digital value network', *Book of Readings – 24715 Strategic Marketing in Electronic Business*, Sydney: University of Technology.

Razzouk, N. and Seitz, V. (2001) 'The effectiveness of banner advertisement: An empirical investigation', unpublished paper, California State University, Bernadino.

Reichheld, F. and Schefter, P. (2000) 'E-Loyalty: Your secret weapon on the web', *Harvard Busines Review* Jul–Aug: 105–33.

Shu, S. T. and Wong, V. (2001) 'The use of online focus groups in marketing research: A feasibility study', *Proceedings of the Academy of Marketing Conference*, 1–4 July, Cardiff: University of Cardiff.

Stone, M. L. (2000) 'Options increase for opt-in emailers', *Business Marketing* 85.

Sutherland, M. (2000) 'Putting 'click through' in perspective', *Professional Marketing*, Dec/Jan: 38–9.

U.S. Department of State (2000) *Country Commercial Guide – China* Washington, DC: U.S. Dept of State, p. 27.

Vakratsas, D. and Ambler, T. (1999) 'How advertising works: What do we really know?', *Journal of Marketing*, January.

Van Doren, D. D., Fechner, D. L. and Green-Adelsberger, K. (2000) 'Promotional strategies on the world wide web', *Journal of Marketing Communications* 6: 21–35.

Westland, J. C. and Clark, H. K. (1999) *Global Electronic Commerce: Theory and Case Studies*, Press, Cambridge, MA: MIT Press.

Case Study 12 *Can online promotional and marketing campaigns effectively cross national boundaries?*
Ruth Chew and Richard Fletcher

Introduction

Tribe Pty Ltd is an Australian firm with key businesses in the entertainment and media business. It was established in the third quarter of 1998 and its online division began in late 1999. The online division has a concept of being an online search portal for lifestyle topics and events happening in the city. The online search portal has web sites all over Australia, mainly operating in the capital cities, and they are 'city-centric'; e.g. if the site was in Melbourne, the site would be melbournetribe.com and if in Sydney, sydneytribe.com, etc. In addition, the sites generally provide information specific to the city they are in. However, most of the business is in Australia and the online division is headquartered in Sydney.

What is Tribe?

Tribe.com, being a lifestyle search portal, has a wide variety of links and information under the following categories:

- Pleasure contains everything related to pleasure – fashion, self-pleasure, aromatherapy, massage recommendations.

- Music showcases new stuff in the music industry – new releases, albums and promotions.
- Club introduces all the night spots and what the 'coolest' places are for a great party.
- Movies provides movie reviews for movies currently showing and updates on what is coming to the screens.
- City is a generic page which offers topics of interest generic to the country.

These five categories are on all Tribe sites. Apart from Australian sites, Tribe has launched in the UK with londontribe.com, and Los Angeles (LA) with latribe.com.

What is Tribe's positioning?

Tribe aims to target broadly 18 to 30-year-olds, with a core target audience of 24-year-olds. This target audience is usually single and young professionals. Their active consumer spending habits include clothes shopping, magazines and music. Also, this target enjoys going out to bars, clubs and nightclubs. They are lifestyle conscious, socially aware of current affairs and highly street credible. The Tribe target market is also more open embracing new ideas, being less conservative and often risk takers. Tribe has the following marketing objectives:

- To increase web site traffic.
- To increase Tribal surfer registrations.
- To build site awareness.
- To attract new unique visitors.
- To retain existing customers.

Tribe's positioning statement for Australia and Los Angeles is that it is 'Life Support' for clubbers, moviegoers, fashion lovers and music enthusiasts. It is different in London where their positioning statement is 'Urban Insite', with a play on words to reflect their position in the city, as well as the pun for both being a web site and also providing insights into London lifestyle and social life. Tribe wants to position itself as city focused and original with up-to-date content. It is visually innovative and possesses unique features while being highly functional. Tribe comes across as quirky and irreverent but still credible, with 120 domain names registered.

Tribe's promotion and communication

Tribe wants to be in the scene and an interactive web site, providing the latest in the city's social life and lifestyle news. Their communication objectives are:

- To communicate the Tribe brand personality.
- To position Tribe as the first destination for entertainment and information.
- To use messages which speak directly to the target audience.
- To emphasize the locally focused 'city-centric' theme.
- To align the Tribe brand with the youth lifestyle.

In order to achieve its marketing objectives and communication objectives, Tribe aims to create awareness and promote itself as the city's 'Life Support' to the target audience. The main elements of the strategy used to make Tribe's brand known is a clever use of appropriate media which will reach out to the target market and focus on getting them as Tribal surfers and also to align Tribe with their lifestyle search needs. Included in the strategy are:

1. Media advertising
2. Publicity
3. Promotions
4. Search engine positioning
5. Tribal surfer programme
6. dot.combis
7. Media and event sponsorship

For publicity, the objective is to build strong media relationships. This involves identifying media angles to develop strong ideas. Distribution of media kits to related press is done together with the media launch. Promotion activities include movie club event tickets, freebies and prizes on the competition page of the web sites. The promotional activities often surround the products and services advertised on the site by the advertisers or through events.

For media sponsorship, Tribe's approach is to find creative and innovative interactive solutions through community radio, television, street press and magazines. The objectives aim to be unique and interactive with their audience. Some objectives include getting naming rights of radio shows and street press pages, holding media competitions and promotions, online polls, providing 'live' reads, having announcer endorsements and increasing and promoting Tribe news feeds. Event sponsorship is used to balance Tribe's media and to gain trust from the target audience as Tribe seeks and sponsors key events. These sponsorship events encourage cut-through to the web site with exclusive interviews, competitions and chats. Giveaways like free tickets and passes to events are handed out by Tribe.

Under the Tribal Surfer programme, which is an online incentive programme, tribal surfers collect points for surfing the site. Points collected are redeemable for innovative products (these products range from Palm Pilots to handbags). Dot.combis are promotional vehicles that are on the road five days a week. Key youth events are 'ambushed' and merchandise (both Tribe's and their clients') is handed out.

Some problems for Tribe

A market research report commissioned in May 2000 reported some problems arising from the Tribe web sites audience profile. Some issues identified were that Tribe is enjoying great success since its launch in March 2000, having a growing presence and sound financials as their operational divisions' profits exceeded predictions. As Tribe plans to have a partial public float in the later part of 2000, they would require a strong rate,

meaning they have to obtain 1,000,000 impressions a day from the web site. Their strong brand needs to be communicated and created. Upon researching the web site, it is found that, on first glance, the Tribe web sites look colourful with bright and fun graphics. In addition, it looks busy, having lots to discover and lots to offer the websurfer. However, after close inspection, there are two clear segments:

1. The Enthusiastic minority, predominantly female and from the younger end of the age range, who find the site interesting.
2. The Cynical Majority who find the site confusing, busy, unclear and difficult to manoeuvre around.

It was concluded from the research that the sites had presentation and navigation as their greatest barrier to reaching out to their target markets. As far as design and layout of the site of the site is concerned, it needs to be simplified as it came across as cluttered, inconsistent, confusing and difficult to surf. They have fallen into the trap of Internet web sites by being offputting and not user friendly. With the amount of content on the portal, it is important that the design and layout is organized and less complex for the surfer.

Navigating around the site was also a major barrier because the ease of manoeuvring through the site was not present. This is an essential factor to retain interest and keep the target market loyal. Again, the amount of content available on the Tribe sites is massive and an interested Tribe surfer would need to have easy access to each of the pages on the portal. With Tribe's navigation, the terminology was ambiguous and not easily comprehensible. Icons on the site had different styles and several different icons served the same destination with interlinking between portals. This then caused inconsistency with the design of the web site from the variety of icons.

To better improve their web site and web market presence, a look at the Internet's use and capability was undertaken. The Internet has four vital elements:

- information
- entertainment
- communication
- service.

These elements aim to serve different target markets' needs. Each of the above elements do different things for the websurfer. For information, the aim is to seek. For entertainment, interacting is the main objective. Communication helps to connect. Services provided on the Internet serve as a transacting element. The Internet is the new integrated solution compared with traditional channels of media. Traditional channels provide only one aspect such as sounds and visuals on television, whereas the Internet provides information with sounds, visuals and animation. It was concluded that Tribe needs to be more focused in its media content, design and layout in order to be effective and win loyal Tribe websurfers. Specific recommendations arising from the research were:

1. To let design and functionality of the site work together to support the content.

2. To allow each site to be differentiated and yet be linked to the Tribe brand.

3. To segment the broad target market so as to be more interactive, user friendly and effective.

Problems with LA Tribe

LA Tribe was developed while the research was being undertaken. However, the LA office's philosophy and positioning statement originates from Sydney. The LA market is cluttered with similar entertainment and lifestyle search portals. Competition is strong and it is also a hard market to penetrate. Not only that, the US technology in Internet is five years' ahead of Sydney. Having had few problems with data processing and transfer for all other Tribe sites, LA proves to be very challenging. While the information is similar and the design is identical, the infrastructure used to support the web site and its content is different from

that of Sydney's. In addition, financial backing is not stable for the LA site because of the reputation of online web sites, following the stock market crash earlier in the year. There is little definite profit from online businesses, hence the LA office suffers.

The problem lies not only within the LA office but also the actual Tribe web site concept. The LA office would need some research done in order to start working on the solution to their problem. Belinda Lee, the marketing coordinator at Tribe, has to solve these problems. She thinks the problems lie with Tribe's fundamental marketing strategy. She sets out to solve the problems. Broadly, they are Tribe's overall marketing and Internet problems, and LA Tribe's lack of boost.

Postscript

The *Sydney Morning Herald* (13–15 April 2001: (39), reported:

> The fall in the Australian dollar has forced Tribe, the online youth publishing venture founded by Village Entertainment chief Mr. Milt Barlow, to close its Los Angeles and London web sites and retrench staff. Sydney based Tribe raised $30 million from venture capitalists last year to pursue a dream of expanding its six Australian city lifestyle guides into North America and Europe, securing the second round of funding in November. Up to 45 staff had been employed in the Los Angeles and London offices, which opened last August . . . Tribe would now focus on Australia, where it had sufficient funds to survive for at least another 12 months.

Questions

1. Analyse the short-term and long-term results from the current Tribe marketing strategy.

2. Operation of LA Tribe is likened to that of operating in marketspace while its marketing activity and strategy are using

tools which are traditional marketing ones. Outline the characteristics of marketing in: (1) marketplace; (2) marketspace. How can Tribe use some of these to aid in their situation in LA?

3. In Belinda's opinion, the decision-making system for the operation of Tribe's online divisions was too centralized and hindered growth internationally. Suggest a way(s) of decentralizing the system which will retain the Tribe brand and yet be suited for each international market.

4. Set new marketing objectives and strategy for Tribe which would enable it in the future to again undertake international expansion.

Index